Her Victorian grace and her stanch wifeliness charmed many, but to the bureaucrats of England, Mrs. Josephine Butler was a holy terror. One Member of Parliament declared her to be "worse than prostitutes," and a powerful British newspaper editor wrote that she was "a shrieking sister, frenzied, unsexed, and utterly without shame." In time she earned herself the outlandish title of "the single individual most responsible for the spread of syphilis"—a gross slander.

The irony of all this abuse was that Josephine Butler was an extraordinary beauty, a highly educated member of one of England's best Whig families, and the contented wife of a distinguished Oxford scholar and educator. But when in 1864 Parliament passed the legislation it called the Contagious Diseases Acts—ostensibly "reform" laws designed to "regulate" prostitution, that is, make it less hazardous for Britain's garrisoned troops to secure prostitutes for themselves, which meanwhile left any working-class woman subject to police harassment and public persecution—Josephine was outraged, appalled at the injustices to women caused by the acts.

With her husband's blessing, she took up a personal campaign to have the acts repealed, and soon became a very sharp thorn in the side of those who sought to uphold and enforce the odious laws. Police were arresting innocent women on the most meager evidence, forcing them to submit to the humiliating and painful physical examinations for venereal disease that the acts required of suspected prostitutes. Once they passed the tests, the prostitutes were "certified" by the Crown to continue doing business, but the young working girl was left to public censure. No attempt was made to prevent the soldiers from spreading disease back among the women. Going to the clinics became a game, with young children gathering on the pavement outside to play "arrest and inspection" while they waited for the prostitutes to emerge, flaunting their certificates and their talents. Police corruption also facilitated the international trade in British children, and Josephine's "undercover agents" brought back some blood-curdling accounts of the practices in English and Continental child brothels.

Bucking threats and abuse, Josephine stepped up her campaigns with determination and compassion. Eventually she traveled all over Europe for the repeal of similar laws there, unfashionably taking up the cause of the poor and abused and personally helping with the care of those who suffered from the acts. Eventually, after years of Josephine Butler's campaigns, Parliament resignedly gave in and abrogated the Contagious Diseases Acts.

Although Josephine Butler sought to ensure that no biography would be written of her, after her death in 1906 many suffragette and feminist organizations printed pamphlets and books about her, re-creating her, but in their own image. Glen Petrie has been able to make use of these, along with his own extensive researches into his subject's life and work, and, with the increased freedom with which it is now possible to write of the sexual and moral dilemmas of Victorian society, has come up with a most revealing and absorbing new biography.

1869.

Josephine E Butler

# A Singular Iniquity

## The Campaigns of
## JOSEPHINE BUTLER

### Glen Petrie

*New York* / THE VIKING PRESS

To P A T

1618924

# ACKNOWLEDGEMENTS

I AM grateful, firstly, to Miss Hetha St Paul Butler, and to the Josephine Butler Society, without whose co-operation I could not have written this book. More particularly, I am grateful to the officers of the executive committee of the Josephine Butler Society, and to the Librarian and staff of the Fawcett Library, Westminster, for the confidence which they reposed in me in placing unrestrictedly at my disposal the materials – Josephine Butler's letters, journals and unpublished manuscripts – upon which this book is largely based.

I am grateful to the Dean and Senior Members of Christ Church, Oxford, for extending their hospitality to me over a period of three months so that I might work over the more difficult sections of the book in comparative solitude, and tranquillity; to the Principal and Staff of Christ's College, Finchley, for their friendly tolerance at my absences and abstraction over the same period; to Mrs B. Sullivan for typing a large, and largely illegible, part of my manuscript; and to my children for bearing with exasperated resignation the occasional outbursts of temperament which go with authorship (mine, at any rate).

Above all, I am grateful to my wife, who introduced me to my subject, and suggested that I should write about her, and to whose experience and understanding I owe whatever insight I may possess regarding the work, and the charity, of Josephine Elizabeth Butler.

A. G. P.

# CONTENTS

# A SINGULAR INIQUITY

# The Contagious Diseases Acts

## I

IN 1864, the first of three Contagious Diseases Acts was passed through Parliament. Its full title was A Contagious Diseases Act (not concerned with animals),[1] and the preamble read:

'That the peculiar conditions of the naval and military services, and the temptations to which the men are exposed, justifies special precautions for the protection of their health, and their maintenance in a state of physical efficiency.'

To this end, provision was to be made for the surgical examination of prostitutes supposed by the police (presumably through information laid) to be infected with a venereal disease, for their detention in government certified hospitals – 'Lock' hospitals – during a limited period and for the punishment of brothel-keepers who knowingly harboured diseased prostitutes. The implementation of the Act was to be limited to eleven 'military stations, garrison towns, and naval seaports'.

This measure was passed through both Commons and Lords without debate. Few people were aware of its existence in or out of parliamentary circles, and those that were considered it entirely unobjectionable. Its operation was, after all, severely limited, and, in any case, a periodical-reading public accustomed to Mrs Lynn Linton's weekly diatribes against 'posticherie' and the aniline-gay fashions which adorned the otherwise mousy daughters of middle-class Bayswater was unlikely to take kindly to a discussion in the Press of methods designed to contain the incidence of venereal disease among soldiers.

Twenty years previously Lord Macaulay had drawn the attention of the House to the ruinous state of health prevailing in the Armed Services. Macaulay's contention – that conditions in urban areas were so appalling that healthy recruits were virtually unobtainable – was something of an exaggeration. Far more to the point were conditions prevailing within the services themselves. The Liverpool administrations of 1816 and 1821, faced with recurring financial crises and the need for stringent restrictions in government expenditure, employed those same laissez-faire methods towards its paid servants as a factory master would have done with his employees under similar circumstances: it crippled the army with false economies. 'It grumbled', wrote Sir John Fortescue, 'at the cost of recruits, and did its best to kill them off as quickly as possible.'[2] Despite the reports of Florence Nightingale, a Sanitary Commission and the complaints of John Arthur Roebuck in the House of Commons, little had been done for the army after its return home from the Crimean War. The average annual death-rate from disease in the army remained double that of the civilian population of military age, and conditions of service continued to ensure that, a few remarkable exceptions apart, only the foulest-mouthed and foulest-minded recruit could endure such a life.

It was hardly surprising that the army presented a microcosm of the social evils which existed in the more overpopulated alleys and tenements of the industrial towns, and these in an exaggerated form. As the under-skilled and over-worked labourer sought comfort and release in drunkenness and sexual indulgence, so did the soldier. From the penalties of the first he was, to some extent, protected: the necessity for sobriety on duty, enforced with savage discipline and hard physical exercise, mitigated the effect of the rot-gut liquor provided by government contractors. Nothing, however, protected him from venereal disease caught from the prostitutes, often the most wretched of their kind, who flocked into the garrison towns.

In London the problem was not so acute. There, soldiers walking the parks found it easy to pick up healthy girls who were willing to give themselves for nothing: 'dolly-mops' – servant-girls who had evaded the vigilance of their employers in order to seek a brief sexual adventure – and nurse-maids prepared to neglect their charges for a few minutes of excitement behind the bushes, and all afflicted with what Mayhew categorised as 'scarlet fever', the inability to resist a man in the uniform of a line regiment.[3]

In garrison towns such as Aldershot, Chatham, Dover, Rochester or Colchester, there were no such delightful opportunities. Women and girls came to such places with the intention of living off soldiers, and they were those who had been unable to make a living in the more fashionable areas of prostitution. In order to make ends meet – they could expect little profit from an individual soldier – they were compelled to seek out as many clients as they could reasonably entertain before the Last Post was sounded in the barracks and lines. They built themselves shacks as near the barracks' gates as they dared, and if they found themselves to be diseased they were faced with the choice either of infecting as many men as they could, or of retirement to the workhouse. Invariably they chose the former, and Mayhew reported seeing one woman in a music-hall frequented by soldiers who 'only yesterday had two buboes lanced; and yet she was present at that scene of apparent festivity, contaminating the very air like a deadly upas tree, and poisoning the blood of the nation with the utmost recklessness'.[4]

The need for army reform, and particularly the need to improve the health of soldiers, was fully recognised in the early 1860s, but the two-party system on which firm legislation in Britain depended was in ruins, and it was not until the following decade that Edward Cardwell, backed by a strong Liberal administration, could force through, by means of an Order in Council, reforms which had long been seen to have been necessary. In the meantime, if recruitment was not to fade away altogether, the British soldier could not be hindered from having frequent recourse both to the bottle and to women. The Contagious Diseases (not concerned with animals) Act (1864) represented both the least and the most that could be done to protect the health of the army without stirring the fires of political controversy in Westminster.

The principal difficulty in implementing the Act at a time when innumerable servant-girls and labouring women supplemented their wretched wages by selling their bodies lay in determining who was a prostitute and who was not. For this reason, plainclothes officers were seconded from the Metropolitan

Police to the garrison towns, with orders to summon before a
magistrate any woman they had cause to suspect was a prostitute. Should a woman fail to comply with such an order she
could be detained at the magistrates' discretion, and be subjected to imprisonment with hard labour.

The success, in practical terms, of this Act resulted in the
passing of a second Act in 1866, under which prostitutes in
garrison towns were required to submit to medical examination
not less than once every twelve months and not more than once
every six months.[5] Women brought before a magistrate by the
plainclothes police had to submit to medical examination
regardless of evidence as to personal character and reputation:
presumption of guilt was invariable. A second Consolidating Act
was passed in 1868 extending the maximum period of enforced
hospitalisation to nine months, and providing for the compulsory moral and religious instruction of women so confined.

Published statistics proved the success of the Contagious
Diseases Acts, and a considerable body of informed public
opinion, including Henry Mayhew and William Acton, sought to
extend their operation to the civilian sector. Thus was born The
Association for the Promotion of the Extension of the Contagious
Diseases Act (1866) to The Civil Population of the United
Kingdom, which advocated the introduction, for a trial period,
of the Acts into London and other large conurbations. In order
to implement the Acts it was suggested that a Morals Police
should be organised, modelled on the pattern of the Parisian
Police des Mœurs. Many people, however, who were content to
allow a Morals Police to operate in towns whose *raison d'être*
was the presence of the military, were less happy at the prospect
of a plainclothes force operating in civilian areas with unlimited
power of arrest. The founding of 'The Association' resulted,
almost immediately, in the emergence of an opposition movement which questioned not merely the desirability of an extension of the Acts, but, upon reflection, brought the existing Acts
under close and critical scrutiny.

The most pertinent objection raised by the oppositionists
concerned the actual constitution and operation of a Morals
Police. The admiration expressed by members of the Association
for the Parisian Police des Mœurs was based on ignorance of
the true character of such a police:

Satin was full of stories on that subject. In the old days, she used to sleep with a plainclothes man of the 'Police des Mœurs' so that she should be left in peace. On two occasions he had prevented her from being given a card as a registered prostitute. . . . The police arrested as many women as possible so as to get a rake off: they grabbed everyone, they gave you a blow to shut you up if you called out, certain of being backed up and rewarded, even when they picked up an honest girl among the other lots. In summer, a dozen or fifteen of them would operate round-ups on the boulevards; they would encircle a stretch of pavement and fish out up to thirty women of an evening.[6]

Zola, if anything, was underestimating the amount of graft, corruption and brutality practised by the Parisian Police des Mœurs. He goes on to describe how his heroine, Nana, throws herself from a second-floor window rather than experience the so-called medical inspection at the St Lazare prison hospital; such a reaction from a prostitute who was in danger of arrest was no mere product of a novelist's licence to melodramatise. By virtue of the authority delegated to them, the power of the Police des Mœurs over girls of the labouring class was absolute.

There is little evidence to show that the Morals Police in Aldershot or any other garrison town were as venal or as sadistic as their French counterparts, or that the medical examination of women suspected of being prostitutes was as callous and wantonly pain-inflicting as the treatment meted out at St Lazare. The fact remains that a considerable number of perfectly innocent women and young girls, many of whom were little over the age of twelve, were detained on the grounds that they had been seen loitering in public places or that they had been observed talking to a soldier. Such women and girls were thrown into the company of the most squalid of their sex, women foul both in speech and behaviour, and were then subjected to a medical examination which was, in the context of a Victorian upbringing, at best degrading and, for the children particularly, incomprehensible and therefore terrifying.

Nobody will ever know how many innocent women suffered personal tragedy as a result of the Contagious Diseases Acts. When arrest and trial of one particular type of offender becomes routine, justice is neither done nor is seen to be done. One such personal tragedy was that of Mrs Percy.[7]

Mrs Percy was a widow living in Aldershot with her sixteen-year-old daughter. Before her marriage she had been a music-hall entertainer, and when her husband died leaving her virtually penniless she returned to her old profession. Primarily concerned for the welfare of her daughter, she took the girl to her dressing-room in the music-hall every night, and every night mother and daughter were escorted to their lodgings by two soldiers drawn from an infantry regiment which had unofficially 'adopted' the Percys. One night, they were thus being escorted from the theatre, when they were stopped by a police patrol. The two infantrymen were ordered to return to their lines immediately, and Mrs and Miss Percy were ordered to appear the following afternoon for medical examination. Mrs Percy was sufficiently hardened by garrison life not to care unduly on her own behalf – indeed, it is more than probable that she had been forced to endure this humiliation before. She was, however, outraged by the thought that the young daughter she had been so careful to protect from the hazards of life in a garrison town should be so degraded and exposed. Not only did mother and daughter fail to appear for examination, but Mrs Percy wrote a letter of protest to the *Daily Telegraph* which that organ of conservative respectability duly published.[8] The Morals Police were determined to prove themselves to be in the right, and to justify their action by securing a conviction. They determined to force her into open practice of prostitution by withholding from her any alternative means of support. Since the existence of any music-hall depended on a licence issued by the magistracy, it was an easy matter to persuade the management of 'The Queen's Tap', the theatre at which Mrs Percy appeared, to dispense with her services, and, in fact, she was blacklisted at every music-hall and tavern in Aldershot.

She and her daughter moved to Windsor, where, thanks to friends in the profession – she was well known and well liked among her fellow artistes – she easily obtained a billing. After a lapse of some months, a Mr Ritson, one of the leading performers at 'The Queen's Tap', urged her to return to Aldershot in order to appear in a double act with himself. It was decided that she should appear under the professional name of Mrs Ritson: there was no suspicion of any liaison in this – there was a genuine Mrs Ritson. Nevertheless Mrs Percy's compliance with this suggestion was an act of supreme folly – she was well known in Aldershot – and is only explicable in that she was popular both with the company and the patrons of 'The Queen's Tap', and in her widowhood had come to look on them as a surrogate family.

Within the first week of her return with her daughter, the Morals Police informed the proprietor of 'The Queen's Tap' that unless Mrs Percy and her daughter were turned away, he would be charged with knowingly harbouring two public women and thus, by inference, keeping a disorderly house (in law, the presence of two prostitutes under one roof constitutes a brothel). On this occasion the persecution was absolute. Not only were all theatrical managers and tavern keepers warned against the Percys, but so were all registered landladies and lodging-house keepers, who were, of course, equally vulnerable before the law. Mrs Percy and her daughter were driven, quite literally, on to the street. Telling her daughter that she was going a few miles out of the town to look for lodgings, Mrs Percy disappeared. A few days later her body was found floating in the Basingstoke Canal. She had committed suicide.

Help came for the daughter in the shape of Josephine Elizabeth Butler, whose attention had been drawn to Mrs Percy's letter in the *Daily Telegraph*. She took the girl into her own home in Liverpool, where she had offered sanctuary to many other less respectable and less deserving young women, and arranged that she should be legally represented in the Coroner's Court when it sat on her mother's body. If Mrs Butler hoped that the names of the two Percys would thus be cleared, it was a vain hope. No testimony as to the character and reputation of either the girl or her mother was admitted, and the name of Mrs Percy was read into the record as being that of a known prostitute. There can be little doubt that the coroner's attitude was hardened rather than otherwise by the knowledge of Josephine Butler's intervention.

The trouble was that by 1875, the date of Mrs Percy's death, Josephine Butler had become a very considerable thorn in the side of those who sought to uphold and enforce the Contagious Diseases Acts. John Morley, then editor of the influential *Pall*

*Mall Gazette*, a man of radical views and deep humanitarian conviction, complained bitterly at her persistent opposition to the Acts:

'To sacrifice the health and vigour of unborn creatures to the "rights" of harlotry to spread disease without interference is a doubtful contribution towards the progress of the race. This sentimental persistence in treating permanently brutalized natures as if they still retained infinite capacities for virtue is one of the worst faults of some of the best people now living.'[9]

Yet this belief in 'the infinite capacities for virtue' to be found in the most degraded prostitute was exactly Josephine's own. To Josephine, the battle against prostitution was a war against a multi-personed Herod – society – which dragged down the Innocents, and the Contagious Diseases Acts, since their purpose was to make prostitution less of a hazard for its male clients, was an integral part of the dragging-down process. To the majority of her contemporaries, who believed that the harlot was a harlot due to the operation of Original Sin, a consummation avoidable by recourse to Industry and Divine Grace through Prayer (a recourse wilfully ignored by the harlot), Josephine's attitude was perverse and naïve. This perversity was made more obvious by the fact that she was beyond doubt a Christian, if anything a Christian of an Evangelical turn of mind. Her charity was broad enough to embrace Catholic, Calvinist, Latitudinarian, Quaker or Jew as her brother in God. She was completely undogmatic, almost undoctrinal, and her Christian witness was her own life and compassion. Since 1865 she had worked among the prostitutes of Liverpool, and this experience had confirmed her in her view that prostitution was the result of evil social conditions combined with the absurd subjugation of women in society.

At first, because her work was limited in scope, she escaped censure, but in 1870, as a result of a visit to the garrison towns of Maidstone and Dover, she embraced the cause for the repeal of the Contagious Diseases Acts and became its virtual leader. In those two towns she discovered that no attempt was made to prevent men from spreading infection or even to isolate those soldiers who had contracted a venereal disease. When she demanded of a senior ranking officer why those who suffered from such a disease were permitted to roam the streets of Maidstone at night with their fellows, he replied that 'men must have their pleasure'. She found that the clinics where women's ⸙ medical examination took place had become places of free public entertainment: crowds assembled on the pavement outside to jeer or cheer the girls going in; as the more hardened prostitutes emerged having been given a clean bill of health, they waved their medical certificates aloft and loudly invited proposals from the men in the crowd. Josephine discovered that such girls were proud of their cleanliness, framed their certificates and hung them above their beds, and called themselves the Queen's Women, as if the absence of disease was a warrant of respectability.[10]

What appalled her most, however, was the spectacle of children, particularly little girls, playing at arrest and inspection openly on the pavement. She realised that medical inspection and the issuing of certificates to infection-free girls raised prostitution to the level of a state-warranted profession whose diploma-ed practitioners children wished to emulate. Under such a system, the hardened woman flourished, while the honest working girl was subjected to a permanent threat of blackmail – it required only one information laid at a police station, one badly scrawled and unsigned note, stating that a certain girl had been seen with soldiers, for that girl, if she belonged to the working classes, to be summonsed for medical inspection; hundreds of such informations were laid as acts of spite, as acts of revenge for some imagined grievance caused by girls or their parents, or as crude practical jokes. Once within the doors of the clinic, girls were assumed to be common street-walkers by doctors and nurses alike, who were wont to accompany their examination with a coarse and ribald patter intended to put the putative harlot at her ease, or to reassure her companions awaiting their turn on the surgical armchair. This experience was enough to convince a number of hitherto uncorrupted girls that they had been violated beyond redemption, and even if that were not the case, that their neighbours would assume it to be so.

Josephine's attack on the Contagious Diseases Acts provoked abuse from all sides. Sir James Elphinstone M.P. declared that she was 'worse than the prostitutes'. The *Daily News*, in an editorial, stated that women like Mrs Butler 'are so discontented in their own homes that they have to find an outlet somewhere, they have to be noticed at all costs, and take pleasure in a hobby too nasty to mention'. Another journalist described Josephine as 'an indecent maenad, a shrieking sister, frenzied, unsexed, and utterly without shame'.[11]

To all who knew Josephine, and they included the highest in the land, such attacks were risible. Born into the most influential family of the Whig landed aristocracy, and happily married to a distinguished scholar and cleric, her position in society was unassailable. The great Whig political families expected their womenfolk to be intelligent, informed and an active influence in political life, and it never occurred to Josephine that she was supposed to reconcile herself, like her middle-class sisters, to an idle, housebound subservience. Nor was she likely to be disturbed by attacks on her moral character. It has been said of her that 'she knew God, talked to Him, and that in no sentimental fashion',[12] and certainly she followed the Evangelical tradition which had been handed down from Wilberforce and the Clapham 'Saints' through Lord Shaftesbury and, later, William Booth, in that her confidence in her chosen line of action was unshakable once she had consulted the Deity.

Gladstone once remarked of her, having acted as her escort at a dinner party, that she was 'quite remarkably feminine'.[13] Like Elizabeth I, she was not above exploiting her femininity – as she had done on that occasion – for political ends. She was also possessed of an extraordinary beauty which was first remarked on when she came out into society at the age of sixteen, and which, according to those who knew her latterly, did not fade with the advance of age but rather resolved into an appearance of dignity and spiritual strength which impressed all who met her. That she knew she was beautiful is beyond doubt: her one vanity was in her appearance – she was always dressed in the height of fashion, and her magnificent mane of hair coiffeured in the prevailing style, whether she was dining with Lord Hartington, exploring the stews of Liverpool or storming into a brothel in Geneva. Her voice was the natural complement of her beauty: low in key, well-modulated and occasionally husky in tone, it held entranced both the single auditor and the large audience, however hostile either might be initially. There are, in fact, few examples recorded of any individual behaving less than courteously towards her in her presence, despite the acerbity of the controversy which frequently raged around her.

Those who could resist her almost irresistible charm were confronted by her formidable intelligence. She was as fluent in French and Italian as she was in her own tongue, and she had a working knowledge of German, Latin, Greek and Hebrew, and even managed to acquire a smattering of Russian. She had studied music under Sterndale Bennett, considered – incredible as it may now seem – the greatest living English composer, and was still taking great delight in playing Liszt's virtuoso piano transcriptions of orchestral works when she was in her seventies. As a scholar she won the grudging respect of her husband's colleagues at Oxford, and was accorded the unique privilege, for a woman, of using the Bodleian and Queen's College Library. Jowett, the near-legendary Master of Balliol who disapproved of everything she stood for, was forced to concede, in a letter to Florence Nightingale, that Josephine was 'touched with genius'.[14]

For all these qualities and talents, her chiefest strength in her battles against prostitution, and on behalf of prostitutes – the hobby 'too nasty to mention' – lay not in her charm, her beauty or her intelligence, but in the protection afforded her by her social rank. Charles Kingsley once wrote to Elizabeth Gaskell, during the furore which raged over her novel *Ruth*, regarding the double moral standard and its effect on girls who had yielded to seduction: 'What is required is one real lady who would dare to stoop.'[15]

Josephine Butler was just such a lady.

# 1. Youth and Preparation

## II

SHE was born in 1828 on her family's Northumberland estate at Milfield. Her father, John Grey of Dilston, was the descendant of a clan of border barons who had distinguished themselves, or made themselves notorious, from the thirteenth century onwards, by ruling their province with a fine disregard either for feudal overlords or monarchs, and by displaying a perverse talent for embracing losing causes and yet surviving. They had supported Mortimer at the battle of Shrewsbury when the Lancastrians were in the ascendant, and the Lancastrians when the Yorkists were dominant, embraced the Catholic cause when Elizabeth I was harrying the Northern Earls and supported the Stuart monarchy when Cromwell was everywhere victorious. They were deeply involved in the futile Jacobite rising in 1715, and appeared to flourish on it, since by the end of the eighteenth century they were the dominant representatives of the Whig Party (not conspicuous for its Jacobite sympathies) in the North. Josephine's father was known in parliamentary circles as The Black Prince of the North, partly because of his good looks and his excellent horsemanship, but chiefly for his talents as a regional party manager at a time when party organisation in general, and Whig Party organisation in particular, was almost non-existent. In 1832, when the crisis over the great Reform Bill was at its height, his cousin, Earl Grey, the Whig Prime Minister, thought it worth his while to travel to Northumberland to consult him. John Grey himself was sufficiently assured of his own position, and sufficiently lacking in tact, to stand up at a Royal Agricultural Society banquet in London and accuse in fairly brutal terms the Duke of Cleveland – the guest of honour – of neglecting the welfare of the tenants on the Cleveland estates.[1]

This spirit of independence informed the whole Grey family. John Grey's sister, Margaretta Grey, was so disgusted at finding she was not allowed to attend Parliament when her cousin was leader of the Whigs – there was no Ladies' Gallery in either House at the time – that she made it her custom to obtain admission by dressing as a boy. His nephew, Charles Grey – and Josephine's favourite relative – was Equerry to Prince Albert, while Mrs Charles Grey was a Woman of the Bedchamber to the Queen (one of those Whig ladies at Court who so disturbed the Tory leadership in 1841). On one occasion the Queen and Prince Albert, who were very fond of Charles Grey, rode across the park to pay them an early morning surprise visit. The Greys were still in bed and the Northumbrian butler informed the Queen and the Prince that they had called too early to see the Colonel and his lady. The Queen firmly demanded to see them.

'Well, if ye wull see them,' replied the butler, 'ye mun wait. Sit ye doon.'[2]

Josephine's mother was born Hannah Annett. The Annetts, a prosperous middle-class family from Alnwick, were of Huguenot descent and had embraced with the enthusiasm of their sect the religious revival of the late eighteenth century; Hannah Grey prided herself on having been dandled, when a toddler, on the knee of John Wesley himself. For all her strict Evangelical upbringing, however, she was a serene and happy woman with a pleasant sense of humour, and her marriage, like Josephine's after her, was a complete success. From her mother Josephine received her deep religious conviction, and the grace to maintain it with compassion and understanding for those who were (in her view) not so fortunate as to share it.

John Grey of Dilston was determined that his daughters – there were six of them – should be brought up as informed, assured and independent as their two brothers. Josephine, the seventh child, was probably the most intelligent and certainly, to judge from family portraits, the most beautiful, of a strikingly handsome and intelligent family. She appears also to have been her father's favourite child, though this, if it be true, inspired no jealousy in a family which was bound strongly together in affection.

In 1833, John Grey was appointed to take charge of the very extensive estates owned by Greenwich Hospital. These had been the property of the Jacobite Lord Derwentwater, who had been executed after the rebellion of 1715, since when they had been considerably extended, largely as a result of various Enclosure Acts. John Grey welcomed the appointment since it gave him the opportunity to put into practice the theories regarding agricultural improvement and estate management with which he had been experimenting on his own estates at Milfield. Agriculturalists came from all over Europe to visit him, and Josephine remembered 'among our pleasantest visitors there were Swedes, Russians, and French, who came to England on missions of agricultural or other enquiry, and sometimes spent weeks with us. Dilston was a house the door of which stood open as if to welcome all comers through the live long summer day (all the days seem like summer days when looking back).'

Josephine, far from being confined to the nursery quarters when important visitors were present, was encouraged to meet them and talk to them. Nor were their guests all agriculturalists. One of her earliest recollections was of being introduced to Clarkson, the leader with Wilberforce of the anti-slavery league, and of listening quietly to him describing to her father the appalling horror of the Middle Passage – she was then five years old. On another occasion she remembered her father exploding with anger at some Whig Party representatives over the Poor Law Amendment Act (which was, of course, a measure initiated by the Whig administration, a fact he found hard to reconcile with his party loyalty): 'Do you think to treat men or women exactly as you do one pound bank-notes, to be used or neglected as you think proper?'

Her four oldest sisters were married off when she was still a child, and the weddings were held at Dilston with considerable style. When Mary Anne, the second daughter, was married to Edgar Garston, a hero of the Greek War of Independence, an early form of 'son et lumière' was arranged in the ruins of Lord Derwentwater's castle, adjoining the house. The ruins were lit by torchlight; a guest, dressed in the clothes of a lady's maid of an earlier age, wandered about the galleries singing Northumbrian folksongs; another guest wandered about the battlements clad as a ghost, wailing horribly; and cannon and fireworks were exploded in semblance of a siege.

As her elder sisters left home, and her brothers, already grown men, went off to manage the family estates, Josephine was thrown more and more into the company of Harriet, the sister nearest to her in age.

'My sister Harriet and I were a pair, in our family we were never separated except perhaps for a few days occasionally, until her marriage and departure for Naples. We were one in heart and soul, and one in all our pursuits.'[3]

Together they learnt to ride, and both of them became accomplished, not to say reckless, horsewomen. When they were young they decided that the vocation they would follow 'above all others' was that of circus-girl. Taking off their boots they would try to stand on the unsaddled backs of their horses, and would 'essay to trot and then to canter round the fields'. After many falls, and with admirable perseverance, they achieved the desired result only to discover that their ambitions 'were turned to other directions than that of the vocation of circus-girl'.[4]

When they had both reached the age of sixteen they attended the great county balls at Alnwick Castle.

Those balls were not like modern ones [Josephine remembered in her old age]. They were stately affairs and, in fact, political gatherings. I recollect my father and old Lord Grey, Lord Howick, and Lord Durham, all standing in a group in the very middle of the ballroom floor, regardless of the dancers all round them, deep in some liberal intrigue. Then the Duke and Duchess would arrive with the Taubervilles who were Conservatives, and the liberal group would break up. I used to dance with Lord Tauberville, though my father did not quite like me dancing with a Tory. Hattie and I were great belles in our showy book-muslin frocks, and natural flowers wreathed on our heads and waists.[5]

'The Grey daughters', confirmed an independent witness, 'were the belles of Northumberland.'

She became as renowned for her hard riding as she was for her beauty. In her teens she would spend the hunting season with her brother George on the home estate at Milfield. George allowed her to ride his fiercest hunters on condition that she keep neck and neck with him in the field – in those days a proviso hardly suited to a young lady. At least one strait-laced gentleman, from the Scottish side of the border, voiced his disapproval at her 'fast' behaviour when out hunting. When he was informed, however, that she was 'Grey of Dilston's daughter', he muttered, 'Ah well, the girl cannot help it. It's in her blood.'

At the age of seventeen, when her success in fashionable society was assured, she suffered a major religious crisis. As always with Josephine's confrontations with the Deity, it was of some months' duration although set off by a single event. She was alone, riding Apple Grey, her favourite horse, through Dipton Wood, a particularly dark and pathless wood near Dilston. Suddenly Apple Grey shied violently and refused to go a step further. Peering into the gloom, Josephine saw the body of a dead man hanging from a branch, and recognised it as that of the valet of a neighbouring gentleman, who had recently been dismissed. At first she was entirely preoccupied in reassuring her mount, but as she rode out of the shadows of the wood into the sunlight on the open hill-side, she found herself in a state of shock.[6]

All her life she had been acquainted with human suffering, for her father had made no attempt to conceal from her the truth regarding the many social causes he chose to espouse. For all his innate mistrust of Tories, he had embraced Lord Ashley's campaign for a Ten Hours Act, and Josephine, even in her earliest teens, was aware of what had come to be known as the 'Condition of England Question'. With her father she read the government 'Blue Books' – the reports on the conditions of work endured by children and young girls in the mills and the coalmines, some of the worst of which were to be found not far removed from the tranquillity of Dilston; she read the reports of Thomas Walkley, the West Middlesex coroner, exposing the abominable treatment of the destitute in Sir Edwin Chadwick's new union workhouses; she read Sir Edwin Chadwick's own report on the sanitary conditions obtaining in the urban slums. Other young women were sheltered from, or were expected to shrink from, such evidence of social distress and degradation. John Grey expected Josephine to appreciate it and evaluate it with compassion. As she rode with him from estate to estate she was introduced to the realities of agricultural poverty: the servile field-work engaged in by labouring women and girls, and their sexual exploitation by gentry and farmers; the fear of

eviction and the seemingly inevitable end in the union workhouse; the omnipresent fear of starvation which made the
repeal of the Corn Laws – at least in the opinion of John Grey –
as essential to the agricultural worker as to the factory operative.
And in contrast to all she heard, saw and read, was the security,
and even glamour, of her own life.

Her first personal encounter with death – for that was what
the Dipton Wood incident represented – came late in her life
compared with that of the average Victorian daughter. The
experience was disturbing, particularly since she related the
valet's suicide to social problems of which she was acutely aware
(it was popularly rumoured in the district that the man had been
dismissed for fathering a child on to a servant-girl). At the same
time she was passing through a phase of religious doubt. Tolerant,
broadminded and enlightened John and Hannah Grey certainly
were, but, certain of their own Christian faith, they never saw
the need to question their beliefs, and were therefore ill-equipped
to resolve Josephine's doubts. This she realised, and therefore
never expressed them. Nor was the local parson of any help:

Two miles from our house was the parish church, to which
we trudged dutifully every Sunday, and where an honest man
in the pulpit taught us loyally all that he probably knew himself about God, but whose words did not even touch the
fringe of my soul's deep discontent. It was my lot to be
haunted by the problems which more or less present themselves to every thoughtful mind. Year after year, this
haunting became more tyrannous.[7]

The effect of the hanged man in Dipton Wood was to bring
together into one single experience of mental agony her sense of
social guilt and her religious uncertainties.

Sin seemed to me the law of the world and fate its master. I
could not love God who appeared to my darkened and foolish
heart to consent to so much which seemed to me cruel and
unjust. I asked of the Lord one thing, that He would reveal to
me His one, His constant, attitude towards His lost world,
that as I showed Him my heart, He would show me His heart,
so much of it as the finite can receive from the Infinite.
Continuing to make this request through day and night,
through summer and winter, with patience and constancy,

the God who answers prayer had mercy on me; He did not deny me my request of His own heart's love for sinners, and when He makes this revelation He does more; He makes the enquiring soul a partaker of His own heart's love for the world.[8]

Since she confided in nobody, the mental isolation which preceded the consummation which she described above aggravated her suffering. In her autobiographical writings she only hinted as to what had happened: she never spoke to her children of this period of her life. A few weeks before her death in 1906 she described the experience fully for the first and only time. Writing to one of her oldest and dearest friends she said:

There were extensive pathless woods near the house. So great was the burden on my soul about the inequalities, injustice, and cruelties in the world, that I used to run into these woods where no one followed me; and kneeling on the ground, I used to *shriek* to God to come and deliver me! This is awfully true. My sisters thought me a little mad. Perhaps I was; but God turned the madness to a purpose He had.[9]

Objectively examined, her particular syndrome holds few surprises. She was an intelligent and sensitive girl passing through the normal tribulations of post-pubertial adolescence. But clearly the repression which she had imposed upon herself had caused her for a few terrible months to doubt her own sanity. She emerged from this nightmare by God's grace – or so she believed – triumphant, but it was a memory so fearful in its desolation that nothing save the need to evaluate her own life, which came with the sense of impending death, would drive her to relive it in memory. She never doubted the value of the experience. For the remainder of her life she was utterly convinced of the living presence of God, and of the efficacy of prayer. Prayer, indeed, came easily to her: she spoke to God unselfconsciously and informally, expecting Him to answer her, and on one occasion, reproaching Him for not having done so adequately. Above all she believed that she had been passed through the refiner's fire in order that she might be His chosen instrument, and that she had only to wait on His guidance to discover in what field she was to be instrumental.

Little of this showed in her outward behaviour. Unlike many

who believe that they have found their personal Saviour, Josephine never expected others to be burdened by her own religious devotion, and she never found such devotion to be a burden, but rather a constant source of happiness and good humour.

'A friend once wrote to me the prophetic words, "Be ready, for whenever one of God's people is called to climb up to a higher faith position than he ever attained before, Hell from beneath is moved to prevent it. Satan knows that it means a great blessing to many, and he summons up all his infernal force to prevent it." '10

Such had been her own experience, so she believed, and it was the measure of her greatness of soul that she could harbour such a belief without displaying either spiritual arrogance or priggishness.

In the autumn of 1851, Josephine took her last holiday with her family. She was twenty-two, and engaged to George Butler, a tutor at Durham University who was waiting to take up an appointment at Oxford as Examiner of Schools. The Greys went to London to combine the purchase of her trousseau with a visit to the Great Exhibition in Hyde Park. Most of the time, Josephine and Harriet were escorted round the sights by Charles Grey and his wife, a series of excursions which left Josephine, in retrospect, almost breathless with pleasure. Not only did they pay extensive visits to the Crystal Palace, but received an entrée into the private apartments at Buckingham Palace, and were graciously permitted to use the Royal Box at Covent Garden. Finally, Colonel Grey presented his adoring cousin with a new Broadwood grand piano bought at the Crystal Palace, as his wedding gift. She treasured it, and used it, for the rest of her life.

A few weeks later she was married to George Butler in the parish church of Corbridge where all her sisters had been married, and left Northumberland to make her home in Oxford. She returned only rarely, yet throughout a life spent away from her native north country in ceaseless work and travel, a love of the Cheviot Hills and the border marches remained with her. In a letter to her son, written in 1898, when she was seventy, she remarks on a holiday he had taken with his children:

Your description of those places has taken me into a long

dream of the past. I know every place and view by heart. I never went by the new railway [it was, in fact, forty years old] but many times we drove over that precise route from Morpeth or Alnwick to Wooler and Milfield. My father used to drive Hattie and me from Dilston to Milfield in a high small open gig. We used to stay a night at Cambo and reach Milfield the next night. I can see now, in memory, the view you describe, and the descent from the high ground to Wooler, in balmy summer evenings when the shadows were long and the bean-fields scented the air.[11]

## III

GEORGE BUTLER had just turned thirty. His father had been a distinguished headmaster of Harrow, a reforming headmaster whose work had anticipated that of Arnold of Rugby. He was now enjoying semi-retirement as Dean of Peterborough Cathedral – such was the attitude of the Established Church in the disposal of its higher offices.

At the age of eighteen, George Butler had followed family tradition by going up to Cambridge (the Butler family has consistently served and been served by the university, and Trinity in particular, over the last two centuries, and the doyen of the Butler family today is the present Master of Trinity). His stay at Trinity, however, hardly added to the family's *réclame*: according to his future wife, 'the sense of duty and responsibility for the use of opportunity and gifts which he possessed lay dormant within him'.[1]

According to himself he attained an excellency at shying stones which enabled him to hit and smash 'high and difficult chimney-pots with wonderful precision, to the annoyance of the owners of the chimney-pots'.

This attainment combined with an incorrigible laziness resulted in his being sent down after a year, though to the chagrin of his tutor he succeeded in taking with him a number of prizes which he won through an apparently effortless facility in writing Greek iambics. In recounting George's misdeeds, Josephine reported that her father-in-law 'often thanked God' that his errant son 'had escaped the contamination of certain influences which leave a stain on the character and sometimes tend to give a serious warp to the judgement of a man in regard to moral questions'. By which she meant, of course, that he had not yielded to the temptation of sexual indulgence which undergraduates, being for the most part wealthy and subject to few restrictions, found easy to gratify (as did George's contemporary, Charles Stewart Parnell) at the expense of the farm-girls of the region, then to justify it by appealing to the prevailing double standard in sexual morality which was to be Josephine's chief target of scorn during her active life.

Three aimless years later, George discovered that he had a natural bent towards academic study and sat for the Hertford Scholarship at Oxford, which he won with ease He later gained a double first, and remained up at Oxford to research for a higher degree, maintaining himself through private tuition. In 1848 he was appointed to a Readership at Durham University, and met Josephine shortly after.

His father was anxious that George, having proved himself, should be ordained into the ministry, but George, though by this time a devout Christian, was put off by the fact the ministry was the most direct route to academic preferment. With characteristic, if tortuous, honesty, he could not decide whether he had a real vocation to the priesthood, or whether acceptance of ordination would simply be pandering to his own very real ambition. His doubts were aggravated by the low opinion in which he held most of his father's colleagues:

'If ever I should take orders, I don't mean to be a mere parson: for if I were like some of them whom I know, I should cease to be a man.'

It was the sort of moral conflict with which Josephine, scarcely convalescent from her own spiritual trials, readily sympathised. Her own opinion, however, was formed by the positive and constructive nature of her character. George was a good man, an honest man and a believing Christian. The ministry would scarcely suffer from having such a man in its midst, and if the end result was that George became vice-Chancellor of Oxford or Cambridge so much the better. When, finally, he accepted orders (soon after their marriage), it was entirely the result of her persuasion, and thanks largely to the confidence he placed in her opinion, he never regretted having done so.

George and Josephine Butler were profoundly suited to one another, to an extent which almost defies belief. They were both in some sense 'beautiful people', enormously talented, good-looking and sharing a particular Christian vision which informed all they thought or did. They seem never to have doubted one another's love for an instant, and had a complete respect and reverence for one another's personality and purpose. They offered advice to each other frequently, criticism rarely. The strongest condemnation uttered by George concerning any of his wife's activities was a quiet, 'I rather think you were wrong', and then, wrote Josephine, she knew that she had been very wrong indeed.

By the time they had been married five years, George had recognised that Josephine was going to be the more active partner. His sole concern regarding what would have seemed a humiliating situation to most Victorian husbands was for her health, which had given her trouble since the occurrence of a lesion on her lung when she was eighteen, and was to continue to trouble her throughout her life. He wrote to her in 1856 – she was spending a few weeks with her father – immediately after reviewing Tennyson's 'Maud' for *Fraser's Magazine*:

Reading love stories which end in death or separation make me dwell the more thankfully on my own happiness. I think we are well suited to one another; no words can express what you are to me. I hope I may be able to cheer you in moments of gloom and despondency when the evils of this world press heavily upon you, and by means of possessing greater physical strength and considerable power of getting through work, I may be enabled to help you in the years to come to carry out plans which may, under God's blessing, do some good, and make men speak of us with respect when we are laid in our graves.[2]

In 1890, when she was trying to reconcile herself to the fact of George's death, Josephine wrote,

In the springtime of life, men dream, speak, write, and sing of love – of love's gracious birth and beautiful youth. But it is not in the springtime of life that love's deepest depths can be fathomed, its vastness measured, and its endurance tested.

There is a love which surmounts all trial and discipline, all the petty vexations and worries, as well as the sorrows and storms of life, and which flows on in an ever deepening current of tenderness, enhanced by memories of the past and hopes of the future – of the Eternal life toward which it is tending.

The truth of this, experientially discovered, did not prevent her recalling her early years with George at Oxford in a haze of nostalgic joy:

During those first two years we spent there, my father kindly provided me with a horse, a fine, well-bred, chestnut. My husband and I explored together all the rising ground round Oxford. Behind our own little garden there were tall trees where nightingales sang night and day for a few weeks in spring. But it was in Bagley Woods and in Abingdon Park that those academic birds put forth all their powers. We sometimes rode from five in the evening till the sun set and the dew fell, on grassy paths between thick undergrowths of woods such as nightingales love to haunt, and from which issued choruses of matchless song.

Josephine had yet to discover her mission in life. For the time being she was content to be wife, mother and George's academic assistant. George had launched out into a series of lectures in Geography, a discipline hitherto deemed fit only for junior classes in charity schools. The senior college lecturers were amused and somewhat scornful at the project, but were broadminded enough to sit in on, and afterwards to approve of, his lectures. Since the university totally lacked wall-maps – the only maps suited to a lecture hall were fifteenth-century *Mappae Mundi* – Josephine turned cartographer, reproducing accurate large-scale maps by copying and enlarging those in George's books. On one occasion, to her great delight and amusement, a senior lecturer in Biblical Studies who was watching her at work asked her to show him the location of Egypt.

In 1853, George persuaded the Vice-Chancellor to allow him to give a course of lectures in the Taylorian Institute on the Fine Arts – another field of study utterly strange to the university. As a result of these lectures he was invited to become art critic for the *Morning Chronicle*, which gave Josephine and him an excuse for paying regular visits to London art galleries. Once again Josephine was conscripted into helping her husband, this time by copying and enlarging drawings, and by sketching details from paintings. Because of this she received her first commission – to write in conjunction with her husband a bibliography, and to draw a full set of copies of Turner's drawings for the Taylorian Institute. **1618924**

Her success as a bibliographer resulted in her being invited to assist George in preparing an edition of Chaucer's works based on the fifteenth-century 'black-letter' manuscripts in the Bodleian Library. For this she had to study comparative palaeography, and thus she was admitted both to the Bodleian and to Exeter College Library. For the first time, the silent, vellum-smelling masculinity of Duke Humphrey's Library was desecrated by the rustle of starched petticoats.

At the same time, the Rev. F. D. Maurice, leader of the Christian Socialist movement, invited George to give a course of lectures on art to the London Workingmen's Association, where Dante Gabriel Rossetti was teaching in his usual enthusiastic if haphazard way. George and Josephine struck up an acquaintance with Rossetti, and occasionally visited him and the beautiful and tragic Guggums at his studio. Unlike Mrs Gaskell, another occasional visitor at this time, Josephine could not regard his private life and heavy flirtatiousness with amused detachment, but she became a devoted admirer of his work, at a time when such admiration was far from fashionable. Such was Rossetti's respect for her linguistic ability – and perhaps his anxiety to establish a relationship with a couple who might be expected to provide him with a little of the 'tin' of which he was usually in dire need – that he submitted to her the manuscript of his translations from Dante's *Vita Nuova* and Cavalcanti's sonnets for correction and criticism. He received both corrections and criticism from Josephine, who was flattered that he should have thought so highly of her gifts, but no 'tin'. Like Mrs Gaskell she thought him a fine painter and poet but 'hardly a Good Cause'.

Through Rossetti's Italian contacts, George was introduced to Aurelio Saffi, the friend and colleague of Garibaldi and Mazzini, and one of the leaders of the ill-fated Roman Republic, who was now living in exile in London. He invited Saffi to come and stay with them at Oxford, and to lecture on Dante to a select audience of senior members of the university assembled in the Butlers' drawing-room. Twenty-seven years later, Aurelio Saffi repaid them for their hospitality, inviting them to be his personal guests at the congress (over which he presided) held at Genoa to commemorate the establishment of the Kingdom of Italy. In fact, through her father, her husband and her beloved sister Harriet, who was married to a Swiss banker living in Naples, Josephine was establishing these contacts all over Western Europe, which were to prove so valuable to her in later years.

Her chief form of relaxation at this time, excluding riding, lay in music. Three of George's colleagues formed with her a string quartet which met every week. With rare discrimination they eschewed the more popular works of the day – Benedict, Spohr or Raff – and concentrated on the chamber music of Haydn, and Mozart, and even studied Beethoven's posthumous quartets, thus displaying either unusual musicianship or temerity.[3]

This pleasant and fruitful life at Oxford had, as Josephine put it, 'its shadow side'. Hitherto, it had scarcely occurred to her that there was a 'condition of women' question. Her father, like her husband, had shared with her his interests, his knowledge, his perplexities. Her own family respected not merely her intelligence but also her intellect, as did the Butler family. It came as something of a shock to her when she realised that permission for her to work in the Taylorian Institute and the Bodleian Library was a matter for controversy, and only grudgingly conceded. She was forced to appreciate the fact that her husband's colleagues were, for the most part, celibates who rarely stirred from the twin sanctuaries of study or senior common room.

'A one-sidedness of judgement', she remarked, 'is apt to be fostered by such circumstances, and a conventional mode of looking at things.'

This was brought home to her in conversation during the frequent dinner-parties and social gatherings she had both to preside over in her own house and to attend outside. While her husband's friends could hardly ignore her – she was far too attractive and lively a personality to be ignored – they addressed only small-talk in her direction, reserving more serious matters for George's sole attention. Her reserve, born of good manners, prevented her from intervening in a conversation from which she had been deliberately excluded. On one occasion, however, she found herself incapable of restraining herself. George was showing his guests a reproduction of a drawing by Raphael of a girl at prayer. Josephine remarked that the girl's face looked insipid. One of the guests replied that any woman's face when so engaged looked dull and stupid. Josephine, with deceptive sweetness, asked whether her face became dull and stupid when she was talking to her husband's friends – 'men of intelligence and exalted thought'. The guests assured her that she did not. Why then, she demanded, should they suppose that she looked stupid when she was speaking to 'the greatest intelligence of all'? The silence which greeted this riposte, she recorded, did not signify a point well taken, but astonishment that a young wife should display such audacity and impertinence. From thenceforward she showed more tact. But this, she sadly remarked, merely confirmed men's opinion that her mind was not capable of grasping the lofty speculations of her husband and his colleagues.

Less irritating, but no less embarrassing, were those occasions when she was involved in a *tête-à-tête* with some eminent academic whose experience of women was so slight that he became tongue-tied in her presence. One example of this extraordinary gaucherie she reported in a letter to her father.[4] She had been out on a picnic with some lady-friends in the woods which cover the pleasant uplands between Oxford and Abingdon, and the evening being agreeably cool, she decided to walk part of the way home. She set off ahead of her friends, who agreed to pick her up in their carriage when they caught up with her. She had walked a considerable distance, night was falling, and the carriage had failed to appear, when she realised that she was lost. She was feeling very tired when, with some relief, she found that she had reached the crossroads on the crest of Boars Hill where Ripon College now stands. Believing that sooner or later some kindly gentleman in a carriage or gig would pass by on the way to Oxford, she sat down, carefully spreading her crinoline about her, on the grass verge beside a dry ditch. At length, a solitary pedestrian loomed out of the dusk. It was the Master of Balliol, Dr Benjamin Jowett. Solemnly raising his hat to her, he sat down beside her with his feet dangling into the ditch, and did not utter a single word. Politeness forbade that a young lady still in her early twenties should initiate conversation with the greatest classical scholar of the age, but Dr Jowett was so clearly incapable of formulating an opening gambit that Josephine felt that for her to usurp the privilege would be an act of Christian charity. Just as she was about to utter some commonplace or other, Dr Jowett suddenly launched himself into a lecture on frogs, which continued without pause for question or reply until, half-an-hour later, the carriage containing Josephine's friends who had been looking for her, made its welcome appearance.

In this essentially anti-feminine environment, Josephine was drawn towards the course of her life's work by a series of events – a progression which is perhaps presented too neatly in her own writings, since she, needless to say, saw in each event the hand of God leading her forward to His purpose. The first of these took the form of an after-dinner discussion of Mrs Gaskell's novel, *Ruth*, then – in 1853 – newly published. The scandal which this explicitly Christian work aroused is scarcely credible today. The plot concerns a seventeen-year-old seamstress in a sweat shop who is seduced and deserted by a young gentleman of means. She is taken up and protected through the resultant pregnancy by a kindly nonconformist minister, his sister and their housekeeper, who pass her off as a young widow. Her secret is discovered by the priggish warden of the chapel, and both she and the minister are subjected to a moral crucifixion which bids fair to wrecking the lives of the heroine, her protectors and her young son.

George's colleagues found this theme totally immoral – their sympathies were clearly on the side of the chapel warden and the village gossips, and they resented the fact that Mrs Gaskell's sympathies were with her eponymous heroine. One young lecturer declared that he would not permit his own mother to read such a book.

'This led to expressions of judgement which seemed to me false – fatally false,' wrote Josephine. 'A moral lapse in a woman was spoken of as an immensely worse thing than in a

man, there was no comparison to be formed between them. A
pure woman, it was reiterated, should be absolutely ignorant of
a certain class of evils in the world, albeit those evils bore with
murderous cruelty on other women.'

For all her upbringing at the hands of her father she had been
strangely sheltered in one respect: it was her first real experience
of the operation of the 'double standard'.

The second of these events, which she saw as being decisive,
occurred when a travelling circus arrived in Oxford. Josephine
was introduced to a young girl – an acrobat – who, when the
circus-manager was not looking, 'went secretly to chapels and
churches'. The girl told her that her dearest wish was to quit the
life into which she had been sold, 'the most innocent part of
which was her acrobatic performances'. Josephine, in a moment
of unconsidered compassion, promised that she would do all she
could to help her. A few days later, the weather having been hot
and sultry, she was sitting at the open window of her drawing-
room enjoying the cool of the late evening, when she saw the
girl running between the trees beyond the garden, obviously
trying to make for the house. She disappeared into the shadows
of the gathering dusk, and Josephine heard a dreadful wailing
cry, the cry of a young girl 'aspiring to Heaven, and dragged
back to Hell'. She wanted to rush out to protect the girl, but
was restrained by George (as so often happened when she was
in one of her more impetuous moods), who pointed out the hard
truth that she would have the support neither of society nor the
law. Later she found out that the girl had indeed tried to escape
from the circus, to which she had been legally apprenticed, but
had been recaptured by the circus-manager's bullies. Josephine
wrote later that as a result of this incident she saw 'the great
wall of prejudice, built up on a foundation of lies, which surrounded a whole world of sorrows, griefs, injustices, and crimes
which must not be spoken of. And I met again the highly
educated, masculine, world in our evening gatherings more than
ever resolved to hold my peace – to speak little with men and
much with God.'

While it is certainly true that she spoke much with God, it is
unlikely that the ebullient Josephine really spoke little with
men. Her resolution was clearly shattered by the third of these
events.

She had learnt of a young mother who was imprisoned in Newgate for the murder of her illegitimate new-born baby. The putative father of the unhappy infant was an Oxford don – a Balliol man. Josephine stormed up Carfax and the Broad, and, banging peremptorily on the door of the Master's lodge, demanded an immediate interview with Dr Jowett. Having been ushered into his presence she expressed the hope 'that he would suggest some means, not of helping the girl, but of bringing to a sense of his crime the man who had wronged her'. Dr Jowett, who by this time had come to know and to like Josephine, replied kindly 'advocating silence and inaction'. Josephine, appalled and furious, retaliated by quoting Blake – whose paintings were known, but whose poetry was almost forgotten – at the astonished Master:

> *The harlot's curse from street to street*
> *Shall weave old England's winding sheet.*

He was, no doubt, somewhat shaken by the close juxtaposition of 'harlot' and 'street' proceeding from the lips of a lady. Writing to Florence Nightingale a few years later, he described Josephine in very friendly terms but added that 'she is very excitable and emotional, and of an over-sympathetic temperament'.[5]

Josephine's immediate reaction to Dr Jowett's gentle rebuff was an announcement to George that she was going to travel to Newgate to see the girl and to tell her that 'there was a God who saw the injustices which had been done to her, and who still loved her'. George was of the opinion that this would not be news to the girl, or, if it was, it would do little to comfort her. Instead he suggested a more effective line of action. He wrote to the chaplain of Newgate stating that he needed a general maid-servant, and would he send the girl to him on expiry of her sentence. Thus, a few months later, the girl was established in the Butler household, a living reproach to university opinion.

'Mrs Butler takes an interest in a class of sinners whom she had better have left to themselves,' commented Dr Jowett sourly.[6]

## IV

IN 1857, George Butler was invited to take up the post of Vice-Principal of Cheltenham College for boys. He accepted readily. He had been disappointed by his failure that year to be elected to the Chair in Latin at Oxford, a failure due almost certainly to the fact that he was married, and he was concerned about the effect of the notoriously damp Oxford climate on Josephine's lung. Josephine herself was enthusiastic at the idea of a change. Their house in St Giles was becoming too small for their growing family – there were the three boys, George, Stanley and Charles, and she was pregnant again with their youngest child, Eva. She was, moreover, delighted at the thought of leaving behind her the celibate narrow-mindedness of the senior members of the university. If she believed that Cheltenham would provide her with a more congenial ambience – her aristocratic upbringing had scarcely equipped her for life in a provincial middle-class milieu – she was sadly mistaken.

The American Civil War broke out in 1861, and in 1862 the abduction of the Confederate agents, Mason and Slidell, from a British passenger ship, the S.S. *Trent*, by sailors from a Federal cruiser, brought Britain to the verge of intervention on the side of the Confederacy. Feeling, particularly among the upper classes, who believed that the Southerners consisted largely of landed gentlefolk like themselves, ran high indeed. George, however, shared the view of the Manchester school of Radicals that the war was between slave-owners and abolitionists, and Josephine, indoctrinated by her father and his abolitionist friends, was passionately of the same opinion.

Since they were the only supporters of Lincoln and the Union in Cheltenham, they found themselves ostracised. They were held to be, recorded Josephine, 'persons of unsound judgement, if not of low and vulgar prejudices. We were compelled to give up visiting, finding ourselves out of sympathy with the persons we met daily, among whom we were scarcely welcome and by whom we were looked on askance, as audacious dissenters from the verdict of august authority, Society.'[1]

Goldwin Smith, one of George's erstwhile colleagues at Oxford, travelled down to Cheltenham to persuade him to write a book

refuting the doctrine newly revived by Confederate sympathisers that the institution of slavery was ordained under Scriptural
authority. In 1863, the book *Does the Bible Sanction Slavery?*
was published. Containing the prefatory statement, 'The
Bible has been quoted in favour of every abomination that ever
cursed the earth', it was a splendid polemic, but did nothing to
restore either George's or Josephine's popularity among their
neighbours.

It was against this background of social isolation that the
psychological blow struck them which Josephine in her more
Evangelical moments was to see as God's final demand upon her.
George and Josephine were making ready to pay an afternoon
call on one of their few remaining acquaintances, and Josephine
was in her room, dressing for the occasion, when Eva came
running in to show her a caterpillar which she had found in the
garden, and to demand a box to keep it in. It was a bad moment
for a child to disturb her mother at the best of times, and
peculiarly bad in the days of the imperial crinoline, which
Josephine had enthusiastically adopted. Understandably, she
was impatient with the child – 'Now trot away, Eva, for I am
late for tea.'

At seven o'clock that same evening, George and Josephine
returned home. As they came through the front door into the
hall, Eva rushed out of her bedroom and leaned over the landing
rail to call down to them. Suddenly, she slipped, lost her
balance and, screaming, plunged head-first on to the tiled
floor almost at her parents' feet. Forty years later Josephine
found the greatest difficulty in recounting the tragedy.[2]

'It was pitiful', she wrote, 'to see her helpless in her father's
arms, her little head drooping on his shoulder, and her beautiful
golden hair all stained with blood, falling over his arm.'

Forty productive years on, during which time she had served
mankind better than it had any right to expect, she could still
blurt out, 'Would to God that I had died that death for her!'

She bore herself bravely until after Eva's funeral, and then
she surrendered herself utterly to her grief. She recalled over and
over again incidents in the child's short life: how she had disliked lessons with her German governess, and how Josephine had
heard Fräulein Blumke saying, 'Arbeit, Eva, arbeit!' and Eva's
indignant reply, 'But I *am* arbeiting, Miss Blumke, as hard as I

can!' how she embarrassed her father with interminable presents of pink and white striped pincushions, pen-wipers, mats and kettle-holders – Josephine was to find them all, after George's death, locked up in his desk in the compartment where he kept confidential papers relating to his work; how, one evening, she had gone to kiss Eva goodnight, and Eva had said, 'Mummy, if I go to Heaven before you, when the door of Heaven opens to let you in, I will run so fast to meet you, and when you put your arms round me, all the angels will stand still to see us.' 'I never thought for a moment,' wrote Josephine, 'that she would go first. She was so perfectly truthful, candid, and pure.' And again and again she would return to the thought that her last words to Eva had been a rebuke. Once again she stood before her God, forging her faith in Him in the fire of her refusal to be reconciled:

Do the words 'accident' or 'chance' properly find a place in the vocabulary of those who have placed themselves and those dear to them in a special manner under the daily providential care of a loving God? [she asked]. Here there entered into the heart of our grief the intellectual difficulty, the moral perplexity and dismay which are not the least terrifying of the phantoms which haunt the 'Valley of the Shadow of Death' – that dark passage through which some toil only to emerge into a hopeless and final denial of the divine goodness, the complete bankruptcy of faith.

One evening she found George alone in his study, his face drawn and pale, his hands deathly cold. She knelt beside him and began to comfort him, and as she did so, she realised that he too was suffering and that she had contributed to his loss both by her refusal to be comforted and by her complete emotional withdrawal from him. After this she came to him every evening, after school hours, and sat beside his chair at the fire-side. Sometimes they sat in silence, Josephine resting her head in his lap while he stroked her hair, sometimes they talked of their dead child. Gradually, the bitterness of loss receded.

Scarcely had it done so when another misfortune confronted her. Her second son, Stanley, contracted diphtheria, and she nursed him by day, and George by night, for a critical week.

Throughout these misfortunes, it must be remembered that

the Butlers, because of their political views, were almost totally
without the support, or diversion, of friends. 'The feeling of
isolation was often painful,' wrote Josephine, with unaccustomed stoicism, 'but the discipline was useful.' Useful or not,
when Stanley had recovered, George decided that his wife had
experienced enough lonely misery, and packed her off to pay a
prolonged visit to Harriet, living in Naples.

She travelled overland to Genoa, where she was met by
Hattie, and the two of them took ship for Naples. Hattie described the journey in a letter to her niece:

Dearest Edith – I must try and tell you our sad adventures,
as you will be anxious. When you left us at Genoa I felt
nervous, but we went to bed. Josie awoke from a short sleep
with a feeling of oppression. The cabin walls felt like the man's
prison walls which contracted daily till they suffocated him.
She got up and lay down in the passage for air. I put a pillow
under her head, and ran up and got old Grumpy to give me a
bottle of champagne, a tumbler, and some vinegar. With the
latter I bathed her head. Old Grumpy was not such a bad
fellow after all. He routed out the maid and she brought us
some tea. The hot liquid removed the oppression on her heart
and she returned to her shelf again. I stayed awake to watch
her. The vessel stopped at Leghorn at seven next morning,
and we got up and came on deck. The air seemed to revive
her greatly, and she enjoyed the sight of the snow-line of the
Apennines far away inland.

We had breakfast, and then I wrapped her up in cloaks on
the deck, and she enjoyed the sunshine and fresh breeze. It
was fine until about noon; but when we got further out to sea
there was one warning heave which made my heart sink, and
I knew we were meeting the Sirocco. Josie was sitting very
quiet. After a while she said faintly, 'I feel ill'. I put my arm
around her and supported her to the saloon. . . . I saw the
captain outside, and thought it would be a good opportunity
to go and coax him for leave for her stay that night in the
saloon, where there was so much more air. He was very kind;
he said it was against the rules, but if I brought her up at
eleven o'clock, when other people had gone to bed, she might;
otherwise he would give her his own cabin, which was very

airy. While we were speaking together Johnny came up with a face of terror, and shouted, 'Mama, come to Aunt Josie.' I went, and found her in a convulsion. Her face was grey, and her hands rigid and blue like those of a corpse. Her eyes were quite closed. By-and-by she said, 'I think I am going. Dear George! Dear George!' Then she became rigid and unnatural, and her eyes which were wide open saw nothing. They gazed right through me, and through the ceiling far beyond, and she said, but not in her own voice, 'My little darling, she went so quick, so quick.' She looked as if she was going quick after her.

I said to the captain, 'Oh, could you not land us?' I saw she was not dead yet, and thought if we could land she would get round. The mountains were still in sight on the left hand. I said, 'Could you do it for £500? for £1000?' He said, 'No I cannot land you on a bare rock in the middle of the sea, and I cannot turn back, it is against the rules.' [It was a government mail-steamer.] I did not feel angry for he said it so kindly. He spoke as if he pitied us, and I thanked him, and felt that the time had come when there was no help in man. I thought of her dying and felt I could bear it, because she would so enjoy heaven; but I have fancied a quiet death, and have thought more of what comes after. It came upon me with horror to see that dear face, always so full of feeling and intelligence, petrified like that of the Greek priestess slain with terror at the sight of Medusa's head. That was the sort of look she had – splendid, but horrible – and quite unlike herself.

So the hours went on, the sea heaving, heaving more heavily every moment, the solitude among strange faces and foreign tongues, the impossibility of landing, the feeling that when she was dead she would still have to go on heaving for twenty-four hours in that gilded saloon. All the time I was kneeling and rubbing her hands and feet, trying to warm them; and while my imagination was realising all the terrors, my heart was praying desperately to God that He would make a way of escape. And He did!

I felt a hand on my shoulder. It was the captain. He said: 'I saw the other mail vessel coming north, and I have signalled her. You shall go on board and return to Leghorn. Make haste!'. . .

We were soon at the other steamer. Misery is stronger than sea-sickness, and I did not feel the tossing. I ran up to the saloon and found Josie lying on her mattress on the floor. She did not seem to be dead, but was locked in the convulsion still. The people were very courteous and delicate. They all went away, except the jolly stout captain of this vessel, and the delicate little maid with whom we had travelled back to Naples last October, and a middle-aged gentleman with a beautiful countenance, and his little, pale, wife. I learned they were Venetians. Venetians are such sweet people.

The captain and the little lady knelt one at each side, rubbing each an arm and a hand as hard as they could, and I her feet, the maid constantly renewing the hot blankets. We worked on for more than half an hour and at last, with trembling joy, I felt her feet less stiff, and watching her face I saw it unlock as if something melted. She was too weak to speak, but I saw she was coming round.

At last the vessel stopped. The jolly old captain was so fatherly; when Josie could listen he stroked her hand and cooed over her, and said 'Bisogna avere coraggio, my dear,' bringing out the two English words he knew triumphantly, as if they were a spell. I took the liberty of being Ludwig's connection to send for Pietro Capanna and told him to go to the Washington Hotel and order a large fire, and to bring a doctor to superintend moving her. After a while, we wrapped her in Pietro's greatcoat lined with yellow fox skins, and put blankets around her. The captain gave us his own boat to land us nearly opposite the hotel and so escape the Customs House. . . . Two of the sailors then carried her up, Queen's fashion on cushions. . . . They brought her quite up to her room, and we laid her on the bed, the doctor remaining awhile. Presently I was called out of her room by the re-arrival of the devoted Pietro, panting and puffing and too blown to speak, but producing in triumph out of a red silk bundle two gorgeously embroided night gowns, stockings, etc. with treble rows of stiff goffered frills. He had been to his home and rifled the wardrobe of Signora Pietro. The very simple minded way in which Italian men do these things saves one's feelings!

That night I thought when we were lying on our steady beds together how it would have been were we still in that heaving saloon, perhaps watching a dead face, with all George's sorrow on my heart, and having to tell Tell [Tell Meuricoffre – Harriet's husband] the dreadful news when he came aboard. The anguish felt so great that I felt almost ten years older that night, but, oh, so full of thankfulness.[3]

Whether Josephine was genuinely critically ill in the physical sense, or whether she was afflicted by an ephemeral nervous exhaustion exacerbated by seasickness and mid-nineteenth-century tight lacing, it is difficult to assess. Certainly both she and Hattie believed that she was dying – and Hattie, considerably less excitable than her elder sister, was not given to alarmist attitudes. Both of them regarded Josephine's restoration, if not to health, at least to convalescence as a near miracle, and Josephine, of course, saw it as a sign that once again God had preserved her for a purpose of His own. This sense of mission was profoundly influenced by Hattie. An enthusiastic supporter of the Italian Risorgimento, she had worked tirelessly as a nurse among Garibaldi's troops during the invasion of the Bourbon Kingdom of the Two Sicilies. Listening to Hattie's account of the sufferings of the troops lying wounded on the battlefields of the Mezzogiorno, Josephine was filled with the desire to emulate her sister's devotion.

'I became possessed with an irresistible desire to go forth and find some pain keener than my own, to meet with people more unhappy than myself, and to say (as now I knew I could) to afflicted people, "I understand: I too have suffered".'[4]

The opportunity came the following year.


V


GEORGE BUTLER was appointed Principal of Liverpool College in January 1866. It was a post which pleased him; the College was a new and thriving public school established to give the sons of the ever-increasingly prosperous merchant and professional classes of Liverpool the classical education becoming to gentlemen, and it afforded him the opportunity both to build on the reformist views which he had inherited from his father, and to expand the traditional public school syllabus well beyond the bounds fixed by Arnold of Rugby two decades previously. To Josephine, anything was preferable to Cheltenham and here was an environment that presented a challenge. In her strong sense of purpose and her contempt for the idle life of the wealthy, Josephine was undoubtedly influenced by her aunt, Margaretta Grey. Following her death in 1858, her private diaries passed into Josephine's possession. Among the expected trivia contained within them were her views on the age in which she lived, unusually shrewd and perceptive observations which she would clearly have liked to have published but for the fear that she was isolated in her opinions:

It appears to me that, with an increase of wealth unequally distributed, and a pressure of population, there has sprung up among us a spurious refinement, that cramps the energy and circumscribes the usefulness of women in the upper classes of society. A lady, to be such, must be a mere lady and nothing else. She must not work for profit, or engage in any occupation that money can command, lest she invade the rights of the working classes, who live by their labour. . . .

Women have almost universally a broken, desultory education, made up of details, of which the secondary and mechanical often have the precedence of the solid and intellectual. Those studies are left out or vaguely pursued that strengthen the faculties, and give vigour and perseverence to the thinking powers. . . . Life is too often divested of any real and important purpose. . . .

When at any time has society presented on the one hand so large an array of respectably educated people embarrassed for want of a proper calling, and on the other, so ponderous a multitude of untrained, neglected poor, who cannot without help rise out of their misery and degradation? What an obstruction to usefulness and all eminence of character is that of being too rich or too genteelly connected to work at anything! . . .

What I plead for is, that those who are led by a necessity of duty made up of choice, adaptation, and general circumstances, to desire a life of philanthropic usefulness, may have the means opened before them of adopting a profession, acquiring the skill, and following out the practice of the particular line of service for which they are fitted.[1]

It seemed that Providence had prepared the line of action that Josephine should take. Her cousin, Charles Birrell, a noted Evangelical reformer who was trying to organise effective Christian missions to union workhouses, was in Liverpool when she arrived, and he drew her attention to the vast workhouse at Brownlow Hill. Against the advice of friends, and her husband's colleagues, she decided to pay it a visit.

The Brownlow Hill Union was not demolished until 1931, and there are plenty of photographs, including an aerial photograph, extant, to testify to its sinister grimness. Tall, grey, soot-stained, multi-storied blocks, grouped into a complex of ruthlessly Benthamite symmetry, glowered over the working-class suburbs of the city, reminding their population to what sickness, trade-recession or the simple fact of old age, might drive them. Inside, the sexes were rigidly segregated, and families split up for ever, according to the rules laid down by the Poor Law Commissioners. Across passages, galleries and staircases, massive iron grills were embedded in the masonry in a seemingly arbitrary manner, to separate male paupers from female. On the female side lived five thousand women and girls. The majority lived in the huge gallery wards whose walls and ceilings were dank with the steam and impregnated with the stench from the laundries and bone-pulp cauldrons in the gallery beneath; food was inadequate and frequently disgusting; the aged, the utterly depraved, the incurably sick, and the incurably alcoholic, the utterly senile, and young children, were herded together, supervised by a staff whose paucity in number was dictated by the exigency of the Poor Law Board. Lying-in wards, and wards for the female insane, were separated from the main galleries by open archways; those who were incapacitated through age, sickness or madness were cared for by those of their companions who happened to be sober at any given time, and then only if the patient was in a position to bribe them with drink, or with the money by which drink could be procured. The noise was continual and appalling: the main wards were filled with the sounds of insane delirium and the cries of women in labour, doomed to an inevitable death from puerperal fever. Beneath the gallery wards was a labyrinthine bridewell where destitute prostitutes, reduced by crippling sickness, disfigurement and winter cold, sought shelter. Here the female refuse of a mid-Victorian city performed work which no other element of society would undertake in order to obtain the barest minimum of food, and the bleakest, most uninviting shelter. The work was of the sort usually to be found in prisons, and then confined to prisoners sentenced to hard labour: oakum-picking, by which tarred rope was picked to fragments to provide material for the caulking of wooden boats. Since the authorities refused to provide tools for such work, the women were forced to use their finger-nails.

When Josephine arrived at Brownlow Hill she insisted against the wishes of the workhouse keepers on visiting the oakum-picking sheds. She was taken to the bridewell, and shown to the door leading to the basement. Passing through alone she found herself at the top of a steep flight of stone steps. Below her was a vast cellar whose vaulted gloom was lit by half-a-dozen sooty gas-jets. There was no furniture of any kind, neither tables nor benches. Some two hundred girls were squatting on the bare flags of the floor, picking the yarn out of the tarred ropes with cracked and bleeding fingers, and singing, laughing and screeching in the foetid semi-darkness.

Screwing up her courage she descended into this inferno, sat down on the floor in the midst of the girls, and began to pick oakum with them. The girls stopped working to stare at her in sheer, silent amazement. She must have presented an extraordinary spectacle in such a place; in her mid-thirties she was at the prime of her physical beauty, and, as always, perfectly groomed, and dressed in the height of fashion. Then, as she fumbled with the rope, the girls burst into high-pitched ribald laughter.

'They told me my fingers were no use for that work, which was true. But while we laughed, we became friends.'[2]

She spent the entire afternoon in the cellar, talking to the girls. Just before she went she asked those of them who were literate to learn their favourite verses from the Bible in order to recite them to the others when she paid her next visit.

Contrary to middle-class opinion, such an evangelistic approach to a mob of girls of this sort was as fraught with danger as it would be today. A considerable number of the working poor were entirely ignorant of any form of religious belief; a survey among the children of labourers in the Birmingham area had come up with the result that most of them thought that 'Jesus Christ' was merely a swear-word.

Josephine knew no other way. When she returned a second time to the cellar and asked whether any of them had done as she asked she was greeted with a stony and hostile silence. Suddenly, a tall, dark, handsome girl, obviously originating from a better class than most of them, stood up and began to declaim the fourteenth chapter of St John's gospel, beginning with the words, 'Let not your hearts be troubled . . .' As she reached the passage, 'Peace I leave with you, my peace I give unto you: not as the world giveth, give I unto you,' the crowd of girls fell silent.

'They listened', wrote Josephine, 'in perfect silence, this audience – wretched, draggled, ignorant, criminal some, wild and defiant others.'

One or two girls were sobbing in the darkness. Josephine called out, 'Now let us all kneel, and cry to that same Jesus who spoke those words.' At first, one or two, then groups and finally the whole crowd, knelt down, and Josephine led them in the Lord's Prayer.[3]

From then on she was a regular visitor to the bridewell at Brownlow Hill. On one occasion (it was an incident which, typically, she never reported, but was remembered by one of the Brownlow Hill staff long afterwards)[4] she was told that a riot had broken out in the girls' punishment wing. A hundred or so of the inmates had defied the ward-staff and had thrown them out by force, and had then barricaded the doors. When Josephine appeared on the scene she found a number of the girls standing out on the window-ledges performing 'every kind of indecency' for the benefit of their besiegers. She announced her intention of going in by herself, and, despite warnings that the girls were quite capable of injuring or even killing her in view of the state of hysteria into which they had worked themselves, she walked up to the main door, and, calling some of the girls by name, induced them to let her in. As the door slammed behind her, the onlookers heard a deafening barrage of screams, whistling and obscenities from inside the wing. As the minutes passed, the uproar slowly subsided. Then, at last, there was complete silence. The doors opened, and Josephine emerged, beckoned to the staff 'to go in and resume their office' and returned, cool and unruffled, to her carriage.

Not all the girls she encountered at Brownlow Hill were prostitutes – in fact, Josephine was amazed by the number of girls reduced to the most pitiable condition who refused to sell their bodies, and she considered them to be moral heroines. Most of these were Irish Catholics who prided themselves on their virginity, if not their sobriety. They earned a precarious livelihood by selling sand for sanding floors, and refuse left at night in the markets to the poorest households, or by scraping up excrement from the courts and alleys of the slums. Barefoot, bonnet-less and without top-coats, they were driven by the winter cold into the workhouse; others had been committed to do 'a week or a month' by the local Justices for drunken brawling. A second category, more pitiable than the first, were the daughters of neglectful parents – drunken, brutal or both – and the issue of venereally-diseased unions. They were, wrote Josephine, 'humanly speaking, useless, not quite all there, poor, limp, fibreless, human weeds'.[5]

Her first attempts at material succour were offered to these. With the help of her sister, Emily, who had recently been left in prosperous widowhood, she acquired a house near her own, where these pathetic and innocent relics of social and individual neglect could await easeful death in warmth, comfort and security.

It was, however, among the dock-side whores – the Maggie Mays – she discovered her real vocation. She encouraged those she met at Brownlow Hill to take her at night to the quays, alleys and basement-areas of Merseyside. Here, plying their trade from gin-shop to gin-shop, or loitering in the shadows of the pierhead gates, transacting their business in doorways and alleys and backyards, were the girls Josephine had come to find; and their name was legion. No one could have supposed that they obtained pleasure by their trade, or that they had adopted such a way of life from choice; here was that variety of prostitution whose existence middle-class opinion was reluctant to admit. These were not the girls who had discovered that they could earn in one night on the street more than they could earn in six weeks at the loom. These were the derelicts who battened on their own kind, the penny-whores who would give themselves for a piece of bread when sober and a small gin when drunk. Drink indeed, wrote Josephine, was both the cause and effect of the way of life for most of them. It was 'the great, the hopeless obstacle which I found among them'.[6] Although by no means a teetotaller by conviction, her first action, before attempting rescue work, was to sign the Pledge at one of the lodges of the Grand Templars.

Already detesting the blinkered attitude of many of her contemporaries, she readily convinced herself that the girls she encountered were more sinned against than sinning, and this conviction of their essential innocence became, combined with her profound Christian convictions, the driving-power of her future activity. To think of them as evil, as irredeemably depraved, was, to her, quite impossible. She had no experience of the fashionable hetaira of Jermyn Street, St John's Wood and Maida Vale – the 'dévergondées en evidence' condemned by Mrs Lynn Linton in the pages of the *Saturday Review*. The prostitutes she knew were tired, hungry, ragged, dirty children, girls whose appearance, unlike that of the Thaises and Phrynes of Hyde Park, would never be emulated by the respectable young ladies of Bayswater, and whose gaiety was, she remarked with an unaccustomed edge of bitterness, 'scarcely clouded by the frequent deaths which came generally as a happy and not unexpected release'.[7]

She began, to the unconcealed disgust of the neighbours, to take home some of the more desperate cases she came across, lodging them in the spare room, and in a basement which she had furnished for the purpose. George Butler accepted the validity of his wife's vocation from the onset; in his own sphere, he too had defied others' prejudice by introducing the study of Classical Hebrew into Liverpool College for the benefit of the Jewish boys. In order to make it clear that this was not a method of ingratiating Christianity to them, he encouraged visits to the school by local Rabbis. With regard to Josephine's often disgustingly filthy and vermin-ridden protégées, according to Josephine, 'he made a point of meeting each girl at the door, and, giving her his arm, he led her gently upstairs as he would any lady-visitor, speaking courteously to her'.[8]

Josephine has left us accounts of only two of the many girls she took into her home,[9] and she wrote about them solely because they proved to her own satisfaction that God extended His Grace to such creatures as fully as to anybody else. The first of these was Marion, daughter of a well-to-do farmer in the Midlands. Four years previously, when she had been fifteen years of age, she had been seduced by an elderly gentleman, a senior member of the local squirearchy, who had persuaded her to run away from home to spend a holiday with him, and had then abandoned her without warning or money. Too frightened of her parents to return to her father's farm, she had drifted from place to place, and from male 'protector' to male 'protector', until she finally ended up in a Liverpool brothel. Within a few months of her arrival in the brothel she was discovered spitting blood by one of the clients, and was thrown out, penniless, on to the streets. Josephine found her in the bridewell cellars at Brownlow Hill, and was attracted to her because of the intensity of her gaze, 'a wildly-seeking look', probably a symptom of tuberculosis in its final stages. Josephine, as impulsive as ever, went straight to her, took her by the hand and said 'Will you come with me to my home and live with me? I had a daughter once.' When they reached the Butlers' house, George, as usual, came out into the hall to welcome the new guest. Recognising her physical condition, he picked her up bodily and carried her upstairs, where he laid her on the bed in the spare room, propping her head up with pillows so that she could see out of the window overlooking the College gardens.

Marion died three months later, and during those three months she spent her time reading and studying the New Testament. Not surprisingly, there was much in it she found difficult and incomprehensible, and when she came to passages she could not understand, she would say, 'I will ask Mr Butler about it this evening.' As a result, George found himself spending a part of every evening up in the spare room, discussing points of Scripture with her, and during the course of these sessions, he became more and more convinced that the girl, far from being hopelessly depraved, was a saint. A well-known preacher of the day was spending a weekend with the Butlers during the last few weeks of Marion's life, and in order to have his own impression of the girl confirmed, George asked his guest to go up and talk to her,

telling him that the girl was mortally sick, but telling him
nothing of her past misfortunes.

'When he joined us again', wrote Josephine, 'his face was
radiant, and he spoke of the help and privilege it was to himself
to have held communion during a short half-hour with a dying
saint, so young yet so near to God.'

The morning before she died, George went in to see her before
leaving for the College. Marion could hardly speak, but she
managed to whisper to him, 'God is with me, sir. I have perfect
peace.'

Josephine was filled with profound indignation. 'If she had
not been destroyed, what a brightness and blessing she might
have been in the world!' she wrote. She was far too committed a
Christian to feel that Marion had lost anything by dying – her
anger was directed against a society which could thus waste in
destructive judgement a life which might have illumined it. Of
the gentleman who had originally seduced Marion, she wrote,
'It might have been good for *that man* to have been forced to
step down from his high social position and to look upon her,
and to have known the abyss from which she had been drawn,
to the verge of which *he* had led her when she was a child of
fifteen.'

Before Marion's funeral, Josephine filled her coffin with
white camellias – the symbol of essential purity – and banked
them around the girl's body. They represented an enormous
expense in early March, with snow still on the ground, but
to Josephine it was a gesture of defiance, a declaration of
war.

In some ways it was the second of the two young prostitutes
whom Josephine cited who is the more interesting. This one was
barely seventeen when Josephine took her directly off the
streets, and she was completely without even the rudiments of
education, coarse, foul-mouthed and utterly brutalised. To both
Josephine and George she presented an almost insoluble problem. Like Marion, she was in the final stages of a wasting
disease. She had not the remotest knowledge, let alone any
conviction, of religious belief; she was also stupid, with the
stupidity of the mentally and physically deprived, embittered
and cynical. Both Josephine and George were anxious to offer
the girl the consolations of religion, yet neither of them were of

the type who would wish to frighten or bully her into a superstitious religiosity. They confined themselves to trying to comfort her through her last days, and to persuade her that a happier, if unspecified, world awaited her. In her last extremity, the girl sat up in bed and shouted out, 'I will fight for my soul through hosts and hosts and hosts!' Josephine knelt beside her bed and tried to tell her 'that she would find Someone waiting for her who had fought through all those hosts for her . . . I cannot explain what she meant. I have never been quite able to understand it; but her words dwelt with us.'

Josephine's reputation spread among the 'unfortunate' girls of Liverpool. Many of them came to the Butlers' house for help, and she had no further need to scour the alleys for them. The necessity for founding some form of institution was almost forced upon her. By exploiting her rank and influence, and through sheer importunity, she persuaded groups of Liverpool merchants to subscribe generously to the purchase of a 'very large and solid house with some ground around it' to serve as a home and refuge, the first of a number she purchased during the course of her future life for such purposes. She appointed a matron to run it, under strict instruction that she should be a mother to the girls rather than an overseer. The work differed little in kind from that done in the Good Shepherd convent by would-be 'reformed' prostitutes, laundry-work and sewing of the simplest type, but Josephine impressed on her girls that, by so working, they were contributing to the cost of their residence, and permitted them to see the fruit of their labour in the form of additional comforts, which in fact, since the house ran at a heavy loss, came out of her own pocket. Primitive though her ideas might appear, they were a far cry from the hodden-grey uniforms and austere boredom of church establishments with their penance-stools and bread-and-water diets. She sought, also, to train her girls in work somewhat more skilled than menial household drudgery, and to this end began a small envelope-making factory, which certainly pleased the girls, though it is doubtful whether it ever achieved even a limited commercial success.

For the two existing refuges in Liverpool, the Good Shepherd convent, and a Church of England penitentiary, her scorn was absolute. In both establishments the attitude prevailed that the inmates were entirely to blame for their degradation and should, therefore, be purged of their guilt for their souls' sake by hard, humourless discipline. It was a view entirely rejected by Josephine:

'I believe there are many who have the love of souls in their hearts, who yet fail to win the lost for want of *humanness* – of human love. Now look at Jesus. He never talked about love of *souls*, and never judged people as a class. He always took the man, the woman, or the child as a person. Jesus respected that sacred thing, Individuality. The making of prostitutes into a class has ruined all rescue work.'[10]

## VI

IN 1866, Anne Jemima Clough returned to her native Liverpool in order to campaign in the northern cities for the further education of women, and, in the following year, she introduced herself to the Butlers, hoping to recruit the distinguished Principal of Liverpool College to her cause. To her astonishment, for she had enjoyed little success in Liverpool up till then, both George and Josephine embraced her views almost as soon as she had given them expression. Josephine in particular appeared to sense an affinity between Anne Clough and herself and a shared personal experience.

Like Josephine, Anne Clough believed that she was drawn to her work because of a decisive event which she interpreted as a call from the Deity. On the death of her father in 1844, she and her mother had moved to Ambleside in the Lake District where, largely from necessity, she had opened a school which she ran successfully for several years. This aroused her interest in the education of girls, but, on her return to London, her entirely unjustified belief that she lacked intelligence, a result of over-exposure to the influence and example of her brother, the poet, Arthur Hugh Clough, and her own brilliant friends in the Langham Place circle, inhibited her from engaging in any serious activity in the educational field:

'I am not clever like many,' she recorded in her diary in 1847. 'I have not the power of taking things in in a moment, but I will try, at least, to be less shy and heavy.'[1]

This sense of inferiority pursued her until 1861. In that year her brother died. As in the case of Josephine on the death of Eva, Anne believed her life to be utterly blighted, such had been her devotion to Arthur Hugh, and then, as the sense of bereavement became less bitter, she saw in her loss a token from God calling her to active work.

She joined with Emily Davies, who had been a member of the Langham Place circle and editor of the *English Woman's Journal*, and was now editor of the more influential *Victoria Magazine*, in fighting to extend the Cambridge Local Examinations, to include girls as well as boys, a campaign which achieved success in 1865. She deposed to the Schools Inquiry Commission set up by Robert Lowe that there should be established central schools in all large towns, 'staffed with competent teachers, and equipped with good libraries, lecture halls and playgrounds, to which batches of girls from the various schools in the district should be sent periodically for special instruction'. She also suggested that 'university men should lecture to the teachers and senior girls in the central schools on English Language and Literature, History, Science, and Art, thus linking the schools with the universities'.[2] These views she repeated in an article published by *Macmillan's Magazine*, whose editor, Professor Masson of Edinburgh University, endorsed them in one of his own articles.

It was the publication of these views in *Macmillan's Magazine* which marked the break between Emily Davies and Anne Clough. By founding a house which she hoped would become the first intra-mural ladies' college at Cambridge, Emily Davies was attempting to force an entrance into the university world. Anne preferred the more cautious approach of founding local associations of teachers and senior girls, and inveigling university lecturers into taking part in these associations. It was ironic, in the light of the bitterness which the conflict between Emily Davies and Anne Clough aroused, that both methods achieved success almost simultaneously; Emily Davies's house was established as Girton College at much the same time as Anne Clough's University Extension Scheme resolved into the foundation of Newnham College.

It was with the intention of founding one of her local associations that Anne sought the assistance of George Butler. George recommended that a Northern Schoolmistresses' Association should be propagated by means of a series of inaugural meetings and lectures to be held in Liverpool, Manchester, Leeds and Sheffield. He undertook to deliver a preliminary address at each meeting if Anne would provide a university lecturer who was prepared to speak to an audience of women on some branch of higher learning. To this end, Anne wrote to her chief ally in Cambridge, Henry Sidgwick, a Fellow of George's old college, Trinity. The result was the arrival in the Butlers' home of James Stuart, the youngest Fellow at Cambridge, who was to become one of Josephine's most devoted and loyal friends, and, as Professor Stuart, her most influential advocate in academic circles.

James Stuart, as a young graduate, had fallen under the influence of F. D. Maurice and Frederic Myers, both of whom knew Josephine: F. D. Maurice from her Oxford days when George had lectured on Art to the London Workingmen's Association, and Frederick Myers from his days as a schoolboy at Cheltenham when, or so he believed, he owed to Josephine 'my very soul'.[3] Through them, Stuart had become involved, somewhat belatedly in the history of that movement, in Christian Socialism. Following the example of Maurice in his London Workingmen's Association, and with the idea of building on it, he devised a plan for what he described as a 'peripatetic university' which should open the opportunities for academic learning to the working classes.

The question which initially engaged the minds of Anne Clough, the Butlers and James Stuart, as they planned their lecture scheme, concerned the subject matter of the lectures, and the way they should be presented. They were determined to excite as little opposition as possible, a clear indication that Anne Clough and George were the prime movers, rather than Josephine. Josephine, indeed, was too deeply involved in her rescue work at this time to become involved in what was for her an entirely new field of activity. The subject, it was decided, should be astronomy, over which there could be little controversy regarding its suitability for ladies. It was thought best that at each lecture Stuart should be introduced by a man, and that a male speaker should propose the vote of thanks at the conclusion of each lecture, despite the fact that the entire audience would be comprised of women. There was also some doubt as to the propriety of allowing members of an audience, many of whom would be young unmarried girls, to put questions to a speaker who was an eligible young bachelor. Stuart records in his *Reminiscences*, published five years after Josephine's death, that he considered it essential for the success of the scheme as a whole that he should evoke some active response from the audience:

'I solved the difficulty by bringing to the first lecture three or four questions in print, which I distributed with the statement that if answers were sent to me by post, two clear days before the next lecture, I would then return them corrected.'[4]

This idea was more significant than at first appears, for, by soliciting essay-answers to questions arising from his talks, James Stuart was effectively inaugurating an extra-mural university extension scheme. And if it seemed that the organisers of the first series of lectures were over-eager to avoid stirring up controversy, the introductory addresses by George Butler destroyed such an illusion. At Leeds, where he delivered the one speech which Josephine thought worth preserving, he spoke uncompromisingly to the point:

A community of women, established purposely to educate girls and to train teachers, was not known to Christendom till the institution of the Ursulines by Angela da Brescia in 1537. So unheard of at this time was any attempt of women to organise a systematic education for their own sex, that when Françoise de Saintonge undertook to found such a school in Dijon she was hooted in the street, and her father called together four doctors, learned in the law, 'pour s'assurer qu'instruire des femmes n'était pas un œuvre du démon'. Even after he had given his consent, he was afraid to countenance his daughter, and Françoise, unprotected and unaided, began her first school in a garret. Twelve years later, she was carried in triumph through the streets, with bells ringing, and flowers strewn in her path, because she had succeeded. So take courage, ladies. You must fight your own battles still. At all times, reforms in the social position of women have been brought about by efforts of their own, for their own sex, supplemented by men, but always coming in the first instance from themselves.[5]

The lectures were extremely well attended, and when Josephine, who was speaking in public for the first time, hinted at the possibility of establishing a lecture-scheme on a permanent basis, she found herself the recipient of a vast quantity of mail, much of which consisted of requests that she should intercede with the organisers of the lecture series in order that they might perpetuate the scheme. This was what Anne Clough had hoped would happen. In order to fulfil a need spontaneously expressed by upper- and middle-class ladies in the northern cities – or so it seemed – a North of England Council for Promoting the Higher Education of Women was founded. Anne became its secretary, and Josephine, since her speech had stimulated the demand, its president. In case the suspicions of anti-feminists should be aroused, the function of the Council was given out to be the establishment of lecture courses on subjects which would be suited to, and would edify, gentlewomen. A list of the names of the founder-members of the Council suggested a different purpose. It included James Bryce and Thomas Markby – both Cambridge examiners (Markby was secretary to the Cambridge Local Examinations Syndicate) – and, perhaps most significant of all, Miss Wolstenholme, the reformist secretary and founder-member of the Northern Schoolmistresses Association.

Within a year the North of England Council had extended the lecture courses into what was to be named in 1870 the University Extension Scheme. The selection of subjects for the curriculum was largely the work of Trinity College, Cambridge, in the persons of Henry Sidgwick and James Stuart. It consisted of English Literature and Language, History, Arithmetic and Algebra and Political Economy, the latter being deemed suited to women as a result of Harriet Martineau's influential if ill-judged popular manuals advocating laissez-faire economics. A Memorial was drafted on behalf of the North of England Council, addressed to the Council of Senate at Cambridge, praying that women over the age of eighteen be admitted to the Higher Local Examinations.

This Memorial clearly marks Josephine's wholehearted participation in the campaign, for it is couched in the high Butlerian style which she always adopted when she believed History to be peering over her shoulder. It was just as well, since her somewhat high-flown phraseology impressed the members of the Senate

Council, coming as it did from the pen of a woman. They were particularly taken by the passage in which she begged that there should be 'such examinations as shall adequately test and attest the higher education of women'.[6] A number of them went out of their way to compliment her on it.

Josephine, in her capacity as president of the North of England Council, travelled to Cambridge to present it to the Senate, and in order to consult in person Henry Sidgwick, and to renew her acquaintance with Frederic Myers, who had dedicated his popular epic poem, 'St Paul', to her. Her impact on the university was considerable. She engaged in deliberate lobbying on behalf of her Memorial, meeting and attempting to proselytise every member of Senate to whom she could obtain an introduction, and, as always when she exerted her charm, to great effect. The experience taught Josephine an unwavering confidence in the impact of her own personality: from then on she exploited the personal encounter as the chief weapon in her armoury.[7]

Despite a few half-hearted objections to the idea of extending the Higher Local Examination to women ('the study of Mathematics would be seriously injurious to their minds'), such was the success of Josephine's exhaustive, and exhausting, lobbying that the Memorial was accepted, and the examination opened to women the following academic year.

From Cambridge, Josephine travelled to London to meet Jessie Boucherett, who had been campaigning during the last ten years for the wider employment of women – unmarried women in particular. During the long conversations she had had with Miss Boucherett, Josephine formulated the theories on women's education which she expressed in the pamphlet *Education and the Employment of Women*, written within a few days of her London visit:

'At the bottom of the whole question of the employment of women we should always come upon their inefficiency through want of education. Until we can get technical training for women equal to the apprenticeship that boys get, we shall be defeated. The women's want of training is so generally called "*incapacity*".'[8]

Jessie Boucherett introduced Josephine to Emily Davies, who had carefully avoided encountering Josephine in Cambridge. She regarded Josephine as an agent of renegades, whose work in Cambridge had set back by years her own endeavour to obtain absolute educational equality between men and women. Even had she made some attempt to disguise her hostility towards Josephine – and she did not – the two women were temperamentally opposed to one another. Josephine's strength of will was concealed beneath an overlay of gentleness and feminine charm quite alien to Emily Davies's somewhat masculine brusqueness of manner. 'These masculine-aiming women *will* fail, but I dread their failure because it clogs the wheels and blocks up the path of us who are driving towards a different and higher goal. I pray for Miss Davies constantly, and for all like her, that a wise heart may be granted them in time, and that God may gently turn them back from error. I believe it is difficult for men to think gently of *women* like Miss Davies.'[9] Josephine was not a feminist except in the broadest sense; she never demonstrated much interest in the legal rights of married women, and absolutely no interest whatever in the question of female suffrage (her only contribution to that debate being the remark made in the last year of her life, 'Fancy me not having a vote!') Her sole preoccupation was her own somewhat limited view of simple social justice. The meeting was not a happy one.

From London, Josephine went on to Oxford in the hope of winning support from her many old friends and acquaintances there for the North of England Council. It was a sad, disillusioning occasion. Her husband's old colleagues had not broadened their attitudes over the ten years since she had been away. They knew her too well, regarded her with affection as something of a pet and considered her reformist zeal as an endearing eccentricity not to be taken over-seriously. Also, she was tired, and believed, as she tended to believe after a period of severe exertion, that she was on the verge of physical collapse – a form of hypochondria endemic among more active Victorian ladies.

She was relieved and glad to return to Liverpool, but there was no escaping the desperate sense of gloom which threatened to engulf her. She had never managed entirely to shake off the misery caused by the loss of Eva, nor, it must be admitted, had she made much effort to do so; but added to this there was the death of her much-loved niece, Hattie's daughter, so much like

Eva in appearance and personality. And then, in January 1868, her father died.

John Grey of Dilston was eighty-three years of age, but he had continued to be an active, even radical, reformer to his last day. Only a month before his death, he had been accused by the Agricultural Commissioners of providing his own tenants with cottages of such a size that the rent to be paid on them and the cost of heating them must have been a serious burden on their limited resources. He had been forced to admit that such tenants paid no rent on their actual dwelling-places, and that he subsidised the coal they received, believing, as he did, that no family could live decently without at least three rooms at their disposal.

In an era when land-holding gentry were not conspicuous for their consideration of their tenantry, John Grey stood as a model of humanity and virtue. Years later, when his daughter was actively campaigning in Yorkshire, far from the family estates, she had only to say that she was Grey of Dilston's daughter to win a respectful and sympathetic hearing from agricultural workers.[10]

Josephine and her children had been frequent visitors to Dilston, and her father when he was well on in his seventies and even when he was eighty had travelled extensively on the Continent, particularly in the Jura and Switzerland, taking with him his grandchildren, whom he adored and who adored him. Josephine had always been very dear to him, and he had recognised how emotionally vulnerable she was, and how much she needed not only affection, but also tokens of that affection. The same month in which he died, learning that she was not in good health, he made arrangements to provide her with what he knew, from past experience, to be a sovereign remedy for the sort of ailments which afflicted her: a particularly fine and well-bred mare by the name of Sylph. It arrived in Liverpool a fortnight after his death, a reminder to Josephine of how much its donor had meant to her.

Once more Josephine threw herself into her rescue work. She procured 'an old shabby large open carriage' capable of holding herself and half-a-dozen of her ailing girls, and, taking advantage of the warm sunny days which sometimes come in early March as a presage of spring, packed them in, 'covering them all over with rugs and cushions',[11] and drove out with them into the country on a number of occasions. Then one of them, a girl to whom she had felt more than ordinarily attached, died of tuberculosis.

> After midnight, I awoke with the feeling that one of the souls under our care was passing away. I got up and prayed for some time. The matron told me that Fanny herself had prayed then for two and a half hours. She said to her that she would wear herself out with it. Poor Fanny whispered, 'I am weaving a crown for Mrs Butler. Tell her, when I get to heaven I will be so busy. I will ask for a place to be got ready for Mr and Mrs Butler.'[12]

There can be little doubt that in our own day Josephine would be considered quite unsuited by temperament to be a social worker. She allowed herself to become far too deeply involved emotionally with the subjects of her casework. Following the death of Fanny she was on the verge of complete breakdown. The memory of Eva seemed to possess her beyond hope of solace.

But it was hypochondria which was her darkest foe. To Albert Rutson she wrote:

> I cannot get rid of the phantoms of sin and sorrow, and false and wicked customs which haunt the mind. My sufferings are very great at times: so great that I cannot wish much to live, though surely God has given me more to live for than many people have . . . Please never mention to me consulting doctors. . . . Every doctor has told me that God is my only Physician (which I knew) and that my ailments were so complicated with the spiritual and intellectual being that it would be an impertinence in them to think they could manage me.[13]

As a last resort she consulted Elizabeth Garrett:

> I must say of her that I gained more from her than from any other doctor . . . *because* I was able to *tell* her so much more than I ever could or would tell to any *man*. . . . O, if only men knew what women have to endure, and how every good woman has prayed for the coming of a change in this. How would any modest *man* endure to put himself in the

hands of a woman medically as women have to put themselves into the hands of men? and are women less modest than men? God forbid. They are *not*, and believe me, the best and purest feelings of women have been torn and harrowed and shamefully wounded for centuries, just to please a wicked *custom*, while those women who are not intrinsically noble and good, are debased, insensibly, by such custom.[14]

So far was Josephine a child of her age. The difficulty, impossibility in some cases, for a genteel woman to confide in her medical adviser such matters as her menstrual periods, frequency of bowel-movements, must have resulted in a plethora of false diagnoses and aimless prescription of opium derivatives – and Josephine was a deal more broadminded than the majority of her middle-class sisters. We may see here, at the same time, the origin of that almost physical revulsion she was to feel towards the Contagious Diseases Acts: the thought of army surgeons probing with surgical instruments into the deepest recesses of a woman's privacy was intolerable.

Her enthusiasm for Elizabeth Garrett either as a person or a doctor was of short duration; three years later they were locked in a bitter, and very public, quarrel, over the desirability of the Contagious Diseases Acts. As Miss Garrett's most recent biographer has stated, a woman of her type and character was incapable of believing that a girl would submit to the sort of medical inspection laid down by the Acts against her will.

It was not Elizabeth Garrett who cured Josephine on this occasion, however relieved Josephine may have been at being able to talk openly about her more feminine ailments, but a Mr F. Harrison who wrote to her attacking her views on the education of women:

> I have this morning the most *terrible* letter from F. Harrison. Please excuse the word, reading it really made me tremble all over. . . . He says *no* occupations should be opened to women, not even light trades, they ought *never* to work, nor have the means of working. I am glad rather to have such an open avowal from a Comtist of social immorality, of cruelty and unmanliness. You must not mind if he tells you I have written him a rude letter, for I must tell him the truth. I cannot pass by such Satanic theories; and if he hates me for speaking out,

it does not the least matter. I do not *wish* to be his friend. I believe [his views] to be the fruit of the rejection of Christ.[15]

To Mr Harrison, of course, she did not write a rude letter, but a courteous and careful presentation of her views.

ᴸ There are more than two million and a half of unmarried women in England, *working* for their own bread. It is not their *choice* for the most part. They would marry, but they cannot; there are many more women than men in the country. Men do not marry invariably, and women cannot ask them or force them to marry them. According to your theory of shutting them out of trades, and not suffering them to work at all for subsistence, you have two millions and a half of women for whom there is no alternative but starvation or prostitution. Thousands are now actually starving: I do not mean of the *lower* classes, but of the middle class. Thousands are driven to prostitution, a profession which theories such as yours do more to encourage than any amount of actual profligacy. Here in Liverpool there are 9000 who follow this profession, because there is *none other* open to them.[16]

She had been commissioned by Macmillan's to edit and to introduce a symposium entitled *Woman's Work and Woman's Culture*, a commission she had been neglecting because of the state of her health. Spurred on by her indignation at Mr Harrison's views and those of men like him, she forgot that she was supposed to be at the point of death, and furiously elaborated on the letter she had written to him. In her introduction, which became the most widely read and well-considered section of the book, she states her sincerely held belief that the place of women is in the home, but points out that the proportion of married women to unmarried is only three to two, and that society provides no outlet for the gifts and energies of the latter, many of whom could be of inestimable value to society were they properly educated. As it is, they represent total waste. She suggests that many social evils of the day are the result of rapid advance in industry, discovery and science, linked to old-fashioned concepts regarding social conventions and ideals. Because of this dichotomy between modern realities and attitudes, women are prevented from obtaining adequate training for skilled employment. It is a handicap which strikes hardest at the daughters of the artisan and labouring classes, and it is these who, suffering from chronic economic insecurity, form the vast majority of recruits for the armies of prostitutes infesting the great cities. Josephine proposes that the problem of prostitution must be dealt with in its origins as well as in its unfortunate effects. The prevailing attitude, that such females should be regarded as a nuisance inevitable in the modern city, against which decent people should be protected, is both unchristian and unscientific. Any theory which fails to take into account the individuality within such dense masses of the female sex is to be utterly condemned. Yet here is a problem – the root causes of urban prostitution – which no individual, public body or government department has attempted to face up to.

'The timid among us are glad to be able to forget the existence of this great shame in our midst; and there is no one fact of life which they more easily succeed in forgetting.'[17]

She states that she is as eager for the salvation of prostitutes as anybody else engaged in rescue work: 'But by salvation I mean something more than penitentiaries, or sanitary measures for the protection of the Army, Navy, and those to whom it is a present advantage to be able to sin with impunity.'[18]

This was the first time she had commented openly on the Contagious Diseases Acts, and it was no more than a single sentence in a long, closely argued article. But as the circulation of *Woman's Work and Woman's Culture* widened, it was duly noted by opponents of the Acts anxious to win new and influential members for their hitherto small and obscure circle.

# 2. The Battleground

THE extent of the problem confronting Josephine, or any woman of the mid-nineteenth century who undertook the rescue and permanent reclamation of prostitutes, can only be assessed within the context of the institution of the latter's way of life as it then existed and the prevailing attitude towards it. A number of prostitutes of the 1850s and 1860s spoke with the authentic voice of the whore down the ages:

> I was very fond of dress, and I could not at home gratify my love of display. My parents were stupid, easy-going old people, and extremely uninteresting to me. All these causes combined induced me to encourage the addresses of a young gentleman of property in the neighbourhood, and without much demur I yielded to his desires. We then went to London, and I have since that time lived with three different men. We got tired of one another in six months, and I was as eager to leave him as he was to get rid of me, so we mutually accommodated one another by separating. Well, my father and mother don't exactly know where I am or what I am doing, although if they had any penetration they might very well guess. Oh yes! they know I am alive, for I keep them very pleasantly aware of my existence by occasionally sending them money. What do I think will become of me? What an absurd question. I could marry tomorrow, if I wished.[1]

Mayhew's interviewee, quoted above, manifests the characteristics of many, perhaps most, of the mid-twentieth century women of the streets. She did not embrace the life of the prostitute by taking a single determining and considered step, but drifted into it through 'an increasing irrelation to society' – a period of floating promiscuity which a modern social psychologist has suggested to be the normal gateway to a life of prostitution. Like the modern whore, she protects herself from any suspicion of her own social inadequacy by resorting to a code of non-values expressed in a series of cliché-worn value-judgements. Her parents – 'stupid and easy-going', yet at the same time strict and repressive – represent the essentially dishonest world. The prostitute sees herself as the only realist in a world deluded by moral hypocrisy.

The *majority* of mid-nineteenth century prostitutes could hardly be described as drop-outs from society since they had never been fortunate enough to have been dropped into society. The difference in role can be judged from the difference in street-cry. The modern prostitute, driven by the Street Offences Act (1959) into her doorway, calls to the passing male, 'Feeling lonely, sweetheart?' or some other phrase indicating that, for a small consideration, she is prepared to confer a favour on him. Her predecessor of the 1860s invariably called out, 'Feeling good-natured, Charlie?' – the wheedling cry of the beggar. Nor did the prostitute of the 1860s experience an irrelation to society, since, in the expanding urban areas, she was but one member of a vast floating community which appeared to centre on the institution which she represented. Thus an article published in *Household Words* in 1857 describes that region embracing Piccadilly, Regent Street and the Haymarket:

> It is always an offensive place to pass, even in the daytime: but at night it is absolutely hideous, with its sparring snobs, and flashing satins and sporting gents, and painted cheeks, and brandy sparkling eyes, and bad tobacco, and hoarse horse laughs, and loud indecency. . . . I have never witnessed such open ruffianism and wretched profligacy as rings along those Piccadilly flagstones any time after the gas is lighted.[2]

On the pavements of Regent Street, girls huddled under the gas-jets, dressed in ill-fitting and often dirty satin crinolines hired from night-houses or cheap dress-shops, their faces yellow with 'slap', their eyes blackened with kohl and in such dense numbers that innocent pedestrians had to walk out into the roadway not so much to avoid their solicitation but rather to make their way through them. In the Strand, reported 'Walter', the odious author of *My Secret Life*, prostitutes could be seen squatting on the edge of the pavement, inadequately masked from public view by groups of their colleagues. 'I have seen them pissing almost in rows, while their pissing in the by-streets was nearly continuous.'[3] They retired in droves to the parks and gardens for which London squares are justly famous, and there, in those places 'on which dead leaves and sweepings are shot down',[4] they would evacuate their bowels in full view of the residents – thus providing one of the reasons for the fencing in of such gardens.

'All the houses except one or two', wrote Taine after visiting Shadwell, 'are evidently inhabited by harlots. Every hundred steps one jostles twenty harlots; some of them ask for a glass of gin; others say "Sir, it is for my lodgings." This is not debauchery which flaunts itself, but destitution – and what destitution!'[5]

Many girls were driven on to the streets not so much by the threat of destitution but by the actual and immediate presence of destitution. Such was the case of the girl whom 'Walter' called Kitty.[6] He met her in the Strand as he was walking home from his club. She was not 'got up in any showy way but looked like the child of a decent mechanic'. He offered to buy her sweets, then changed his mind, gave her three and sixpence and took her up to an accommodation room above a cigar-divan.

'How long have you been gay?' he asked her.
'I ain't gay,' she replied.
'Yes you are.'
'No I ain't.'
'You let men fuck you, don't you?'
'Yes. But I ain't gay.'

Her father had died – she was, in fact, still wearing mourning for him – and her mother was ill with rheumatic fever. Kitty was compelled to provide for her mother and her young brother and sister. Prostitution was a temporary expedient only, and therefore she did not consider herself 'gay'. Even so, she could only provide gruel and salt and bread 'sometimes' for her family. Her brother and sister, aged eight and six respectively, had to be kept locked in their room all day while she was out on the street, and, though it was mid-winter, without a fire. She cried when she talked about her family, and she was sufficiently lacking in experience to cry when 'Walter' took her. 'Walter' was, of course, not to be taken in by the tears of a harlot. Equally, he was determined to force her to admit to being 'gay'. Finally, he wrung out of her an admission that she bought a little food for herself which she did not share with the others.

'What do you like?' he asked.

'Pies and sausage rolls,' she answered. 'Oh my! Ain't they prime, – ah!'

'That's what you went gay for?'

'I ain't gay.'

'Well, it's what you let men fuck you for?'

'Yes.'

'Walter' went to Kitty several times afterwards, during the following months, and observed with that detachment and total lack of compassion which makes *My Secret Life* almost unbearable to read, how she gradually came to put on the faded satin of the truly 'gay', how she was initiated into drinking gin and brandy and how her appearances on the Strand became less and less frequent as she became too drink-sodden to seek out the more fashionable clientèle of the West End. He expressed no regrets at her decline and fall. Why should he have done? There was a host of children travelling the same wretched road, and for the same reasons.

Kitty took to the streets because there was nothing else she could do. For tens of thousands of others there was the chance of alternative employment, but alternatives so menial, so pitiful in their servility, so fatiguing in the demands they made, that a girl who was fortunate enough to be tolerably good-looking might be forgiven if she realised – to quote the old proverb – that she was sitting on a fortune. Moreover, girls of the labouring class were brought up in an environment so squalid, so promiscuous and so disfigured by drunkenness – that universal panacea against the misery of hopeless poverty – and their conditions of work were so degrading, that it was highly improbable that any concept of 'virtue' or 'purity' as understood by middle-class England ever occurred to them. Thus the manager of a glass factory in St Helens, Lancashire, deposed to the Children's Employment Commission (1865) regarding his girl-operatives:

'Many cannot read or write. Most of their conversation is

horrid to listen to, some curse and swear like troopers; not a few have illegitimate children. There is one who sleeps with one man or another nearly every night of her life.'[7]

Concerning conditions of work, the foreman of a London garret tobacco factory declared to the same Commission that the attic windows of the workshop would not open, and that there was no ventilation whatsoever: 'The girls have fainting or hysterical fits now and then, but I think they are in connection with their monthly periods and not with the effect of the tobacco.'[8]

There has been a tendency of recent years among social historians to deny that the mid-nineteenth century factory was a breeding-ground for sexual profligacy and prostitution: it is claimed that the genteel classes mistook unavoidable dirt and raggedness in clothing, coarseness of speech and frankness in behaviour, to indicate complete promiscuity in sexual relationships. But this is itself a proof of the contention. People see themselves 'as by reflection, by some other thing', and the factory-girl saw her reflection as being that of a potential harlot. No novelist concerned about industrial conditions dared to allow a significant character, least of all a heroine, earn her bread in a factory. Mrs Wilson, in Mrs Gaskell's *Mary Barton*, is the sole representative of the class, and she exists to denounce the employment of women in industry:

> 'Father does not like girls to work in factories,' said Mary. 'No, I know he does not; and reason good,' replies Mrs Wilson. 'They oughtn't to go out after they're married, that I'm very clear about. I could reckon up' – counting on her fingers – 'aye, nine men I know as has been driven to the public house by having wives as worked in factories; good folk too, as thought there was no harm in putting their little ones out to nurse and letting their homes go all dirty and their fires all out.'[9]

Mrs Wilson's view was confirmed by a Leeds factory inspector, Robert Baker, writing in 1860. The family as a stable social unit had virtually ceased to exist among the labouring class in the industrial towns, he maintained, and this was primarily due to 'the want of domestic qualification on the part of the factory-girls; their utter incapacity to make a home more desirable from its comforts than external amusements and associations; their extravagance in purchasing new and tawdry articles of dress, partly from a love of finery, partly from their incapableness of mending old clothes; their general waste or misapplication of their earnings in the purchase of provisions'.[10]

The breakdown of the family unit was bound to lead to a breakdown of the moral stability which stemmed from it. It was bound to lead to a shifting, and shiftless, series of relationships, devoid of any responsibility. The housing conditions which prevailed merely exacerbated a situation which was already likely to drive a girl to the streets.

It comes as no surprise to discover that an appalling number of very young girls were initiated into sexual experience through acts of incest whose promiscuity was so staggering as to outdo the imagination of a hardcore pornographer. One of Sir Edwin Chadwick's investigators reported to Somerset House on working-class housing in Manchester:

'I could enumerate a variety of instances in which I found a promiscuous mixture of the sexes in sleeping-rooms. I may mention one; a man and his wife and child sleeping in one bed; in another bed, two grown-up females; and in the same room, two young men, unmarried. I have met with instances of a man, his wife, and his wife's sister, sleeping in the same bed together.'[11]

Chadwick asked his investigators whether the sexual practices resulting from such over-crowding were 'deemed extraordinary or culpable amongst that class of persons?' 'It seems not to be thought of,' was the reply. One of the investigators cited an example of a collier and his young sister, 'not by any means of ill-fame', who indulged in improper intercourse, as a result of which the girl became 'more and more depraved and at length was thrown upon the town because, having lost her character, the town has become her only resource'.[12]

Investigators in Leeds summed up their impression of the conditions in which *the generality* of labouring folk lived:

> With broken panes in every window-frame, and filth and vermin in every nook. With walls unwhitewashed for years, black with the smoke of foul chimneys, without water, with corded bed-stocks for beds and sacking for bed-clothing, with floors unwashed from year to year, without out-offices, while

outside there are streets with stagnant puddles here and there, with their foetid exhalations, choked up with filth and excrementitious matter, undrained, unpaved, unventilated . . . Those who might advocate a better state of things depart; and those who remain, by repeated exhibitions of indecency and vulgarity, and indeed by the mere fact of neighbourhoodship, sink into moral degradation and vicious habits.[13]

In rural England the conditions of labour were, if possible, even worse. Among girls and women recruited into gangs for field-work, sexual promiscuity was part of the way of life:

In a gang it necessarily follows that even those who were steady and respectable when they joined it must become corrupted. The dress of the women is to a certain extent almost of necessity immodest. When the crops are wet they tuck up their dresses between their legs, often leaving the legs much exposed. The long absences and distance from home often render it necessary that the women should attend to the calls of nature, and this they do in the presence of the lads, boys, and men. . . . Thus the gang system is the cause of a moral pestilence. . . . To say that a girl has been employed in the fields, in gangs or otherwise, is sufficient to cause anyone to reject her application for domestic service.[14]

The agricultural labouring girl was denied that which was considered the unalienable right of every Victorian – the right to better herself by her own unaided efforts, to effect the doctrine enshrined in Samuel Smiles's *Self Help*. From field-work there was no escape save either the Union Workhouse via rheumatism and malnutrition, or, assuming she retained some vestige of her looks, prostitution.

Among farmers and young gentlemen agricultural labouring girls were notoriously easy. The ineffable 'Walter' was advised by a young squire, 'You can always have a field-girl. Nobody cares'.[15] The initial rape was frequently the prerogative of the gang-master himself, who considered the exercise of this right the natural reward for having taken on the girl in the first place:

Mr C. pulled me down and pulled up my clothes, only to my waist. I think there were a dozen in the gang, it was in sight of the gang, we were sitting down to our dinners. The other boys and girls in the gang were round me. I called out, the others laughed. He said, 'Open your legs more'. He had a stick.[16]

The magistrate who accepted this deposition remarked, 'I'm afraid these cases would come oftener before the magistrates if the children dared to speak.' Since the girls would lose all hope of employment if they did report a gang-master, such an eventuality was not likely to occur.

Many girls – prostitutes initially at least of the more prosperous sort for the most part – were those who, though not in a condition of desperate poverty, had been directly exposed to the glamour of wealth. Of these, the majority were, or had been, in service. Over-worked, subjected to continual if petty humiliation – few were allowed 'followers', some were not permitted even to go to church of a Sunday – lodged in attics deliberately furnished with ascetic bleakness lest they should get ideas above their station in life, frequently subjected to sexual advances on the part of their male 'betters' – junior domestics found that the young men of the families for whom they worked expected to gain sexual experience from them – and often dreadfully isolated from possibility of real friendship by the rigid hierarchies which existed in the servants' hall, the young housemaid or kitchen-maid observed daily the reality of middle-class prosperity: the operation of the laws of conspicuous consumption. In becoming a 'dolly-mop', and – by natural progression – a part-time prostitute, the junior servant was motivated sometimes by a genuine need for companionship, but more frequently by a desire to share, to some very limited extent, the luxuries enjoyed by her 'betters'.

Frequently she was driven into prostitution because she was dismissed, often for some real or imagined sexual offence, without the very necessary 'character'. Such was the situation faithfully recorded as always by 'Walter'. His wife, on one occasion, discovered that a newly-acquired maid had lost her virginity in her previous position. As a result, the girl was given a week's notice. 'I could not, of course, interfere,' wrote 'Walter'. 'It would not have done to have passed over fornication. Had I done so the habit would have spread throughout the household. The girl went quietly, in tears.'[17] To his horror, he discovered that his wife had actually given her a 'character'. Immediately, he set about rectifying this appalling indiscretion by ensuring through his very considerable influence that the girl would never be able to obtain a post through the more reputable agencies.

Among a less depressed but equally over-worked class, that of apprentice-milliners, dressmakers and shop-assistants, temptation worked with equal strength. Engaged in the creation of personal finery or in its display, their appetite for it was naturally aroused. Frequently such girls were in immediate contact with their would-be seducers, and the offer of a small private *pied-à-terre*, and the chance to dress in the quality of gown they were employed to make and to sell, seemed infinitely preferable to life in the promiscuity of an attic dormitory above the shop and an eighteen-hour day during the 'Season'.

A number of West End dress-shop managers actively encouraged their girls into a way of life that was little better than high-class prostitution, and hired out dresses to prostitutes as a means of advertising their product. The majority, however, fell into line with the manager of 'Madame Elise's Establishment', Regent Street:

> Letters come with coronets and elaborate monograms for the young ladies. Such things have but one meaning and commonly but one end. We do not encourage the young ladies in our show-rooms to wear silk. If any are known to dress beyond their means, they had better go. The wearing of silk stockings and 'military boots' are out of place with us.[18]

As with maidservants, respectable employers tended to assume that any intercourse between work-girls and the male sex was prima facie evidence of moral delinquency:

> I have unfortunately had to dismiss two or three girls [wrote the so-called superintendent of a dress-shop dormitory in 1864] They were receiving notes from gentlemen, and making appointments to meet them. It might be all innocent, but for the sake of the rest, we had to send them away. They were particularly pretty and well-mannered girls. I had great doubts what I ought to do, for to dismiss them was, perhaps,

to take away their last chance: but the example to the others was too dangerous.[19]

The 'two or three' young seamstresses, robbed of all chance of honest employment, no doubt joined the army of ex-house-maids who thronged the pavements of the Haymarket.

The cause beyond all others of recruitment for 'The Social Problem' – the favoured mid-Victorian euphemism for prostitution – was one which was apparently insoluble. This was the chronic unemployment caused by the enormous surplus of unmarried women of all classes. In 1851, there were 2,765,000 unmarried adult females; in 1861, 2,959,000; and by 1871, the figure had risen to 3,228,000.

Industry and domestic service could not absorb such numbers, and for these women who were not on the lowest rung of the social ladder, life in the factories or below stairs was, of course, quite unthinkable.

> It is in vain [wrote Andrew Wynter in 1869] that we sing 'The Song of The Shirt', and get up annual subscriptions for down-stricken seamstresses. It is in vain that we hold midnight tea-meetings to tempt Lorettes from their evil courses; as long as we shut young women out from honourable means of employment, so long will their labour be a drug on the market, and their degradation but too facile a matter for the tempter.'[20]

Unmarried daughters of professional men earning less than £1000 a year were 'a constant source of anxiety, and should they not get married there is every probability of their being, sooner or later, obliged to enter the battle of life utterly unprepared and unfitted for the fight'.[21] They sought to become governesses – the only genteel occupation open to them, and one in which they were almost as vulnerable to the advances of their male employers as were the lower members of their sex in the household. For they too could scarcely afford dismissal without testimonial – in 1849, one advertiser requiring the services of a governess received ninety-eight applications for the post. It would be absurd to suppose that unemployed and unemployable girls of the genteel classes took immediately to the streets, but such was their need for protection by a gentleman that many were easy prey to the experienced seducer. Having been seduced and betrayed, there lay before them only one way.

Associations existed to promote opportunities for the honest employment of unmarried females of the gentler classes, but these were confronted with a wall of prejudice best summed up in the pages of the strongly anti-feminist *Saturday Review* (1859):

> The end of education is to fit its subjects for that station and those duties in which, the chances are, that their future life will be spent. Our girls, whom it is sought to put down in the desk and the counter, will have to abandon them when they become wives and mothers. All the time, therefore, that they employ in the counting-house is so much time lost – it does not only not fit them, but positively unfits them, for their future duties.[22]

## VIII

THE causes of prostitution in the second half of the nineteenth century were comprehensively examined by contemporary social investigators, and their findings, particularly the reports of Mayhew and Acton, reached a wide public. The chief obstacle to the would-be reformer lay not in a general ignorance regarding prostitution itself, but in the fear, sexual prejudice and quietism which the hosts of prostitutes evoked among the 'respectable' classes. The face of poverty, particularly poverty on a massive scale, is ugly and repellent in a very actual sense. Poverty and exploitation do not bring out virtue in those who are afflicted by them, but result in ever-increasing moral debilitation. The concept of a 'deserving poor' is a hare which was all too readily and frequently started by the mid-Victorians, and has not been unknown in our own times. The poor inevitably become less 'deserving' as they become more conscious of the hopelessness of their condition, and the face they present is disfigured not merely by anxiety, hunger and apathy, but is also ravaged by febrile bouts of self-indulgence: cul-de-sacs offering faint glimpses of impossible joys. This ugliness, frightening in its complete lack of human dignity and spiritual beauty, is amply revealed in the drawings of George Cruikshank, 'Phiz' and Gustave Doré. Too often such pictures have been taken to be caricatures rather than the authentic face of nineteenth-century urban poverty.

The physical as well as moral revulsion felt not only by the prosperous middle classes, but also by the skilled operatives – artisans and engineers – towards the destitute and the near-destitute, explains to a great extent the apparently callous attitude which they adopted towards them, and the moral standards they sought to enforce. We observe how Charles Dickens depicts Oliver Twist as one of nature's little gentlemen, a natural member of the middle classes even in his speech, when everything that his creator tells us about the boy demands – since he is exposed neither to any experience of love nor any decent social standards of behaviour – that he should be a coarse, foul-mouthed, amoral delinquent. Had Dickens depicted his hero true to human experience, his readers would have rejected his entire thesis. The very fact that Dickens makes him talk and behave like a well-brought-up little bourgeois makes the possibility of his corruption more terrible to the reader, and it is a real possibility.

'I wish I had been struck dead in the street,' cried Nancy, 'or had changed places with them we passed so near tonight, before I had lent a hand in bringing him here. He's a thief, a liar, a devil, all that's bad from this night forth. Isn't that enough for the old wretch, without blows?'

When Nancy, who, Dickens explicitly states (in the preface to the first edition), is a prostitute, defends Oliver, and latterly dies for him, the author skilfully ensures that the reader's pity and compassion is extended to a girl who would otherwise, given the ethos of the age, appear entirely undeserving of pity. The juxtaposition of Oliver and Nancy emphasises the nightmare perversion of innocence, and when Nancy makes herself instrumental in the return of Oliver to the care of good Mr Brownlow, his escape from her world is seen to be a very close thing, and the reader is touched on the raw nerve of social guilt.

The 1850s saw a massive expansion in industrial development as a result of the expansion in rail communication and the effective application of steam-power to ocean-going shipping. Wealth, in the form of dividends, poured into the pockets of the share-holding middle classes, giving rise to the so-called 'law of con-spicuous consumption'. As industrial growth and middle-class bank accounts expanded, so did the population of the urban centres – and the prosperous amounted to a mere fraction of that population, compared to the vast armies of labouring poor who floated helplessly on the tides and currents of uncontrolled laissez-faire capitalism. The prosperous settled in suburbs, class-colonies from which contact was made with the labouring classes only by employing them in small numbers for domestic service of the most menial sort, or by doling out charity in timid sallies into the less unsavoury labouring-class areas.

At the same time, the new-rich – and most of the urban middle classes were to a greater or lesser extent *nouveaux riches* – were compelled to seek a viable social identity. They may never have seen an urban slum, but their roadways and pavements were infested by beggars, cheap-jacks and whores, to remind them of the degradation into which the human condition might descend. To them a promiscuity of living which had been ac-ceptable in the spaciousness of a rural society became horrifying in the new conurbations, and they retreated into a stifling pri-vacy of which lace curtains, heavy velvet pelmets and double front-doors were the outward and visible sign. Ladies who, living in a rural village, were not above continuing a conversa-tion with the escorting males while they squatted in a wayside ditch to relieve themselves, were justifiably appalled by the spectacle of such behaviour in the cramped and over-populated towns. Defensively, they hid their limbs under layers of cotton and lace, and hid the performance of their natural functions in tight-lipped taciturnity, tortuous euphemism and a lavatory as far removed from eye and ear as the ingenuity of an architect could devise.

In an age rich in the possibilities of accumulating wealth there was also the possibility of losing it rapidly. While it was true that Peel's Bank Charter Act had brought to an end the epidemic of collapsing private banks which had disrupted economic life in the 1820s and 1830s, ill-judged speculation on the money mar-kets was still rife, and the threat of sudden poverty in the midst of plenty was real enough. Socially insecure, haunted by the spectre of sudden impoverishment, they sought to protect themselves and their social position by adopting a stifling rigidity in manners and etiquette. At the same time, they sought to protect themselves spiritually with the one certainty they had brought with them from their village and market-town origins, their particular brand of puritan Christianity, which tended to harden into conventionalised attitudes the more it was beset by intellectual doubt or social guilt. The idea that God helps those that help themselves, enshrined in the works of Samuel Smiles, was not only a way of dismissing the problem of urban poverty by suggesting that the destitute were destitute because of some moral weakness, but was also a confirmation of the conviction that their own prosperity was in some measure dependent upon the stereotyped moral rectitude which they observed within the orbit of their own homes.

The home, and within it the family, was the one certainty, the ultimate bastion, in an age of cultural and economic revolution, and the family was centred emotionally around the mother, as it was centred financially about the father. The stability of home and family depended on the absolute fidelity of the wife to her husband; daughters must be so trained that their fidelity towards their future husbands would be unquestionable. The best way of ensuring this seemed to lie in the preservation of ignorance regarding sexual matters among women, complete in the case of unmarried girls, and enlightened only by experience within the marriage-bed in the case of wives.

Since the presence of a positive sexuality in women suggested that they might be tempted by nature to be sexually promiscuous, the very existence of a female sexuality was denied:

I should say that the majority of women (happily for society) are not much troubled by sexual feeling of any kind. Many of the best mothers, wives, and managers of households, know little or are careless about sexual relations. Love of the home, children, and of domestic duties are the only passions they feel. As a general rule, a modest woman seldom desires any sexual gratification for herself. She submits to her husband's embraces, but principally to gratify him; and were it not for the desire of maternity, would far rather be relieved from his attention.[1]

Sexual promiscuity in a man was undesirable, but essentially *natural*; in woman it represented a perversion of nature. Women were divided into two categories: innocents and whores. The road to whoredom, according to medical science, was masturbation, which men, having no reason to suppose otherwise, believed to be as prevalent among adolescent girls as among boys (despite the absence of female sexuality). In boys, masturbation led to insanity – a belief which survived well into the twentieth century, and probably still exists in some households. In girls it led to nymphomania and the brothel. In the 1850s girls certainly strangers to, and probably entirely ignorant of, the practice of masturbation were strapped into Dr John Moodie's 'girdle of chastity', an ingenious device which permitted the wearer to urinate freely while making it impossible for her to touch her sexual parts. Such devices were still marketed in the 1930s, but even more popular (and Dr Moodie made a fortune with his 'girdle') was clitoridectomy. In 1858 clinics existed in many major cities entirely devoted to this simple operation.

Victorian medical opinion considered *all* seminal emissions to be physically debilitating and liable to produce disturbing mental effects, thus the use of the word 'spending' as a synonym for orgasm. As late as 1918, so learned and respected a pioneer of Freudian psychology as Ernest Jones could write that 'true neurasthenia will be found to depend on excessive seminal emissions'. Most Victorians believed that women emitted seminal fluid *in orgasm* and could thus be described as 'spending', with the physical effects and mental disturbance which obtained in men, only made worse because of the essential unnaturalness of the act. Neither in men nor women could the sexual act be entirely divorced from guilt, if enjoyed – though, clearly, the guilt was more intense in women. Middle-class men tended to have recourse to prostitutes or semi-prostitutes – servants or lower-class factory-workers – because sexual intercourse, when enjoyed, was essentially a conspiracy to do something wicked, and was therefore unsuited to 'respectable' people. In marital sexual relations it was often as incumbent upon men as it was upon women to conceal satisfaction in the act. At the same time there was a natural, if frequently subconscious, male resentment at female frigidity, and here lay the paradox which so bedevilled Victorian sexual attitudes. The man who would have been shocked and disgusted by any display of enthusiasm on the part of his wife resented his inability to arouse her to that enthusiasm. He was compelled to have recourse to prostitutes in order to enjoy sex without inhibition; he was compelled to despise his partner in sexual pleasure because she shared in, stimulated and compounded, his guilty enjoyment of the act; he was compelled to seduce the daughters of his social inferiors in order to prove his own virility.

Even if he was callous enough to wish his wife to participate with him in a conspiracy to enjoy sex, the Victorian middle-class husband was unlikely to meet with any success. A typical example of a late-Victorian bride wrote to her mother from her honeymoon, announcing that she was engaged in lengthening 'his' nightshirts so that 'I shan't be able to see any of him'. A less amusing example was provided by Sir Richard Burton in the introduction to his book *The Customs and Manners of the East* when, in comparing the attitudes of western and oriental brides, he cites the case of an English girl who retired before her husband on her wedding night, and chloroformed herself, having pinned a note to the pillow which read, 'Mama says you are to do what you like.'

Doctors were frequently confronted with young husbands who were afraid either of debauching their wives or were worried lest their brides' reluctance would reduce them to impotence. William Acton cheerfully put them at their ease:

'It is a delusion under which many a previously incontinent man suffers to suppose that in newly-married life he will be required to treat his wife as he used to treat his mistresses. It is not so in the case of any modest Englishwoman. He need not fear that his wife will require the excitement or in any way imitate the ways of a courtesan.'[2]

Acton had, in fact, arrived at his view regarding the sexuality of women through his considerable study of prostitution, in which he had shown himself to be both percipient and realistic. He had observed that the majority of prostitutes pretended to a sexual satisfaction with their clients which they did not in fact experience. From this perfectly valid observation he deduced that if 'public women' were for the most part frigid, it was ludicrous to suppose that decent women were not.

Confronted by the insipidity of an 'Angel in the Home' who

had been instructed by innumerable books, tracts and women's magazines to devote herself to, and to comply with, every wish of her husband save one; confronted by her simpering frigidity, it was hardly surprising if the husband sought more vital companionship. Indeed, his own sexual instruction would draw him towards the prostitute. It was recommended that a young gentleman should derive his sexual knowledge by observing the habits of dogs in kennels, while his practical initiation would either be at the hands of a prostitute or a complacent (or frightened) junior maidservant – an initiation fraught with difficulty as a result of his observation in the kennels. Since there was little hope of his arriving at sexual expertise within the context of friendship and affection however temporary, sexuality and love were irrevocably separated. The man thus initiated was incapable of perceiving a compatibility, let alone an enhancement, in his respect for a woman and the enjoyment of her body.

'It seemed to me', wrote 'Walter', 'scarcely possible that the sweet, well dressed, smooth-spoken, ladies who came to our house could let men put the spunk up their cunts.'[3]

An obvious *reductio* of such a situation led to the acceptance of prostitution as being necessary to the health of men, to the respect due to virtuous wives and to the stability of the home. The prostitute, wrote the eminent historian Lecky in 1862, 'is ultimately the most efficient guardian of virtue. But for her, the unchallenged purity of countless happy homes would be polluted, and not a few who, in the pride of their untempted chastity, think of her with an indignant shudder would have known the agony of remorse and despair.'[4]

At the same time, by recourse to a prostitute, a normal healthy young man could postpone marriage until such time as he could keep a wife in the manner befitting an 'Angel in the Home': 'The man who marries before he is in receipt of an ample income and has to face the struggles which await the poor, is considered to lose caste. Parents will sooner contrive at illicit amours in the case of their sons.'[5]

So wrote John Forster, Charles Dickens's friend and biographer. Such statements were unusually frank declarations of the true meaning of the 'double standard' in morality, a view generally – almost universally – accepted, though shrouded in a vast conspiracy of silence. The onerous duty of any reformer who wished to strike at the roots of prostitution as practised in mid-Victorian England was to shatter that silence. In doing so her actions must, inevitably, be harshly opposed and bitterly resented, for it must seem that she was striking at the very fabric of society.

# 3. The First Crusade

ALTHOUGH 'The Cause', as Josephine christened the campaign, was ostensibly limited to the Contagious Diseases Acts, it was in fact a war against the entire concept of officially institutionalised vice and the regulation by the State of prostitution. The establishment of *maisons tolérées* and the regulation of them by a special Police des Mœurs had begun in Paris in 1802, and had spread to the Low Countries and Switzerland with the introduction of the *Code Napoléon*. Similar laws were implemented, in those parts of Italy ruled by the House of Savoy, by Cavour in the 1850s. Josephine, a frequent visitor both to Paris and to Italy, had long been acquainted with the practices of western Europe, but it was not until 1866 that she came to appreciate the danger existing in Britain. In that year, two Members of Parliament, Henley and Ayrton, who had become increasingly concerned about the implications of the Contagious Diseases Acts, protested against them in the House of Commons. Josephine read – was, indeed, one of the few people who did – the ensuing debate as reported in *Hansard*. It occurred to her, as it had occurred to Henley and Ayrton, that sooner or later the French method of regulating vice would be introduced into Britain. 'The depression which took possession of my mind was overwhelming,' she wrote. She felt a presentiment that, do what she would, she was doomed to 'enter into this cloud'.[1] More immediate matters – her work at Brownlow Hill, and her association with Anne Clough – pushed the Contagious Diseases Acts to the back of her mind. Four years later, when returning from holiday in 1870 and passing through Dover and Maidstone, she witnessed for herself the effects of the Acts on the women and children of garrison towns. Even then she was less than eager to embrace a new sphere of activity. 'Like Jonah,' she wrote, 'when he was charged by God with a commission he could not endure to contemplate, "I fled from the face of the Lord".'[2]

One might be forgiven for doubting whether even Josephine could seriously believe that working with Liverpool prostitutes constituted 'fleeing from the face of the Lord'. But Josephine was well aware of her own talents; she knew that, while others were capable of engaging in direct rescue work, she possessed the influence in political and academic circles to work for, and perhaps win, a nation-wide struggle against the Acts. In any case, like Jonah, she was not allowed to flee for long.

Harriet Martineau, an immensely respected figure, had fired the first round on behalf of the women. To the *Daily News* she had written:

> If the soldier is more immoral than his contemporaries of the working class, it must be because the standard of morality is lower in the army than out of it. Shall we then raise it to what we clearly see it might be, or degrade it further by a practical avowal that vice is in the soldier's case a necessity to be provided for, like his need for food and clothing? This admission of the necessity of vice is the point on which the whole argument turns, and on which irretrievable consequences depend. Once admitted, the necessity of a long series of fearful evils follows of course. There can be no resistance to seduction, procuration, disease, regulation, when once the original necessity is granted.[3]

But Harriet Martineau was old, and in semi-retirement, a massive voice from the past. Josephine's own North of England Council had taken up her argument, and had passed resolutions opposing the Acts during Josephine's absence on the Continent (she had been having a long holiday with her family, meandering about Italy, Switzerland and Bavaria). Josephine's cousin, Charles Birrell, had been to London to present a memorial protesting against the Acts to the Government – neither he, nor the ladies of the North of England Council, were likely to forget that Gladstone was a personal friend of the Butlers, and had been their house guest on a number of occasions both at Oxford and in Liverpool.

Josephine's book had been widely read, and her oblique attack on the Acts had been duly noticed. A considerable number of

letters were waiting for her in Liverpool on her return, including
one from a number of distinguished medical men, begging her to
take up the campaign, and more continued to pour in. 'I read
all that was sent to me, and I vividly recalled all that I had
learned before of this fatal system and its corrupting influence in
Continental cities.'[4] But she was still reluctant to involve herself
in it.

It is easy, with the advantages of hindsight, to see in Josephine one of the great leaders of the late-nineteenth-century
women's movement, and most of her biographers have approached her as such. It must be remembered, therefore, that
in the conventional meaning of the word, she was not a 'feminist',
and, as we have seen, found it difficult to have sympathetic relations with the more forthright feminists. She was, if anything,
profoundly conservative, and believed, for all her activity, that
her first duty was to her husband and her children. She was no
more endowed by nature to be the presiding general of a public
cause than she was to be a social worker. She was too sensitive
to opposition and too excitable to enjoy the rough-and-tumble
of the public forum – that had been proved by her intense depression after her failure at Oxford. She loathed being the recipient of abuse, whereas the born fighter would have been
stimulated by it.

It is no exaggeration to state that Josephine was appalled
at the prospect of entering into the debate over the Contagious
Diseases Acts. For a man publicly to oppose the Acts was bad
enough; for a woman to do so was, if she was younger than
Harriet Martineau, a certain invitation for doubts to be cast on
her sexual integrity. Josephine, though better protected than
some due to the eminence of her social and academic circle of
friends, was in one sense at least peculiarly open to attack.
Although in her forties she was an immensely attractive woman
who, secure in her own chastity and in her husband's trust,
travelled widely and unescorted, and frequently encountered
members of the opposite sex *tête-à-tête* and in private. Undoubtedly, she had a sexual impact on many of the men who met her
and were attracted to her. The near idolatry with which they
wrote about her contains no reference to physical glamour – we
would hardly expect Frederic Myers or James Stuart to admit
to having fallen in love with her physical attributes, since they

regarded her as their saint and, in the case of Myers, his muse.
On John Addington Symonds, however, the effect of her attractiveness was unclouded by thoughts of worship. Her presence –
he met her during her ill-fated visit to Oxford – he found most
disturbing: 'a traumatic sexual experience', according to a later
post-Freudian commentator. The form taken by this trauma or
disturbance was that 'his reproductive equipment swelled'.[5]
While this, it is to be hoped, was an extreme reaction, it explains
why a number of her more vehement critics chose to abuse her
by describing her, without a shadow of justification, as 'worse
than a prostitute'. Hell knows no fury like the scorn of a man
who has been humiliated in debate by a sexually attractive
woman. Josephine herself was well aware of the form abuse
would take, and she dreaded it.

'For three months I was very unhappy,' she wrote later. 'I
can only give a very imperfect impression of the sufferings of that
time. The toils and conflicts of the years that followed were light
in comparison with the anguish of that first plunge into the
full realisation of the villainy there is in the world, and the dread
of being called to oppose it.'[6]

In fact, she went to some trouble to try to avoid it. She protested that she had no influence socially – no more, at any rate,
than the next woman. 'I have lived among the middle and lower
classes. I know nothing of fashionable society or aristocracy or
grand London people.'[7] Coming from the girl who had been the
regular dancing partner of Lord Tauberville and the Earl of
Durham, or the woman who had been hostess to Mr Gladstone,
such a protest was something less than the whole truth. She wrote
to her friend Daniel Cooper, the Secretary of the Rescue Society,
suggesting that his Society had not done all that it might to
oppose the Acts. He replied at length, pointing out that the
Rescue Society had done all in its power, and thereby knocking
the ball back into Josephine's court:

'We were rejoiced beyond measure when we saw the announcement of your ladies' Association. . . . We felt that Providence
had well chosen the means for the defeat of these wicked Acts.
The ladies of England will save the country from this wicked
curse . . . Go on; give the country no rest till this law is
abolished.'[8]

What worried Josephine more than anything, once she had

really made up her mind, was the effect it would have on her husband and children. She need not have concerned herself. Though she was extraordinarily and unnecessarily nervous about telling George – 'I went to him one evening when he was alone, all the household having retired to rest; I hesitated, and leaned my head against his closed door; and as I leaned, I prayed' – his reaction was one of encouragement: 'Go, and God go with you.'[9] In fact she needed, and obtained, his active support and encouragement in everything she did; she depended on him in a very real sense.

Having made up her mind, and having obtained George's blessing on her undertaking, she had no second thoughts on the matter. It had become, she said, a warfare 'in which He who conquered Death and Sin and Hell goes before us and is our *rereward*'.[10] Carefully she selected the scene for her first public appearance in the Abolitionist cause. It was to be Crewe Junction, where there was 'a manufactory of locomotives', and therefore a large concentration of skilled operatives organised into a craft-union.

A friend had introduced her to local union officials in Liverpool, and they had arranged that the 'Popular Hall' of the railway engineers at Crewe should be placed at her disposal. She was sufficiently acquainted with the political scene since the Second Reform Act (1867) to be aware of advantages to be obtained from addressing a massed audience of skilled working men. Not only did they represent the class on whose womenfolk the Contagious Diseases Acts fell most heavily and most unjustly, they also constituted a new and significant element in the electorate. Again and again during the ensuing months, Josephine would address herself to them, and in terms which revealed a considerable skill in appreciating the areas of sensitivity in their political outlook.

Travelling to Crewe to make her first public speech against the Acts, and to a type of audience with which she was unfamiliar, she was both nervous and ill-prepared. By her own account, she had little idea of what she was going to say, but, as usual, took refuge in prayer, and came to the conclusion that she would rely, like the Society of Friends, on the direct inspiration of the Holy Spirit. Whether or not as a result of the operation of the Holy Spirit, or because of the friendly and even enthusiastic reception she received on mounting the platform, her speech was entirely successful. After the meeting was officially closed, a group of railway engineers came to her, and explained why the audience had, from the start, been predisposed in her favour. They had been seconded to Paris for some months, they told her, to assist in the development of the French railway system during the Second Empire. They had been shocked and appalled, not by the blatancy of prostitution as practised in Paris – it was no worse, and probably better, than in London – but by the inhumanity, corruption and blackmail exercised by the Police des Mœurs, and the terror in which they were held by the wives and daughters of their French colleagues. They were genuinely horrified by the idea of such an institution being imported into Britain.

As a result of this informal conversation, Josephine was provided with introductions to groups of engineers all over the North of England, and during the ensuing three weeks she addressed mass meetings of artisans in Leeds, York, Sunderland, Newcastle upon Tyne and Carlisle. Her Carlisle speech was recorded by the local press:

I believe we are called, in this our day, to labour for the abolition of harlotry – that great and soul-devouring evil, that huge Typical Sin. But now, the first obstacle we find is these chains imposed by legislation upon the frail and fallen (of one sex only, and that the weaker) to bring them under a legal bondage, to a recognised and superintended shame.

You know that it is much easier to disperse a loose rabble than well organised troops. These Acts of Parliament have changed prostitution from a rabble into a well drilled army, fenced in by regulations, and so completely in the hands of official persons as to make the efforts of God's voluntary and free-hearted evangelists hopeless in that direction. We wake up to the awful nature of the Social Evil, and to the corruption of our national life through its influence, just at a time when authority and power have set their seal upon the abomination, just when our Parliament – the first in all the world which has done such a thing – has spoken with awful and unmistakable voice the words (which it is unlawful for any human judge to utter), 'He that is filthy, let him be filthy still'! For such is the verdict gone forth![11]

This is fine rhetoric and, delivered with the calculated passion which was Josephine's oratorical style, it must have had an electrifying effect on the audience for which it was intended. On the other hand, it offered few arguments against those presented by the men who upheld and who wished to extend the Acts on the basis of the belief, expressed by John Morley in the *Pall Mall Gazette*, that 'fleshly instincts will outlive all moral crusades', and that it was therefore right and proper to take precautions against the possible result of any yielding to 'fleshly instinct'.

Having won the sympathies of her audiences on the emotional level she took care after each meeting to organise *ad hoc* committees among the artisans ostensibly to agree on a programme of action, but, in fact, to endorse the Declaration of Policy which she was engaged in drafting during the long and often arduous railway journeys from meeting to meeting, and which the editor of the *Daily News* had promised to publish.

The Declaration was comprised of eight major points:[12]

(1) The Law, in safeguarding individual liberty outside the home, had not, hitherto, discriminated between men and women. The Acts, however, constituted just such a discrimination. Moreover, a significant alteration to the Constitution which affected over fifty per cent of British subjects, had been passed through Parliament without the knowledge or consent of the electorate as a whole, but also unnoticed by a large number of Members of Parliament.

(2) The Acts placed the liberty, reputation, and persons of young women entirely into the hands of the police.

(3) When an individual is detained by the police, the Law clearly demands that the offence for which he is detained should be publicly stated. The Acts constituted a complete disregard for that demand.

(4) The medical examination and treatment imposed under threat of sentence to Hard Labour constituted a punishment, and it was manifestly unjust to punish one partner only for the practice of a vice which obviously required two participants. Particularly was it unjust since the female partner was all too

frequently the social and moral victim, in effect the consequence of the vice, rather than its root cause.

(5) The Acts were openly designed to ensure that men could have safe and easy recourse to prostitutes.

(6) The specific measures recommended by the Acts had a peculiarly brutalising effect on those prostitutes already committed to their way of life, and tended to harden and to make more abandoned those girls who were still new to prostitution, and therefore more readily reclaimable.

(7) In countries where licensed prostitution was practised, notably France and Prussia where statistics were readily available, there had been little or no diminution in the incidence of venereal diseases – for the very good reason that venereal diseases were carried to prostitutes who had previously been medically examined by their clients, who were subject to no such examination.

(8) By imposing a system of 'regulated' vice, Society was divesting itself of the responsibility of examining the social and moral causes of that vice.

The arguments presented in the Declaration were engrossed into two lengthier statements by Josephine published within weeks of the original statement – 'Justina's Letters in reply to Miss Garrett's Defence of The Contagious Diseases Acts', published in the *Pall Mall Gazette*, and *An Appeal to The People of England on the Recognition and Superintendence of Prostitution by Governments*, which was issued in book form, and it was these two works which thrust her into the full glare of public debate.

Lujo Bassermann, a German journalist turned social-historian, in a somewhat erratic survey of prostitution down the ages, has summed up Josephine, in her largely successful war against the state regulation of vice, as the single individual most responsible for the spread of syphilis in Europe and perhaps the world.[13] Fernando Henriques, in a far more considered and scholarly work, while displaying more sympathy for her aims, has shown himself none too happy regarding her achievements, and for much the same reason.[14]

It cannot be denied that Josephine laid herself open to such attacks by her refusal to consider arguments against her chosen position as sincere, let alone valid. Convinced that she was engaged in God's work she believed that anyone who opposed her

was opposed to the manifest will of God. It is all the more necessary, therefore, in attempting an appreciation of her work and
her attitude to it, to understand what the Contagious Diseases
Acts stood for from her point of view. As a Liberal and a 'republican' (to use her own term), she was deeply opposed to the idea
of any legislation which granted the police special powers of
summary arrest and imprisonment (albeit in a prison infirmary)
without trial and proper conviction; it was unconstitutional, a
denial of all she had learnt from her father. As an enlightened
and educated woman who had enjoyed intellectual advantages
denied to most of her sex, she believed that the Acts constituted
a discrimination in law more grave than anything enacted before,
an enshrinement in the statute-book of the iniquitous 'double
standard'.

As a floating straw indicates the flow of the tide, so there are
certain expressions that have become almost proverbial, and
till lately have passed unchallenged in conversation and in
literature, plainly revealing the double standard which society
has accepted. One of these expressions is, 'he is only sowing
his wild oats'; another is, that 'a reformed profligate makes a
good husband'. Here we are at once brought into contact with
the false and misleading idea that the essence of right and
wrong is in some way dependent on sex. We never hear it
carelessly or complacently asserted of a young woman that
'*she* is only sowing her wild oats'.[15]

The reason for this discrepancy, she went on, is because men

are driven away at an early age from the society of women,
and thrown upon the society of each other only – in schools,
colleges, barracks, etc.; and have thus concocted and cherished
a wholly different standard of moral purity from that obtaining among women. Even those men who are personally pure
and blameless become persuaded by the force of familiarity
with male profligacy around them, that this sin in *man* is
venial and excusable.[16]

The result of this situation, she concluded, is that many men
have convinced themselves that recourse to prostitution for
men is a regrettable necessity, and it is on the basis of this belief
– that there should be a reserve of healthy women who are depraved beyond redemption for the use of such men – that the

Contagious Diseases Acts have been established. But if the offence which is venial and excusable in men, is held to be damnable in women, it argues that regulations which virtually provide women for the enjoyment of men are reducing such women to the level of slaves. It is 'the most open denial which modern times have seen of the principle of the sacredness of the individual human being'.[17]

The reason, of course, for the almost fanatic horror in which she held the Acts, lay in her belief that the women who were exploited so lightly by men were not damned or irreclaimable, had not entered upon their way of life from choice or inclination, but would be fettered to that way of life by the implementation of the Acts. The trouble was that few men, or women for that matter, considered the prostitute worth reclaiming. Most men, said Josephine in an address to an all-male conference in Manchester, believe that

> fallen women are lost, irreclaimable, unsexed, mere animals, harpies, and the like. . . . I was about to say, when I began, that in order to convince people in this matter I must ask them to come with me to haunts of evil repute, and to poor homes and hiding-places of shame, and spend a week with me among these poor women and then say whether they are not altogether human beings like ourselves, with hearts and consciences, sorrows and joys, tender hopes and poignant regrets. But then I reflect that this would be useless.[18]

Useless it might be, but Josephine had not the slightest intention of letting her audience off such an informative excursion:

> Perhaps no one here present has ever experienced the pain of hunger – I mean starvation hunger. I believe it is difficult for us to realise what that overpowering desire for food is. A girl I saw lately, had lived – motherless – in a wretched home with her father, who, in a fit of intoxication, violated her. She fled in horror; she found a shelter where she slept for many nights on a hard bare floor. Hunger and faintness increased. She was young – not sixteen, not wise, not instructed. She lighted by chance on a low house, where the woman said, 'I'll take you in; here are soldiers every evening.' The girl was hungry; the way seemed easy. I asked her how much she

earned thus – how much a soldier paid. She said, 'Sixpence; and out of that I had to pay fourpence to the woman of the house.' Twopence, gentlemen, is the price, in England, of a poor girl's honour. How often have I thought of Hood's lines:

> O God! That bread should be so dear,
> And Woman's flesh so cheap.

And yet we hear it said, 'Women who sell their persons are already so degraded that even registration for sanitary purposes can degrade them no further'; henceforth they are to be no longer women, but only bits of numbered, inspected, and ticketed human flesh, flung by Government into the public market! As well might one say that a woman is irreclaimable who has experienced the bitterness of protracted famine as that she is irreclaimable when once she has sold her person for money.

When you make a law which includes all unchaste women as 'common prostitutes' you err and you oppress; and when you say that fallen women in the mass are irreclaimable, have lost all truthfulness, all nobleness, all delicacy of feeling, all clearness of intellect, and all tenderness of heart because they are unchaste, you are guilty of a blasphemy against human nature and against God.[19]

When she was testifying before the Royal Commission on the Contagious Diseases Acts in March 1871, Josephine was asked how she regarded the girls she had taken into her care. 'As my friends,' she replied, and she meant it. On another occasion she was asked what gave her the strength to continue her work despite frequent bouts of real or imagined ill-health. 'The awful abundance of compassion which makes me fierce,' she replied.[20]

It is this awful abundance of compassion which raises her in some way above criticism either of her views, or her tactics in making those views evident.

The result of the publication of An Appeal to The People of England had been a brief spell of intense publicity for the Repealers, or Abolitionists as they preferred to be called; 'Like a flash of summer lightning in the dark turn of the year,' wrote Josephine. Unfortunately, like a flash of summer lightning, it was short-lived. The Abolitionists, now formed into the male National Association for Repeal of the Acts, and the Ladies National Association for Repeal, formed local associations up and down the country, and canvassed tirelessly for signatures to petitions demanding the repeal of the Acts. The national press, however, lapsed into what Josephine believed to be a conspiracy of silence.

Josephine had become so single-minded and single-purposed that she failed to realise that events both abroad and at home might crowd a subject which the majority of newspaper subscribers considered either of somewhat limited interest or of such a nature that it should not be aired at all, off the pages of the national dailies. The year was 1870. In an apocalyptic atmosphere the First Vatican Council was debating the doctrine of Papal Infallibility, while the House of Savoy was completing the process of Italian Unification. The question of the Spanish Succession had crescendoed, via the Ems Telegram, into imminent war between France and Prussia, a war which could engulf the whole of Europe. Russia under Alexander II had recovered from the defeat of the Crimean War, and was preparing unilaterally to revoke the Treaty of Paris and to remilitarise the Black Sea ports. At home, the Liberal administration was embarked on perhaps the most intensive and radical reforms undertaken by any nineteenth-century government: the Church, Education, the armed forces, the civil service and Ireland were all under review, and the volcano which Disraeli, four years later, was to describe as 'extinct', was in full eruption. With the Continent volatile to an extent unequalled save in the years immediately preceding the First World War, and a Government which had heaped enough controversy on its head to last a decade, it was not a time favourable to private crusading.

There remained one answer to this problem from the Abolitionists' point of view; to take advantage of the controversy which surrounded the Government. Two by-elections were pending, both in apparently safe Liberal constituencies. Taking advantage of the hostility against the Acts which existed among the voters of the artisan class, most of whom would be going to the polls for the first time, and who had been stirred by Josephine's campaign in the North, Abolitionist candidates would stand against the orthodox Liberal candidates on the single issue of the Contagious Diseases Acts.

The first of these by-elections was at Newark in March 1870. The Liberal candidate was Sir Henry Storks. Storks was a man of the highest integrity. A regular soldier of some distinction, he had been High Commissioner in Malta, was an expert on army administration, a zealous and humane army reformer.

He had also been responsible for implementing the Contagious Diseases Acts in Malta (where, if anywhere, it could be argued that they were urgently necessary in the early 1860s), and had been perhaps the most distinguished and weightiest authority to give evidence – in favour of the Acts – before a select committee of the House of Lords in 1868.

Storks's testimony before the select committee had been subjected to the closest scrutiny on the part of the more academic of Josephine's abolitionist friends and allies, due to his somewhat rash boast that, under his governorship, venereal diseases had been completely wiped out in Malta due to firm application of the regulations. It was true that the incidence of the diseases had diminished significantly; syphilis, it appeared, had almost entirely disappeared, but, on the other hand, the incidence of the far more common, if less dangerous, gonorrhoea remained relatively constant. Then it was discovered that one of the surveys upon which Storks, quite innocently, had based his claim, had been taken from a small detachment of sailors and marines who had spent a leave of only two days on the island. It was discovered that the incidence of syphilis, although much diminished since the 1850s, was still present, and subject to yearly fluctuation. Various explanations were offered by Storks and his advisers for this apparent anomaly: in 1865, the rise in syphilis figures was due to the arrival of Greek camp followers (notorious on the Mediterranean Station for their lack of hygiene). The growing presence of syphilis could be put down to the number of Naval officers' mistresses who supplemented the allowances offered them by their 'protectors' by prostituting themselves with members of the Other Ranks; despite this activity, it was still maintained to be indecorous to subject them to enforced medical inspection; yet another explanation lay in the number of women who passed themselves off, or were passed off, as soldiers' wives.

Had the abolitionists not wished to fight by-elections as a matter of policy, the weight given to Storks's views, the absolute nature of his claims and the relative hollowness of his claims in the view of abolitionists (later confirmed by statistics published by the Admiralty), made him a very particular object of attack. If the Contagious Diseases Acts could not effectively be operated in a small, clearly defined area, to which all egress and access could be carefully checked, with the authority of the army medical corps virtually unquestioned and absolute, how could they prove effective in Chatham or Aldershot, or, if the Association for the Promotion of the Contagious Diseases Acts (1866) had its way, in Manchester or the Metropolitan area?

The intervention of the abolitionists at Newark took the Liberals completely by surprise. A safe Liberal constituency, influenced to a great extent by Joseph Arch, they were sure of Sir Henry Storks's safe return to the House of Commons. As soon as Josephine learnt of Storks's candidature she travelled down to Newark, armed with an introduction to Joseph Arch provided by her allies in the craft unions of the North. Joseph Arch had not yet achieved national fame – two years were to pass before his attempted establishment of an agricultural workers' union – but already he was held in high esteem by his fellow agricultural workers in the Newark district. He was a confirmed, indeed by his own admission fanatic, Liberal. Despite this, Josephine persuaded him to withdraw his support from Sir Henry Storks, and as a result of the ensuing outcry, Storks decided to stand down.

Fortified by this initial success, William Fowler M.P., an enthusiastic abolitionist, asked leave in May 1870, to introduce a private member's bill to repeal the Acts – the first of many such attempts. The abolitionists, Josephine included, had woefully over-estimated the effect of their victory at Newark. Fowler's motion was dropped, not for the last time, due not merely to lack of support – and lack of opposition for that matter – but also to the painful fact that not sufficient numbers of Members of the House were interested enough to attend the chamber.

In October 1870, the abolitionists discovered that Sir Henry Storks had again been nominated as a Liberal candidate, this time at Colchester, where the second of the by-elections was pending. The National Association for Repeal of the Acts, on this occasion, put up and financed one of their own members,

Dr Baxter Langley – himself a Liberal – to oppose Storks. They had little hope of victory: Colchester was one of the garrison towns in which the implementation of the Contagious Diseases Acts had met with considerable success. (Among troops stationed there, the incidence of primary venereal sores detected had dropped from 173 in 1866, when the regulations were first enforced, to a mere 32 in 1870.) The abolitionists had to rely on the hostility excited among the lower classes as a result of the enforcement of the regulations. It was to be a bitterly fought campaign, and the single most exciting adventure undertaken by Josephine herself.

A few days before the electors were due to go to the hustings, Professor James Stuart, Josephine and a few of their colleagues 'invaded' Colchester, equipped with posters drawn up by Harriet Martineau and pamphlets written by John Stuart Mill and other distinguished sympathisers. They, and their candidate, Dr Langley, were due to address an abolitionist meeting at the Colchester Theatre. They met for dinner, before going out, at the hotel where Josephine had taken up residence, and even before they left for the theatre, gangs of ruffians and bullies, hired, and in some cases led, by leading brothel-keepers of the town, were assembling in the streets outside the hotel. There was no doubt as to the object of their attention. Vociferously, they demanded that Josephine be handed over to them. James Stuart and Dr Langley insisted that Josephine remain in the hotel, and they and their gentleman friends gave her their watches, wallets and valuables to look after until their return. Almost as soon as they had set foot in the street, the gangs who were waiting for them realised that Josephine was not with them. Instead of pursuing Stuart and Langley, they elected to remain besieging the hotel, their yelling and jeering becoming more and more menacing as they attracted an ever-growing mob of like-minded people to themselves. At length, the hotel manager came to the drawing-room where Josephine was sitting praying for the safe return of her friends.

'I must turn down the lights; and will you, Madam, consent to go to an attic and remain there until the mob is quieter?'
I consented to this for his sake. His words were emphasised

at the moment by the crashing in of the window near which
I sat, and the noise of heavy stones hurled along the floor
which I managed to evade.[21]

Professor Stuart and Dr Langley returned about an hour
later, and Josephine was led out of the maids' attic bedroom
where she had been secreted. She found both of them 'very
pitiful objects, covered with mud, flour, and other more unpleasant things'.

The following day, the manager requested of Josephine that
she should leave his hotel. She complied, and passed the rest of
the day seeking alternative accommodation, being rejected by
one hotel or inn after another. Finally she was admitted to 'a
very respectable Tory hotel' having been reduced to the
humiliating stratagem of registering under a false name. She
was worn out, and after dinner she immediately retired to bed.
Just as she was dozing off she was made uncomfortably aware
of disturbance in the street below her window. As the noise
grew louder and more violent, there came a sharp rap on her
door, and the hotel manager entered her room:

'I'm sorry, Madam, but I have a very unpleasant announcement to make. I find you are Mrs Josephine Butler, and the mob
outside have found out that you are here, and have threatened
to set fire to the house unless I send you out to them at once.'

Josephine appealed to him; suffering both nervous and physical exhaustion, and profoundly ashamed at having been caught
out after concealing her true identity, she was at her lowest ebb.
She was, in fact, reduced to tears. Though shamefaced, the
manager remained adamant.

'They are so incensed against you, Madam, that my house is
not safe while you are in it!'

He did, however, relent to the extent of summoning one of
the maids, who lent her coat and shawl to Josephine and escorted her out of the back door as if they were two servants leaving
for home after the completion of their duties. The girl was, in
fact, intended by the manager only to see his embarrassing
guest safely off the premises, but she led Josephine to the cottage
of an elderly working man and his wife where she was made
very welcome, and where she stayed for the remainder of her
campaigning in Colchester. It is pleasant to relate, and typical of

Josephine, that she corresponded with her hosts, and helped them (as much as they would permit) for the rest of their lives.

Next morning, she was herself again and declared her intention to continue with the women's rally she had planned for that night. Dressed in the coat and shawl lent to her by the maid from the 'very respectable Tory hotel', she was escorted to the hall where the rally was to be held by twenty-four strong-arm men summoned from London by one of the seasoned political campaigners on her staff. She confessed herself uneasy at being protected by this 'arm of the flesh', understandably since they had been instructed to surround her, concealing her from view, and to bawl lustily in support of the Contagious Diseases Acts until they had seen her safely into the hall.

The meeting was successful, despite the jeering and obscenities from the streets outside the hall. The problem for Josephine lay, not in addressing the assembled womenfolk and their husbands – after she had spoken, she heard a small, fragile-looking girl turn to the young man next to her, presumably her husband, and say, 'If you vote for that man Storks, I'll kill you!' – but in escaping back to her lodgings after it was over. The two policemen who had been deputed to attend the meeting went out, ostensibly to clear a path for Josephine, but more probably to warn the bullies outside that she was coming (in Colchester the police and brothel-owners were hand-in-glove). In the meantime, she, together with Mrs Hampson, one of her supporters, dropped out of a window behind the hall, and made off down the narrow streets away from the main street. Within minutes they were lost in a maze of alleys and courts and wandered for what seemed to Josephine to be an age, while, from a distance, they could hear the baying of the mob.

Finally they came out on to a main street, turned a corner and found themselves face to face with the mob which was hunting for Josephine. They turned back round the corner, and, picking up their skirts, fled running as fast as they could with the mob in full pursuit. They came to a dark and apparently unused warehouse. Mrs Hampson pushed Josephine through the broken door and made off, calling that she would either find a cab or obtain help from their friends. The mob seemed to bay around the warehouse, and Josephine hid in the darkness inside, crouching miserably among crates of empty soda-water bottles, with broken glass underfoot. As the noise receded down the street, the warehouse door was opened slightly, and in the light from the street outside, Josephine saw the slight figure of a girl whom she recognised from her tawdry finery to be a prostitute.

' "Are you the lady the mob are after?" ' the girl asked. ' "Oh what a shame to treat a lady so! I weren't at the meeting, but I heard of you." '

She had seen Josephine from her accustomed beat on the pavement near to the warehouse, and had made up her mind to protect the lady from the mob which was now marching up the street, having lost the scent.

About half-an-hour having passed, during which time the little prostitute stood guard at the door, Mrs Hampson returned. She had failed both to find a cab and to find her way back to Dr Langley's inn. Once more they set out to walk, escorted by the prostitute, who elected to show them the way, and once more they walked straight into the arms of a gang of brothel bullies. This time, Josephine took refuge in the doorway nearest to hand. Fortunately for them, the door was open and admitted them into ' a cheerfully lighted grocer's shop, where a very kind, stout, grocer – a Methodist – welcomed us, and seemed ready to give his life for me. He installed me amongst his bacon, soap, and candles, having sent for a cab; and rubbing his hands, he said, "Well, this is a capital thing; here you are, safe and sound!" '
At last the cab arrived, and escorted by Mrs Hampson, the grocer and the prostitute, Josephine was returned to the safety of the cottage where she had taken up lodging.

Even Josephine's most enthusiastic devotees have expressed doubts as to whether Sir Henry Storks endorsed his less reputable supporters' attempts to intimidate her. Certainly he sent emissaries to Dr Langley's headquarters imploring her to withdraw from the struggle, though whether from solicitude for her personal safety or from acute awareness of the harm being done to his campaign among the artisan and dissenting lower middle-class electorate by the behaviour of the street gangs, it is impossible to say. In any case it would have served no purpose for Josephine to have stayed in Colchester to be present at the traditional rowdyism and drunkenness of the actual poll itself. She returned to Liverpool.

The morning after the poll was counted she received a telegram from James Stuart. 'Shot dead', it read, referring to Storks, whom they had come to refer to either as 'the stork' or even less flatteringly as 'the bird'. He had been defeated by four hundred votes and the Conservative had won the seat, the Abolitionists having split the Liberal vote as they had intended. With a suitable sense of gratitude, the new member for Colchester promised to support William Fowler's campaign in the House for the repeal of the Contagious Diseases Acts.

For Josephine, the triumph was blighted by the realisation that the national press had not so much as mentioned the intervention of the Abolitionists, and while it had expressed surprise at the result, it made no attempt to explain it. In fact, the staggering defeat of the Imperial French army at the hands of the Prussians and their allies, and the equally staggering resistance of the French *levée en masse* following the encirclement of Paris, had driven virtually all other news off the leader pages. But the Colchester election had not gone unnoticed by Gladstone and his colleagues – the loss of a safe Liberal seat could not be ignored. There was talk of another select committee to examine the operation of the Contagious Diseases Acts. As soon as Josephine heard that it was in the wind she was determined that the Abolitionist cause should be heard as it had not been previously, and that something should be done to counteract the sort of evidence given in 1868, in which one doctor had claimed to find a whole ward full of infected prostitutes meditating over *Pilgrim's Progress*, such was the irresistible odour of sanctity prevailing in 'Lock' hospitals.

She drew up a memorandum with a formidable list of accounts of innocent girls who had been forced into compulsory examination.[22] Some of these were found to be false; Josephine, as so often happened, though she would never knowingly have countenanced dishonesty, was too impetuous, and too hard-worked, to verify every tale reported to her. One, at least, was well-authenticated: the case of Caroline Wyburgh, of Chatham.

Caroline was aged nineteen, lived in one room with her mother and kept them both by working at the most menial form of domestic service – scrubbing doorsteps and basement areas at a penny or two a time.[23] She was generally held to be a good girl, sober, honest, industrious and never home late. She was also, and it was fatal, 'walking out' with a soldier. Late one

night she was roused from her bed by an Inspector Wakeford
of the Metropolitan Police (he was later to testify before the
Royal Commission on the Contagious Diseases Acts saying, in
answer to the question did he believe that a Common Prostitute
was a woman who earned her livelihood by prostitution, 'If
you confine yourself to this definition your Acts will never succeed'). Inspector Wakeford insisted that she was a prostitute
and that, despite the lateness of the hour, she should go up
with him for examination. Caroline refused, saying 'she was not
one of that lot'. Inspector Wakeford replied that if she persisted
in her refusal he would make sure she spent three months at
hard labour in Maidstone Gaol. At this, her mother, faced with
the prospect of three months without Caroline's pitiful wage to
support her, persuaded her to go. At the police station she was
presented with a piece of paper and ordered, since she was illit-
erate, to make her mark. She did so, carefully stating at the same
time that she 'had always been a good girl'. Since the paper was
the form of 'voluntary submission' her statement was ignored.
She was then taken to the examination room. As soon as she
saw the surgical couch with its tray of instruments, and the
stock-like clamps which were used for bracing apart the legs
of recalcitrant women, she refused absolutely to submit to
examination. She was then dragged to one of the 'Lock'
wards, strapped into bed where she was kept for four days and
subjected to a diet of black tea and dry bread. On the fifth day
she agreed to be examined provided no instruments were used.
As soon as she entered the surgery she was forced into a strait-
jacket, thrust into the couch and her feet were clamped apart in
the required position, while an assistant thrust his elbow on to
her breasts to prevent her from struggling. Struggle she did,
with the result that her body rolled out of the couch while her
ankles remained secure in the stocks, causing her serious injury.
Meanwhile the blood which issued from between her legs told its
own story. According to Caroline's mother, who was present at
this edifying scene, the doctor laughed and said, 'Well, now you
can go home. You have been telling the truth. You are not a
"bad girl".' The matron of the 'Lock' hospital took her to her
office, gave her a hot dinner and presented her with five shillings
after exacting from her a promise – which Caroline understandably decided not to keep – that she would never tell 'any Lady

or Gentleman' about what had occurred. It was such incidents as these which inspired W. T. Stead (Josephine's biographer and editor of the *Northern Echo* and later the *Pall Mall Gazette*) to describe compulsory surgical examination as 'surgical rape'.

To this, Josephine added that she had seen hardened prostitutes having to be removed unconscious from the surgical couch after examination, while in one case she herself had witnessed, the patient, who was pregnant, had suffered a 'flooding' of blood, and had lost her baby as a result.[24]

Circulating these accounts of abuses resulting from the operation of the Contagious Diseases Acts, she obtained a thousand signatures in support of her memorandum that there should be a government inquiry. She then took it to London, in person. A few days later she wrote a letter to all the signatories:

> I had the honour of presenting your memorial to Lord Granville on Tuesday last. I wrote previously to Lord Granville telling him that I should call at his house for this purpose . . . I added, 'I shall be in London for three days, and I will wait, if necessary, those three days *outside* your door, until your Lordship shall find it convenient to choose either to hear our petition, or to order my removal.'[25]

In fact Lord Granville took her challenge in good part, assured her that he had no wish to be subjected to so formidable a siege and invited her to dinner. He was able to inform her that a committee of the House of Lords was already meeting under the chairmanship of Lord Dalhousie to discuss arrangements for a possible Royal Commission to inquire into the Acts.

# X

THE Royal Commission on the Contagious Diseases Acts commenced taking evidence only eight weeks after the Colchester election. It consisted of twenty-three members, including ten representatives from both Houses of Parliament, four from the Bishops and Clergy and six eminent scientists among whom was T. H. Huxley, the most celebrated scientist of his day (Darwin excepted). The composition of the Commission was calculated to produce an impartially considered result despite Josephine's initial hostility towards it. It is true that only one of its members, Peter Rylands M.P., was a committed abolitionist, but others were likely to listen sympathetically to Josephine and her allies – Cowper-Temple, a distinguished member of the Liberal administration; A. J. Mundella (later to be author of the third Education Act), a prosperous business-man, and a friend and spokesman in the Commons for Josephine's principal body of support, the craft unions; and Robert Applegarth, presiding genius of the most authoritative body of the craft unions, the London Junta. Others were already her personal friends, including the Rev. F. D. Maurice, and the Bishop of Carlisle. Only one member was likely to prove as prejudiced in favour of the Acts as Peter Rylands was prejudiced against them – Admiral Collinson.

The Commission took evidence for forty-five days spread over six months, commencing in early January 1871. At first, witnesses were confined to officials concerned in administering the Acts – medical men, magistrates, hospital managers and police officers. The statistics which they produced indicated that where regulation of vice was applied venereal diseases were firmly contained and the incidence of such diseases greatly reduced. For all this, much of the incidental evidence offered by these witnesses bore out the claims of the abolitionists, and was noted by the Commission in its Report as having done so.

Mr Parsons, a Portsmouth surgeon employed in the medical inspection of women, was asked:

*Q.* Suppose the Acts were abolished, you say that women would regret it?
*A.* Certainly. They feel now that when they are diseased they have a home to go to, to be cured. A large portion of their earnings went formally in medical bills and chemists' bills. The money which they formally spent on their cure can now be spent in ways more palatable to them.[1]

Inspector Annis of Plymouth, who, like Mr Parsons, was a fervent supporter of the Acts, was asked:

*Q.* [Prostitutes] are better off and get more employment of this immoral character, and so get a larger income?
*A.* I am sorry to think their income is rather too large now.

But that is the only evil I see.[2]

A senior army officer was asked:

*Q.* Have you been able to trace any of the influence of these Acts on the moral tone of the men in general?
*A.* I think I can recognise distinctly a feeling among the men, that when they get into a subjected district they are safe. They indulge more freely in fornication than they would in places not subjected, because they think the Acts give them security from disease.[3]

At least one member of the Commission could endorse this last statement from personal experience. A. J. Mundella declared that 'members of his own club told him that they themselves resorted to protected districts, and that they could not understand why he had any doubts regarding the Acts'.[4]

Evidence submitted by Police authorities to show that the Acts actually diminished the practice of prostitution was easily refuted. It was claimed that the number of beer-houses in protected areas which operated as houses of assignation – a significant feature of nineteenth-century prostitution – had been reduced drastically. This was true; what was not mentioned was that for every beer-house which had its licence revoked or which was properly patrolled, two private houses of assignation were opened. It was suggested that the incidence of juvenile prostitution was reduced almost to the point of disappearance, a statement known to be untrue by anybody who was remotely familiar with London's club-land. In fact, the statistical evidence was rigged by the simple procedure of entering statistics of girls under the age of fifteen in the column reserved for those under the age of seventeen. Such attempts to mislead the Commissioners were, for the most part, self-defeating. They resulted in Professor Huxley, whose opinion on such matters carried great weight among his colleagues, casting grave doubt on the entire body of statistical evidence, including that relating to the reduction in the incidence of venereal diseases.

In fact, evidence tended to reveal that the operation of the Acts consolidated, if not actually increased, the practice of prostitution in protected areas. Certainly, irrefutable evidence was placed before the Commission that compulsory medical examination tended to harden part-time prostitutes (e.g. of the

'dolly-mop' class) into full-time professionals, and, as a result
of the notoriety gained from having been so examined, to recruit
prostitutes from the hitherto innocent girls who had had the
misfortune to be trapped in the police net. J. A. Phillips, an
officer in the Metropolitan Police who had resigned from plainclothes work in a regulated area (and lost five shillings a week of
his wages – a considerable sum for him – as a result of his
resignation) because he objected to the way in which the regulations were enforced, deposed:

> It was very clear that there was with many going up to
> examination on the first time a considerable amount of shame
> and sensitiveness, and afterwards a marked spirit of boldness
> and hardening influence. . . . [At first] they were often obliged
> to get half-drunk before they could submit to the ordeal they
> had to pass through by the examination.[5]

The necessity for girls to get drunk or 'half-drunk' before
submitting themselves to examination was amply confirmed by
other witnesses.

W. R. D. Williams, a member of the committee of the Rescue
Society, said that he had been authorised by 'Mrs Macdonald,
Matron of the Exeter Penitentiary; Mrs Clayton, Matron of the
Rescue Home at Woolwich; and Mrs Walker, Matron of the
Pentonville Institution', to state that 'the women are quite
unlike what they were before the Acts came into operation, and
the chance of their reformation is very much on the decrease'.[6]
He added that the Rescue Society Committee had been forced
reluctantly to refuse admission to girls from regulated areas to
their Pentonville Institution since such girls had become so
hardened and so brazen that they only obstructed the work of
the Institution.

An interesting, and somewhat ignored aspect, of the controversy was provided by the Editor of the *Medical Times and
Gazetteer*, a confirmed and committed supporter of the Acts:

> There is nothing which tends more to deprive Medicine of
> the rank of a respectable calling than the fact that prac-
> titioners should be found willing to lend themselves to the
> dirty work of examining prostitutes, in order to enable them
> to carry on their trade, and even instructing them in the art
> of injecting, so that they may sin in safety.[7]

On the other hand, military and naval surgeons testified readily enough that, while they would object profoundly to inspecting soldiers and sailors for symptoms of venereal infection as being degrading both to themselves and to the Service to which they belonged, they saw nothing degrading in inspecting queues of young girls for signs of the same diseases.

Josephine was invited to appear before the Royal Commission fairly late in its transactions, at the end of March 1871, when it had been taking evidence for more than twelve weeks. Her own attitude toward the composition of the Commission was at one with the views expressed in a letter to her from a working man, a Carlisle clog-maker, one of many such letters she brought with her to Westminster:

> I consider the Royal Commission to enquire into these Acts anything but a fair one. I understand that it is chiefly chosen from the Government officers, who, it appears to me, are on their trial; and yet they have the choosing of their own jury. I see they boast of having a bishop and two or three Church clergymen, but I hear they never invited a nonconformist minister, independent and free. We know that some bishops advocated slavery, and were amongst the stoutest defenders of that crime, not many years ago.[8]

She herself was worked up into a fury of indignation. She had been granted only a few days' notice, and had had no time to prepare a proper brief. She was also suffering from that real or imagined loss of health which always afflicted her at moments of crisis. She was quite genuinely overworked with pamphleteering, recruiting support for the Cause, ceaseless travelling and lecturing, not to mention letter-writing; she was, by now, the acknowledged leader of the abolitionists. Her nervous tension manifested itself in outbursts of truculence before the Commissioners, and a tendency to stray off the point.

As soon as she entered the committee-room where the Royal Commission was sitting, she glanced around hoping to recognise at least one friendly face in that of the Rev. F. D. Maurice. Unfortunately, he was absent through illness that day:

> To compare a very small person with a great one [Josephine wrote to George that same night], I felt rather like Paul before Nero, very weak and lonely . . . I handed to the Chairman

[The Right Hon. William N. Massey] the large packet of the letters and resolutions from working-men. He said: 'We may as well see them; for no doubt that class takes some little interest in the question.' I should think so! Let them wait until election times and they will see! One of the Commissioners asked: 'Are these bona-fide working men?' I replied: 'Yes, and well-known men. There is more virtue in the country than you gentlemen in high life imagine.' He then asked: 'If these laws were put in operation in the North, do you believe they would be forcibly resisted?' I replied: 'I do.'[9]

The Chairman opened the formal examination by questioning Josephine about her work in reclaiming prostitutes. As later transpired, William Massey was more sympathetic towards her attitude than otherwise, but Josephine's replies to his questions reveal a nervous aggressiveness towards him. She refused to be drawn into a discussion on statistics of success or failure, blandly stating that she 'preferred to forget' such things, and it soon became clear that there was some difference between what Massey took to be success, and Josephine's attitude. Josephine was less concerned with cleaning up the streets – Massey had suggested that reformatories were a better place for fallen women than Josephine's spare bedroom – than with stimulating a girl's individual self-respect.

'Efforts made by private persons like yourself', he said, 'are very inadequate to meet the evil.'[10]

'If there were a sufficient number of private persons to act as I do,' she retorted, 'you would require no government machinery.'

Understandably, Massey suggested that such an eventuality was improbable in the extreme.

'How would you induce so many to be as devoted as yourself in the matter?' he asked.

'By showing them the example of Christ,' she replied.

The examination then moved on to the subject of the Contagious Diseases Acts, and Josephine was allowed to express her predictable views on them.

Did she not think that some control over the spread of venereal diseases was necessary? In reply to a question from Sir John Pakington she agreed that it was necessary. Then she explained why:

I could give as an illustration the case of a girl who died in my house. I will not reveal her father's disgrace by speaking of his name, nor of that gentleman now in London, who was her seducer. She lived in my house until she died of a frightful disease. She was the daughter of the keeper of a lodge belonging to a gentleman of large property. This gentleman, whose name I will not mention, seduced her, and communicated to her this disease, and she died of this. The father of that girl will come to a meeting which I hold, of working men. He hears these Acts are put in force to prevent women infecting men with this disease, and he gnashes his teeth with anger, and says, 'Do not men ever communicate it to women?'

How then, she was asked, would she deal with the problem?

'Legislation alone will not do it,' she replied. 'Seduction must be punished. At present, for the purpose of seduction, and of seduction only, our law declares every female child a woman at twelve years of age. I am ashamed to have to confess to such a shameful state of the law before you gentlemen, but a child is a woman, for that purpose alone, at twelve years of age. I know from my experience amongst this class of women, how many have become so from that cause.'

She went on to point out how abuses arising from the deplorably early age of consent as established by English law were aggravated by equally deplorable social conditions.

Up to now, she continued, any attempt at dealing with the problem of prostitution had been hamstrung by the operation of the double standard in morality: 'It cannot be said that there is no such thing as seduction of young girls by gentlemen of the upper classes.' Surely, members of the Commission asked, there were other motives for a girl taking to the streets than seduction? Starvation, parental negligence and sheer wantonness were mentioned. Josephine agreed:

'And there is one most important cause of all, which is the absolute want of industrial training and paid industries for women; for without them, what is a friendless woman to do?'

She was asked if she did not believe that there was a genuine attempt made under the provisions of the Acts for the reclamation of prostitutes?

'I am aware that it is continually asserted by the supporters of the system,' she replied. 'I grant that you reclaim – how many, would you say?'

'I will suppose thirty per cent,' replied a Commissioner.

'I grant you then that you reclaim ninety per cent of the women, if that will satisfy you, but it is not of the least consequence to my argument, for there is a double motive in these Acts, there are two ends to be served by them, and we cannot serve two masters. There are two motives, one the providing of clean women for the army and navy, the other the reclamation of women. We cannot serve two masters. While you reclaim the women you are stimulating the vices of men. That is the point, and I insist on this Commission hearing it; and what is the use, I ask you in the name of Heaven, to save women while you are stimulating the vices of men?'

On being asked whether she believed that, concealed in the figures on the police registers, there were girls under the age of fourteen who were common prostitutes, she replied:

'Our law declares a girl of twelve a woman. On this Parliament could and should act. The age of consent must be raised.'

One of the Commissioners suggested that working-class girls were themselves responsible for the high incidence of prostitution, and that young men of gentler birth were lured by them into sin. Such an opinion was almost calculated to drive Josephine into a frenzy of anger. Why, she demanded, if working-class girls held a monopoly in original sin, did procurers and procuresses do such a roaring trade in Britain?

I have seen girls bought and sold just as young girls were, at the time of the slave trade. Are you not aware that there are young gentlemen among the higher classes who will pay? When a young gentleman sends to a professional brothel for a girl, he pays for her – is that not paying? . . . I will set a floodlight on your doings – I mean the immorality which exists among gentlemen of the upper classes!

One of her interrogators expressed surprise at Josephine's familiarity with the technicalities of professional prostitution and brothel-keeping, and asked her how a lady of her social standing and breeding could bear to contemplate such degradation and wickedness in members of her own sex. Her reply was magnificent:

'There is no evil in the world so great, that God cannot raise up to meet it a corresponding beauty and glory that will blaze it out of countenance.'

She went on to emphasise the fear engendered among decent working-class families by the thought that the Acts might be extended to the civil population – a fear which ran like an *idée fixe* through the letters she had submitted to the chairman of the Commission. One such letter, from an employer in this instance, fairly sums up the views expressed in a host of others:

I feel impelled as an employer of more than 150 women and 100 men and youths to tell you that no language can express the indignation, dread, and shame with which they view these Acts. There is not one dissentient.

The women say they are at work all day; the evening is the only time that is their own, and unless they remain entirely in the house and debar themselves from chapels, lectures, seeing their acquaintances, or even from fresh air, they must often be out then, and it is abominable that they are to be watched by policemen or any other spies, and at their evidence or suspicion be compelled to submit to treatment too degrading to mention; and all without trial by judge and jury, which the worst criminals are allowed before they can be punished. Many of them, feeling too helpless and friendless to struggle against such laws, look forward to a prison as their future lot, almost for life, if the laws are extended.

Finally Josephine was asked what weight she would place on the findings of the Royal Commission.

'All of us,' she replied, 'who are seeking the repeal of these Acts, are wholly indifferent to the decision of the Commission. We have the Word of God in our hands, the Law of God in our consciences. We know that to protect vice in men is not according to the Word of God. The Acts are abhorred by the country as a tyranny of the upper classes against the lower classes, as an injustice practised by men on women, and as an insult to the moral sense of the people – an iniquity which is abhorred by Christian England.'

As she was resting in the Lobby of the House of Lords, having left the committee room, Cowper-Temple came over to her and asked her if she had not been nervous at having to appear before the Commission. Her reply was a trifle harsh and not entirely truthful:

'Not at all, sir; I was not nervous. But my soul was deeply troubled at the sight of so many men with so base and low a moral standard as you seem to have, and such utter scepticism both about God and human nature.'[11]

She wrote to George that she had been dissatisfied with her appearance, but she had forgotten the impact invariably made by her own personality. One of the members of the Commission wrote to George:

'I am not accustomed to religious phraseology, but I cannot give any idea of the effect Mrs Butler produced, except by saying that the influence of the spirit of God was there.'[12]

Her point regarding child prostitution was taken up, and, during the latter part of their investigation, appears to have distracted the Commissioners from the main point at issue. Certainly, witness after witness was questioned as to the incidence of prostitution among girls under the age of fourteen. When, in July 1871, the Report of the Royal Commission was published, no room was left for doubt regarding their views on the subject:

> The traffic in children for infamous purposes is notoriously considerable in London and other large towns. We think that a child of twelve can hardly be deemed capable of giving consent and should not have the power of yielding up her person. We therefore recommend the absolute protection of female children to the age of fourteen years, making the age of consent to commence at fourteen instead of twelve as under the existing law.[13]

In virtually every other respect the Commissioners vacillated, torn between the view which was held by the majority – that prostitution was inevitable, and, following the opinion of Lecky, perhaps even necessary to the assurance of a stable and pure family life – and the recognition that any legislation required to ensure that the dangers inherent in sexual promiscuity should not infect the innocent was, at the same time, inherently unjust and could, if extended, lead to even grosser forms of injustice. Thus they were caught between two completely rational, acceptable, but entirely contradictory points of view. The result was caution and compromise. The Report recommended a reversion to the first Contagious Diseases Act (1864) and the abolition of regular inspection of women, deemed to be common prostitutes by the police, at periodic intervals. This should be replaced by the old system whereby every common prostitute found diseased following voluntary resort to a doctor or government hospital, or following a complaint made by erstwhile clients that she had infected them, or following arrest by police as a result of her having caused a public nuisance by soliciting, should be detained in a government hospital until discharged by magistrates' order, or by the hospital authorities, or on the expiry of three months. This, it was hoped, would prevent arrests and compulsory examination as a result of common information (often anonymous) being laid, and irresponsible arrest of perfectly innocent girls going about the streets in the early evening. Recommended also was the abolition of the plain-clothes 'morals police' in garrison towns, and that such police, uniformed or otherwise, should be under the direct authority of the Home Office.[14]

Some effort had been made by the Commissioners to meet the views of the abolitionists, at least regarding the worst abuses produced by the Acts. Josephine, however, was far from satisfied. The preamble of the majority report was enough to put her on her guard, particularly the section which read:

'There is no comparison to be drawn between prostitutes and the men who consort with them. With one sex the offence is committed as a matter of gain, with the other it is an irregular indulgence of a *natural* impulse.' The principle of the 'double standard' which she so deeply resented could hardly have been expressed more succinctly.

There were, however, more grave implications to be found in the Report, in Josephine's opinion. On 14 November 1871 she addressed the annual meeting of the Ladies' Association:

The secret information which is to make them [the authorities] believe that a prostitute is diseased can only come from one of three sources:– 1st, the woman herself;– 2nd, the accomplice of her sin;– 3rd, a brothel-keeper. This is a very dangerous power when put into their hands. Under the present Acts, a man whose infamous proposals have been rejected by a girl, may inform the police against her, and on his evidence the girl may be subjected to examination and ruined. Under the law the Commissioners recommend, he would only have to hint she is diseased; before his words could be proved false, the girl would have been brought before the magistrates and condemned to be examined, and, whatever were the result, the man's revenge would be completed by the Act of the Government. A like power would, by such a system, be legally vested in the hands of the brothel-keepers. If one of these wretches should mark a young and friendless girl for his victim – and the more innocent and helpless-looking the higher her value to them – his course would be easy. A secret information could be given to the sanitary officer that the girl had been ruined and was diseased. She could be brought before the magistrate, and ordered for examination. At once every lodging house would be closed to her; no employer would have her; rude men and women would jeer at her. Then the brothel-keeper would have but to meet her, be filled with compassion, take her in, feed and shelter her; knowing well that under this new law, once inside his door he is sure of her.[15]

In an age when procuresses from London brothels dressed themselves as nuns in order to meet Irish immigrant girls off the Fishguard and Liverpool boat-trains, then to lure them to houses furnished as convents so that their suspicions should not be aroused, it was no flight of fancy to assume that brothel-keepers would, and did, recruit girls in the way Josephine described.

A new theme was entering into Josephine's arguments. The parallels between the old slave trade, which had played so strong a part in her childhood and adolescent imagination, and prostitution had always been present in her mind. But now, the parallels were becoming more exact. In Liverpool in the 1860s she had been dealing with mendicant prostitution and girls who had suffered from individual seducers. Now, with the wider knowledge and experience offered as a result of her emergence as a national leader of the abolitionist cause, she was confronted more and more often by the 'traffic in flesh', by prostitution as a capitalistic enterprise condoned if not actually encouraged by an astonishingly large proportion of apparently respectable middle- and upper-middle-class manhood. Josephine could not

know, when she faced the individual members of the Royal
Commission, or a group of high-ranking members of the Liberal
Party known to her from childhood, which of them, for all the
sympathetic hearings they offered her, resorted habitually to
Mrs Jeffries's flagellation houses, or were prepared to pay up to
twenty-five guineas for the pleasure of raping a terrified twelve-
year-old virgin; and it was this which provoked her outcry to
the Royal Commission, 'I will set a floodlight on your doings!'

Rightly or wrongly, Josephine believed that should legislation
be passed on the basis of the Royal Commission's Report, the
situation would be worse than before. The innocent girl who,
when summoned before the government surgeons, might have
had some shred of hope, some fragment of respect, would now
be assumed to have contracted a venereal disease, to be beyond
moral reclamation, and her only resort, the brothel. The only
positive effects of such legislation, she declared, would be 'to
compel the brothel-keepers to see that their girl-slaves are
always kept healthy for the use of their customers'.[16]

# XI

IF the Royal Commission had found it difficult to arrive at a
consensus opinion in order to produce their report, the Government found it even more difficult to draft a bill which would
satisfy public opinion (which, on the basis of the Colchester
election, they were convinced, opposed the Contagious Diseases
Acts) while, at the same time, avoiding controversy within their
own parliamentary ranks. The unhappy result was 'A Bill to
Repeal the Contagious Diseases Acts and for the Better protection of Women'. Among Abolitionists and supporters of 'the
Cause' it became known, and has been remembered, as 'Mr
Bruce's Bill', named after the Home Secretary who introduced it
far from enthusiastically into the Commons on 13 February 1872.

Many in the Abolitionist ranks greeted it favourably. Josephine did not; the Bill appeared to confirm every fear she had
expressed regarding the report of the Royal Commission. For
the Repealers it was a difficult decision to make, whether to
support or oppose the Bill, and certainly both Gladstone and
Bruce had expected their unqualified support. Even today

doubts have been expressed regarding Josephine's adamant rejection of it.

Part four of the Bill – the 'supplemental clauses' – was unexceptionable:

1. The age of consent, as recommended by the Royal Commission, to be raised to fourteen.

2. The harbouring or placing under restraint of any girl under the age of sixteen for purposes of prostitution to be made a misdemeanour, punishable summarily with six months imprisonment, or, upon indictment, with a sentence up to two years.

3. The obtaining possession of any woman, regardless of age, by false pretences to be a misdemeanour punishable as above.

4. The maintaining of women in any house for purposes of prostitution, whether diseased or not, to be subject to the above penalties.

Part one, section two, of the Bill called for the complete withdrawal of the three Contagious Diseases Acts, but Part one, section three, contained the clauses which aroused Josephine's opposition, and which she described as 'rendering that repeal practically nugatory, inasmuch as these clauses contain the leading principles of the present Acts'.[1] These are so crucial to the understanding of her view of the Bill (whether such a view was a responsible one or not) that they should be reproduced in full:

1. Whereas by the Vagrant Act, 1824, it is provided that 'every common prostitute wandering in the public streets or public highways, or in any place of public resort, and behaving in a riotous or indecent manner' shall be liable to conviction to be imprisoned as therein mentioned, and it is expedient to explain the said provision and extend the same to Ireland, be it enacted –

'Every common prostitute who in any public street, public highway, or place of public resort, solicits or importunes persons for the purpose of prostitution, shall be deemed to behave in an indecent manner within the meaning of the recited provision of the Vagrant Act, 1824.'

2. Where a woman is imprisoned in pursuance –

(1) Of a conviction for any offence as a common prostitute,

or,

(2) Of a conviction for any offence by a court, of summary

jurisdiction, at the trial for which offence it is proved that
she is a common prostitute;
and such a woman is found, at the expiration of her sentence
to be affected by contagious disease, she shall be liable to be
detained in the infirmary of the prison, or to be removed to a
certified hospital, in the manner provided by this Act.

3. Every woman detained in a certified hospital or prison
infirmary in pursuance of this Act shall be discharged there-
from as soon as the chief medical officer of such hospital or
infirmary certifies that her detention for medical treatment for
contagious disease is no longer requisite, and in any case at
the expiration of nine months from the expiration of the term
of her imprisonment.

4. Where a justice of the peace is satisfied on the application of a woman who is detained in a hospital or prison infirmary in pursuance of this Act that the applicant intends to
cease to be a common prostitute, such justice may, if he think
fit, make an order in a summary manner for her discharge from
the hospital or infirmary, and she shall be discharged forthwith.

A fifth clause provided a penalty for escaping from certified
hospitals.

Josephine admitted that the Bill, while maintaining the
principles of the Contagious Diseases Acts, modified them and
presented them in a milder form. But this, in her opinion, was
'more than counterbalanced by the enormously greater extent
over which this Bill is to be applied. It applies to the whole
kingdom, whereas the present Acts apply to only thirteen towns.
By this Bill the principle of the Contagious Diseases Acts is in-
sinuated into every town, and in a form peculiarly capable of
development and extension.'

Because she believed the essential principle of the Bill and the
Acts to be the same, many of her detailed objections were also
the same. Prostitutes are to be cured not for their own sakes,
but for the sake of their clients. Under clause four, a woman may
be discharged from hospital whether she is affected by disease
or not, because, assuming that she really does intend to reform
her ways, she will not infect 'wicked and immoral men'. The
argument that compulsory treatment is designed to protect the
innocent and unborn is thereby nullified; the authorities are in

no way concerned about the men the erstwhile prostitute may marry, nor are they worried about the children she may, in the future, bear. They are concerned entirely about the welfare of upper-class men who seek illicit pleasure with unfortunate and poverty-stricken women. 'The object of the Bill is to render it safer for immoral men to associate with these women – the continuance of a practice by men of the vice which produces the disease which the Bill is supposed to eradicate.'

Not even her compassion for the children caught up in the dreadful market in juvenile prostitution, who would almost certainly have been saved a further fourteen years of exploitation had 'Mr Bruce's Bill' been passed, could budge her. 'It was impossible', Josephine wrote twenty years after the Bill was presented to the Commons, 'for us to accept a measure which had at the heart of it the very principle which we had determined to get rid of, though this principle was ingeniously wrapped up in various proposals for the protection of the young and other good things.'[2]

It was a hard line to take, and such was the view of the overwhelming majority of her supporters and associates, at least at first. In Parliament her supporters such as Peter Rylands and Jacob Bright voted for a second reading of the Bill, as did those who had been won over by her testimony before the Royal Commission, Cowper-Temple and A. J. Mundella. The Repeal Association was almost wholly out of sympathy with Josephine, and the Ladies' Association, her own immediate following, was deeply divided and thoroughly demoralised. Josephine was even more depressed. Never daunted by the strength of opposition, she was always saddened when she was made aware that friends whom she loved and admired, and whose opinions she valued, disagreed with her. Only once again, towards the end of her life when she advocated the British stand during the Boer War, was she to find herself at odds with so many of her closest adherents. In a vehement letter to her own Liverpool association she expressed her apologia:

I suspect that the real reason why men are not here treated in the same way as women is that Parliament would not endure that men should be put in prison for solicitation on such slight evidence before a summary court, as is the case with women; for the men of the upper classes would be laid hold of by the Bill, and it would be a terrible thing indeed to the hearts of our present legislators to think that one of themselves or their sons might be touched. . . .

The language of the state now again, through the medium of Mr Bruce's Bill, is as follows – 'It being needful, in deference to public opinion, to abandon the Acts, I can only say to you – immoral men – with whose bodily health I charge myself, that I shall do my best to continue to stand between you and the disease which your vicious actions lay you open to, by falling back upon already existing legal machinery, which I shall make more stringent in its actions upon women of the poorer classes. I shall be able to offer you at the doors of prison infirmaries and certified hospitals, a supply of women who, though not possessing certificates, you may rely on as having passed through the surgeons' hands, and having been made safe for your use. So careful am I that no woman, except such as are made thus safe, shall escape from the aforesaid hospitals and infirmaries, that I have adjudged heavy penalties – arrest without warrant, and imprisonment with hard labour – to any woman who shall attempt to escape. Prison is now the portal to our new system; but there will be no great difficulty in securing that this portal will be made very wide, and that a vast number of women of the poorer classes shall pass through this portal, inasmuch as every penalty shall be enforced with double stringency against all such offences as loitering, begging, "being in any place for the purpose of prostitution, (in the opinion of a policeman)" etc. It is, moreover, open to me to create a host of new offences, such as those which have been created in Paris, in order to bring women into the hands of the surgeons.'[3]

Josephine's chief ally, and the person most responsible for causing the Abolitionists to close their ranks about her, was the Home Secretary himself. In introducing a bill whose supposed purpose was the repeal of the Contagious Diseases Acts, Mr Bruce saw fit to make a speech in which he expressed his regret at their disappearance. He agreed that those who had opposed the Acts were 'persons of serious and thoughtful habits', but added that they were also prone to exaggeration, wilful distortion and in the case of the ladies, somewhat hysterical in their denunciation of the measures. The Acts had cleared the streets of prostitutes in the thirteen regulated towns, he maintained; venereal diseases had been virtually eliminated in those towns; and juvenile prostitution had been almost entirely suppressed. Medical opinion was almost unanimous in its approval of the Acts, while the view taken by some, that the effect of the Acts was to harden prostitutes and to encourage them in vice, was rejected by many authorities of equal or greater standing. Unfortunately, he concluded, 'it is impossible to maintain laws which have not the sanction of public opinion'. The Government would therefore present to the House proposed legislation in which the best results of the Acts would be retained and extended to embrace the whole nation.

The Home Secretary's speech seemed to confirm every warning Josephine had uttered. At the end of February 1872, the National Association and the Ladies' Association held a joint general meeting at the Westminster Palace Hotel to discuss their attitude towards the Bill. There was considerable division in the ranks of the National Association, who were anxious that the Supplemental Clauses of the Bill should be given the force of law, but the Ladies' Association was almost entirely opposed to the Bill. The result was a compromise motion suggesting that the Supplemental Clauses should be retained, but that Part one of the Bill should be rejected. Since this would have resulted in the abandonment of three-quarters of the Bill, it was unlikely to have proved acceptable to the Government. The effect of the motion was, therefore, a declaration of opposition to the Bill.

Under the circumstances, and faced with an important by-election at Pontefract in a matter of weeks, Gladstone withdrew the Bill on the grounds that it was too late in the Parliamentary session to proceed with a measure which was bound to prove controversial.

## XII

DURING the summer of 1872, and as a direct result of the controversy surrounding her outright objection to 'Mr Bruce's Bill', Josephine published her book *The New Era*. In many ways this is the most remarkable of her propagandist works. Unlike much of her pamphleteering against the Contagious Diseases Acts and the draft-legislation intended to replace them, it does not take the form of a sermon couched in biblical phraseology and founded on undebated premisses, but is a careful and incisive presentation of her case. It was written, as its preamble makes clear, as a considered argument against 'Mr Bruce's Bill', but, in fact, it reached the public after the Bill had been withdrawn. It is something of the measure of the book that its late arrival on the market did nothing to lessen either its significance or its value. It was to become, and was to remain until long after her death, the testament of those opposed to the state regulation of prostitution.

She begins by pointing out that Great Britain had remained until the 1860s the one European country free of a 'regulated' system of vice, 'but with all the energy and zeal of a new convert, she has made amends to the devil for her long repose'.[1] As a result of possessing an empire over which the sun never sets, Britain had now ensured that the sun could never set over the system of 'regulated' vice.

At this point, Josephine states that in order to examine the validity of state regulation, both moral and practical, it is necessary to examine the system as practised in a society which has known such a system over a considerable number of years. From the British point of view, Prussia affords the best such example. Prussia is a Protestant nation, with a form of Protestantism not unlike that of the Anglican church. She is a nation with a rapidly expanding industry, and an increasingly influential urban middle class. Most important of all, those British politicians who first framed the Contagious Diseases Acts, and the Home Secretary himself, took the Prussian system as their model.

We find, both in Prussia and Britain, acts 'reflecting the utterance of a people which, between its respect for religious truth and the clamours of licentious men, has constantly aimed at a compromise between the two'.[2] In Prussia by 1717, a religious opposition to the concept of keeping women clean at state expense for the safety of 'revellers' had emerged, not unlike the opposition movement which had emerged in Britain by 1869. The government of Prussia therefore reworded its Berlin ordinance of 1700, giving as the reason for the ordinance the opportunities it afforded for the reclamation and salvation of loose women. Thus hypocrisy was enshrined in law, and if only for that reason, such laws could not hope to tend towards the general good of Society.

But did such enactments really regulate and delimit the traffic of prostitution? In eighteenth-century Prussia it was found that around regulated areas, unregulated vice spread in ever-widening circles, resulting from the myth of safety from infection. Far from containing the incidence of prostitution, the government was forced to extend again and again the operation of the ordinances of 1700 and 1717. In 1792, the Police Director of Berlin presented a memorial to the King of Prussia begging that the ordinances be made effective throughout the city. The King endorsed this request with the words:

> Prostitution is a necessary evil in a great city where many men are not in a position to marry, and is an outlet whereby to avoid greater disorders which are not to be restrained by any law or authority, and which take their rise from an inextinguishable natural impulse in men.[3]

In 1839, the Prussian Minister of the Interior refused to allow the provincial governments of the Rhineland permission to introduce a system of Regulation into their provinces:

> No man has the right to expect himself to be protected from injury and disease while seeking the gratification of his unreasonable sexual enjoyments. The opinion that brothels are hindrances against dangerous arts of seduction in men is erroneous. Had the police ever realised the suppression of other immoralities by the means of regulated brothels, then indeed an opinion might be formed as to the utility, in a sanitary point of view, of brothels; but this has never been the case.[4]

The arguments on both sides, writes Josephine, are precisely the same as those presented pro and contra the Contagious Diseases Acts in Britain. The basis of the defenders' position in both countries is that the opposition refuse to debate over proven facts. 'But what do they mean by facts?' she asks:

> Both they and we desire facts; the difference is that we

desire facts over a wide area and over a long period of time, moral as well as material facts, and facts whose expression has been generalised into great principles; whereas they call for facts of a material kind alone, of a limited extent, and over a short period of time.[5]

At this point, Josephine removes the debate from the area of vice and individual morality. Two years previously she had argued that the Contagious Diseases Acts were contrary to the principles of Magna Carta. Now she states the danger to Society as a whole inherent in the very nature of the Acts and their extension:

the many dangers of the future which arise when men become willing to barter constitutional freedom for liberty in lust; when they make over their citizen-rights and the guardianship of their morals to the police, which grows continually in power and in insolence, until they come to be no longer amenable to those who gave them the power.[6]

Such a decline into police-tyranny would be bad enough if the powers granted to the police proved effective in their intention. But they do not, and here Josephine cites statistics provided for her by William Acton, an arch-apostle of the Contagious Diseases Acts.[7] In 1868, the number of women in Berlin subjected to regular medical examination was 1,639. By the end of July 1869 it had risen by 13,539. At the time of writing *The New Era*, a further 12,000 had been drawn into the net. Thus, no fewer than 27,177 women in Berlin were now subjected to periodic examination, which meant, in fact, one woman in every seven, 'and all with a view to stamping out one particular disease'. Yet, over the same number of years, 1868 to 1872, the incidence of syphilis in Berlin actually rose by 5.7 per cent.

Josephine was very far from being prejudiced against Germans. On the contrary, like most cultivated Victorians, she greatly admired them, and believed that there were close ties of kinship between the so-called Anglo-Saxon peoples. It was for this reason that she believed the Prussian example to be so pertinent to her theme. Yet there is something prophetic, if exaggerated, in the vision which concludes her analysis of the Prussian system. Unerringly she points to the weaknesses in North European Protestantism. While praising its virtues and power for good – she was after all a devout believer in it – she warns against the close proximity between Puritanism and hypocrisy, between respectability and blind adherence to Authority. Perverted by an ever increasing licentiousness and hypocrisy, and utterly dependent upon an unquestioned police authority, Prussia will lose sight of all honesty and truth, will become a menace to other nations, until 'the war cloud gathers around us, which must break over the nations in a deluge of blood.'[8]

Her loathing for the whole concept of state regulation of vice leads her from her particular prophecies regarding Prussia to a Lear-like vision of the effect of such regulation everywhere in which, 'mountains upon mountains of super-added horrors turn men by their weight from immortal beings into beasts, extinguishing our souls, and turning earth into Hell!'[9]

Having relieved her spirit by this brief burst of self-indulgent rhetoric, she returns for the remainder of her book to a cool examination of the social injustice manifested in all systems of regulation. She also discusses, for the first time, whether any attempt to make men and women morally good by legislative action is not doomed to failure, and productive of injustice. From this, she returns finally to the essentially Christian argument that it is only through individual regeneration that a healthy society can emerge.

The importance of *The New Era* lies in the fact that it was the first exposition in depth of the philosophy – if that is not too grandiose a term – of the Repealers and Abolitionists, and was and is Josephine's most satisfactory apologia against her critics. Despite the strength of many of the arguments she presented, or perhaps because of them, supporters of the Contagious Diseases Acts writing in the Press greeted the publication of the book by attacking it with some of the very statements Josephine had refuted. Typical was a critic writing in *The Lancet* who responded to her remark that the only way of dealing positively with the problem of prostitution was 'so to transform the law and customs of society that the social standard of morality for men and women shall be the same', with the words:

We must deal with facts and actions, not with motives and

hypotheses. Prostitution among women falls into the former category; the assumed licentiousness of men into the latter. The outward aspect of a woman who walks Regent Street in lace and satin, is a more immediate cause of the descent of many a girl into prostitution, than all the licentiousness of all the men in creation.[10]

To such a staggering assertion a friend of Josephine's could only reply, 'Since the potency of the lace and satin, displayed in a single street in a single city, is so enormous, we are compelled – though at the risk of the complete overthrow of his tottering intellect – to ask the critic of *The Lancet*: "Who pays for this abnormal lace and satin?" '[11] The sense of frustration induced by the sheer inanity and obtuseness manifested by those who opposed her views does much to explain her occasional lapses into pseudo-biblical denunciation.

# XIII

No sooner had Josephine completed *The New Era* than she felt herself constrained once more to take part in an election campaign, this time in the constituency known as Pontefract, though in fact both campaign and polling centred on the shire town of Knottingley. The sitting member, Hugh Childers, who had been up till then First Lord of the Admiralty, was about to be raised to Cabinet rank as Chancellor of the Duchy of Lancaster, and, by the rules then obtaining, was compelled to seek re-election. This provided, in Josephine's words, 'an opportunity of reminding the government once more that the claims of the Abolitionists could not safely be ignored'.[1] The unfortunate Mr Childers, together with Sir Clarence Paget, who was by far the more active partner in the matter, had been the initiator of the second of the Contagious Diseases Acts – particularly detested by repealers because of its emphasis on periodic examination – and 'it had fallen to his lot to administer the obnoxious regulations in connection with our naval stations'.[2] He presented a target too choice to be resisted.

There were, however, difficulties regarding intervention in the Pontefract by-election which had not arisen either in Newark or

Colchester, and they existed in part because of the very clear distinctions to be drawn between Sir Henry Storks and Hugh Childers. Storks was not a professional politician, but a soldier imposed on a constituency because the Liberal government, and more particularly Sir Edward Cardwell, had need of him. He was also a well-known apologist for the Contagious Diseases Acts, frequently quoted by supporters and would-be extenders of the Acts. Hugh Childers was a career-politician who, for the past twelve years, had represented Pontefract and had served his constituents well. Nor was he known as a particularly enthusiastic supporter of the Acts; his sponsorship of them was a rubber-stamp action resulting from his position as First Lord.

Not surprisingly, no Abolitionist alternative Liberal candidate was forthcoming, and Josephine, her close friend and ally, Henry Wilson, and James Stuart proceeded to Knottingley with the intention of reducing the Liberal vote by encouraging abstentions on polling-day and engaging in secret and temporary alliances with the supporters of Lord Pollington, the Conservative candidate.

Childers was not merely taken aback by the arrival of a small but vociferous party of Abolitionists; he was completely bewildered. Aware that the Abolitionists might heckle one of his meetings, he wrote to *The Times* expressing his view that Bruce's Bill had been a repealist measure, and that he had supported it as such. He added that it was his belief that Bruce's Bill contained a clause by which men were to be penalised for spreading venereal diseases as heavily as women – which suggests that he had never read the Bill in detail – and that he could not understand why the Abolitionists had opposed it.[3] Such was his naïveté, that he clearly thought that publication of this letter would result in the withdrawal of Josephine and her friends from Knottingley.

If Josephine and Fothergill, the Abolitionists' experienced and zealous Parliamentary agent, had determined on obstructing the Liberal vote as a matter of strategy, they decided to obstruct the Liberal campaign as a matter of tactics. On the first evening of official electioneering – the 'canvas' – Childers had booked the town hall at Knottingley for a meeting to be held at nine o'clock. The Abolitionists promptly booked the hall for seven o'clock, promising that it would be cleared in time for

Childers and his officials, but hoping of course that they would come into contact with and perhaps convert a number of his supporters. Childers's agent was quick to reply to this manœuvre: as Josephine, Mr and Mrs Henry Wilson, James Stuart, Fothergill and Joseph Edmondson, who was reporting the election for the Abolitionist newspaper, the *Shield*, were making their way to the town hall, they encountered the town-crier of Knottingley, 'an old lame woman with a voice like an iron bell',[4] who, to their astonishment, was giving out that the Abolitionist meeting was to be held in the town hall at nine o'clock, and that Childers proposed to address the electors of Pontefract from the window of his rooms in the Buck Inn at seven o'clock.

Josephine and her party promptly hurried to the Buck Inn where a large and excitable crowd was assembling. Josephine herself, with Mrs Wilson, procured a place at a window on the opposite side of the inn-yard to that of Childers and his agent, while the men took up positions in the front of the crowd, where Fothergill ensured that they were hemmed in by a bodyguard of 'sturdy working-men' – presumably of the same type as had protected Josephine at Colchester.

In a desperate attempt to stop his meeting degenerating into a free-for-all, the hapless Childers, who had never before had to fight an election with any degree of intensity (Lord Pollington, his rival, was a local landowner devoid of political talent or hope since the newly enfranchised borough voters were totally opposed to the idea of being represented by a colourless offshoot of the old order), attempted to address the crowd. He shouted above the hubbub that he had always avoided involving himself in the controversy surrounding the Contagious Diseases Acts, that they were 'a subject of the greatest possible delicacy, and, to which, in the presence of so many ladies, I dare hardly allude. On such a subject I speak with great reluctance. I never speak about it in Parliament, nor am I aware that I have spoken about it in public. I am not aware that I have ever discussed it even among small bodies of men within the four walls of a room. I shrink from mentioning it in the presence of either sex; I would not raise a blush to the cheek of any woman.'[5]

This last assurance produced jeers and cat-calls from the groups of working-class girls who had gathered in the crowd, some of whom, according to Josephine, were engaged in breastfeeding their babies in the midst of the turmoil. One or two women yelled out, 'To the town hall!' Smiling, Henry Wilson assented to this call. Bearing the massive volume containing the Report of the Royal Commission of 1871 under his arm, and surrounded by Fothergill's cohort and an outer guard of enthusiastic women, he quitted the inn-yard in triumph, 'while Mr Childers and his friends looked with perplexed faces from the windows of the Buck Inn upon their retreating audience'.[6]

However jubilant Josephine may have been over this minor triumph, the form her intervention was taking was both tactless and ill-judged as a number of her supporters were quick to point out. Their principal objection was to the sudden, improbable conversion of the Tories of Pontefract to the Abolitionist cause. Tory speakers were dwelling on the abuses and horrors of the Contagious Diseases Acts, while Tory canvassers solemnly distributed Josephine's pamphlets from door to door with fliers of their own suggesting that the correct action for anyone agreeing with Josephine's views was to vote for Lord Pollington. Thus W. T. Stead, writing in the *Northern Echo* which, under his editorship, was fast becoming the most influential of the northern dailies, remarked:

'That this should be the role of the Tories in the country is the more surprising since, in the Commons, they are the enthusiastic followers of those whose ardent defence of the Acts justified Mr Mundella in remarking that they seemed to think that the way to heaven lay through a Lock hospital.'[7]

The plain fact of the matter was, whether Josephine liked it or not, that the Tories would never repeal the Acts. Her aim was to show the extent to which she could damage Liberal chances in elections, and in so doing, she could hardly expect a sympathetic hearing by the Parliamentary Liberal Party. If both parties were hostile to her views and her actions, it is difficult to see how she could hope for success within the bounds of the constitution. A few days before polling took place in Knottingley, however, the Abolitionist cause was not merely preserved, but enhanced, by the crass stupidity of its opponents.

The best account of this incident is undoubtedly the one written by Josephine herself at the request of W. T. Stead:

Our women's meetings were now stopped, or made more

dangerous. On a certain afternoon, when Mr Childers was again to address a large meeting from the window of a house, I and my lady friends determined to hold a meeting at the same hour, thinking we should be unmolested. We had to go all over the town before we found any one bold enough to let us a place to meet in. At last we found a kind of large hay-loft over an empty room on the outskirts of the town. You could only ascend to it by means of a kind of ladder, leading through a trap-door in the floor. However, the place was large enough to hold a good meeting, and soon filled. Stuart had run on in advance and paid for the room in his own name, and looked in to see that all was right. He found the floor strewn with cayenne pepper to make it impossible for us to speak, and there were some bundles of straw in the empty room below. He got a poor woman to help him, and with buckets of water he managed to drench the floor and sweep together the cayenne pepper. Still, when we arrived, it was very unpleasant for eyes and throat. We began our meeting with prayer, and the women were listening, when a smell of burning was felt, smoke began to curl up through the floor, and a threatening noise was then heard underneath at the door. The bundles of straw beneath had been set on fire, and the smoke much annoyed us. To our horror, looking down the room to the trap-door entrance, we saw head after head appear; man after man came in until they crowded the place. There was no possible exit for us, the windows being high above the ground, and we were gathered into one end of the room like a flock of sheep surrounded by wolves. They were mostly *not* Yorkshire people; they were led on by two or three *gentlemen* (!) one of whom afterwards became a candidate for Parliament.

It would hardly do to describe in words what followed. It was a time which required strong faith and calm courage. Mrs Wilson and I stood in front of the company of women, side by side. She whispered in my ear, 'Now is the time to trust in God; don't let us fear.' And a wonderful sense of the Divine presence came to us both. You understand, it was not so much personal violence that we feared as what would have been to any of us *worse than death*; for the indecencies of the men, their gestures and threats, were what I would prefer not to describe. Their language was hideous. They shook their

fists in our faces with volleys of oaths. This continued for
some time, and we had no defence or means of escape. Their
chief rage was directed against me; half-a-dozen fists were at
my face at once, and the epithets applied were such as one
only hears of in brothels. They filled their foul talk with
allusions to the visits under the Contagious Diseases Acts,
with which they all seemed minutely familiar. It was very
clear that they understood that their craft was in danger.
The new teaching and revolt of women had stirred up the very
depths of hell. We said nothing, for our voices could not have
been heard. We simply stood shoulder to shoulder – Mrs
Wilson and I – and waited and endured. But it seemed all the
time as if some strong angel were present, for when these
men's hands were literally upon us, they seemed held back by
some unseen power. . . . Hope came at last in the shape of two
or three helmeted policemen, whose heads appeared one by
one up through the trap-door. Now, we thought, we are safe!
But no. They had been hired by the government, and they
simply looked at the scene for a few minutes with a cynical
smile, and left the place without an attempt to defend us.
My heart grew sick as I saw them disappear. It seemed now
to become desperate.

Mrs Wilson and I whispered to each other in the midst of
the din, 'Let us ask God to help us, and make a rush for the
entrance.' Two or three working women put themselves in
the front, and we pushed our way, I don't know how, to the
stairs. It was only myself and one or two other ladies that the
men really cared to do violence to; so if we could get away,
the rest would be all right. I made a dash forward, and took
one flying leap from the trap-door on to the ground below.
It was a long jump, but being light, I came down all right.
I was not a bit too soon, for the feet of the men were ready to
kick my head as it disappeared down the hole. I found Mrs
Wilson after me very soon in the street. Once in the street, of
course these cowards did not dare to offer us the same violence. We went straight to our own hotel, and there we had a
magnificent women's meeting. Such a revulsion of feeling
came over the inhabitants of Pontefract when they heard of
this disgraceful scene, that they flocked to hear us, many of
the women weeping.[8]

As in the case of Colchester, Josephine withdrew from Knot-tingley before polling took place. The result of the vote came as a shock to the Liberals: the Liberal majority had fallen from two hundred and thirty-three in 1868, to eighty, without Lord Pollington's poll having appreciably increased. *The Times*, in a leading article, was quick to point the moral:

> The election at Pontefract, yesterday, is remarkable for the comparatively small majority secured by Mr Childers, and the small proportion of voters who came to the poll. . . . A majority of eighty over such an opponent as Lord Polling-ton does not imply a very secure seat against a strong candidate. Mr Childers was contending, not only with the Conservatives, but with the Anti-Contagious Diseases Acts Society [sic], three or four of whose agents actively canvassed the town against him and in favour of his opponents for some days. His loss from this cause was from 100 to 150 votes.[9]

Without doubt, the decisive factor in the decline of Childers's poll was the attack on Josephine's meeting. Thus the report in the *Manchester Examiner*:

> Mrs Butler and the ladies who act with her are influenced by the highest sense of duty, and we cannot but admire the courage, and, as we believe, the pure spirit of self-sacrificing devotion which led them to encounter the rude risks of an electoral campaign in pursuit of the object to which they have consecrated their energies. We only wish that it had been possible to import chivalry into Pontefract along with the Ballot, or that the public spirit of the inhabitants had im-posed some restraint on the 'roughs' who broke up the meet-ing on Wednesday night. It was the one disgraceful feature of the election – unjust, tyrannical, cowardly, and deserving, so far as moral deserts go, of the cat o' nine tails and the pillory.[10]

Such, needless to say, was not the view of the *Saturday Review*, which referred, the day following the poll, to 'Those dreadful women who appear on the eve of every election to foul the ears and minds of simple people with disquisitions on the Contagious Diseases Acts, and flitted through Pontefract and did not disappear without some hooting.'[11] Josephine was con-fident of the value of what had occurred, and was not beyond

pointing out that it was not the first time great things had
happened in an upper room. Childers himself was appalled by
the incident and made every effort, once he had been re-elected,
to apprehend the men responsible even to the extent of writing
to Josephine to ask if she was prepared to identify them. His
relative complacency regarding the Acts themselves was also
shaken. During a debate on the Contagious Diseases Acts in the
Commons in June 1875, he stated that they failed 'in the most
marked degree with regard to the principle of equally treating
the two sexes, which ought to be the basis of our legislation'. He
was not, however, so shaken as to seek for their repeal, but
suggested that their operation should be limited strictly to the
thirteen areas where they were at present enforced, that compulsory periodic examination should be abolished, and where
possible men should be penalised as much as women for the
spreading of venereal contagion (though Abolitionists were quick
to point out that this latter suggestion was easily said but
impossible to implement). In 1886, he joined the majority of
114 members who finally voted for Repeal.


## XIV


F O R the two years following the Pontefract election, Josephine
toured the country, lecturing, addressing meetings, interview-
ing and debating. When she visited the regulated areas she
would force herself to visit brothels and 'Lock' hospitals,
believing that it was her duty to face in person the evils she was
fighting. Although she was escorted by the ever-faithful James
Stuart, or by officials of the Rescue Society, she insisted that
she be allowed to enter the brothels alone. On one occasion she
went into the reception room of a brothel in a garrison town to
find it crowded with young soldiers, 'boys who may have been
eighteen or twenty'. As always, she made no attempt to preach
to them, but sat quietly with them as they awaited their turn
to go to the girls upstairs. When they had recovered from their
surprise at finding 'a lady' in their midst, she encouraged them
to talk about themselves. She then asked them about the girls
in the house, and was assured that they were perfectly all right:
'all the soldiers come here – these are Government women'. One

of the boys sitting near her began to cry. An older soldier came over to her and whispered to her, 'He's a young lad; just joined. Couldn't you get him out of this? He doesn't know what it means.' She led the boy out, her arm round him, his head on her shoulder, still sobbing. 'I am the mother of sons,'she told the Select Committee of 1882, 'and my heart was well-nigh broken.'[1]

In that same area she visited the 'Lock' hospital, where, in one of the wards, a girl lay dying as a result of the injuries she had received from her ponce who had accused her of withholding from him her non-existent earnings. The girl 'was hideous to look at, dying and raging, and though dying she was hungry as, indeed, she had been for years, and was tearing like a wild beast at some scraps of meat and bread'. She spoke to the girl quietly, as always. Screaming obscenities, the girl hurled her plate across the room. Josephine stayed where she was, beside her, still talking quietly to her. Suddenly the girl clutched at Josephine's arm, and 'became silent, gentle; tears welled from her eyes. . . . She knew that she was loved, and believed it, and was transformed. I loved her. It was no pretence.' As she was leaving, Josephine told the girl that she would come back soon. The following day she returned to the hospital, only to be told that the girl had died during the night, at peace and saying to herself over and over again, 'The lady is going to come back.'[2]

It is this facet of Josephine's personality which is extraordinary: her ability, whether in confronting the riot in the Brownlow Hill infirmary or in talking to prostitutes from whom the last shred of self-respect had been stripped, to bring peace, sometimes at the very last. We are tempted to speculate on what Josephine actually said to these girls. She never tells us, and for good reason; the words she spoke were of little importance. Her power lay in the fact that she loved them, and it was no pretence. What still must amaze us however is that the love she offered had the strength to cut through the bitterness, cynicism and hardness of the completely deprived, the totally maladjusted. There could be no sentimentality here. It might be possible to project an image of Josephine as a sentimental figure – indeed it has been done on a number of occasions – but those who do project such an image can have no experience of the sort of girl who responded to her offer of love, the sort of girl whose instinctive reaction would be 'what's in it for her?'

Josephine's solution to this mystery was simple enough – the girl saw in her the reflexion of Divine love and responded to it. Others could do as well if they had the inclination and the faith. Nor did she rate her own power of faith highly, believing that it was lame compared to her husband's. Since not for a moment would she accept that her ability to communicate peace and gentleness was a manifestation of any personal sanctity, it caused her to adopt a somewhat simplistic view of the endeavours of others. No prostitute was so debauched, so depraved, that she was incapable of responding to affection, and for this reason, any attempt to regulate or regiment them by legislation was, to her, immediately repulsive, sick substitute for love and real concern. At the same time, because she saw each prostitute as an individual – a soul, a single individual child of God – her anger at those who used and exploited them was fierce. More and more she came to see prostitution as being the result of a social structure in which there were gentlemen who had the means to purchase what they wished, and women who had nothing but their bodies to sell. As the years went by, the word 'gentleman' became, to Josephine, a private term of abuse.

Frequently on her tours she was threatened, as at Pontefract and Colchester, with physical violence. In Glasgow a public meeting which she was addressing was broken up by a mob of medical students. The University authorities came down firmly on Josephine's side – the Assembly of the Church of Scotland had, for some time, been unhappy about the Contagious Diseases Acts – and the leaders of the riot were handed over to the baillies who charged them with the offence of 'barking like dogs, mewing like cats, crowing like cocks, and whistling and rattling with their sticks'. It was, commented Josephine, an indictment 'more racy than judicial'.[3]

In Manchester, on another occasion, Josephine was due to make a speech at a theatre. The inspector of police did all he could to dissuade her from leaving the hotel, but upon her insisting on keeping the engagement, provided her with a large, if half-hearted escort. Once at the theatre, the escort ceased to be even half-hearted, and lapsed into complete inactivity. Josephine had scarcely mounted the stage when a gang from the stalls rushed her, knocked her down and, to use a more modern

vulgarism, 'put the boot in'. Two hours later a small group of
her sympathisers brought her back to the hotel. She was covered
in flour and excrement, her clothes had been torn off her body,
her face was discoloured and stiff with dried blood and she was
so bruised that she could hardly move.[4]

Such savage onslaughts were rare, and were confined to those
areas where organised vice was so well established that it could
hire mobs and ignore the police. A more depressing and debilitating form of opposition was the vaguely hostile apathy with
which she was almost invariably greeted. Fairly typical of this
was the report in a small provincial newspaper of a meeting she
had addressed in a Welsh mining village. After commenting un-
favourably on both the content of her speech and her propriety
in giving it, a view supported by inaccurate and distorted
examples which purported to have been taken from her
address, the reporter concluded by saying, 'the speech concluded with a tirade of language which, coming from the lips of
a lady, we would rather not reproduce'.[5] The tirade in question,
according to James Stuart who was present at the meeting, was
a direct quotation from the Book of Isaiah. Such misrepresenta-
tion, which was characteristic not merely of the lesser provincial
newspapers, but also of some elements in the national press,
constituted a barely-concealed refusal to consider rationally the
presentation of rational arguments. Set against the obtuseness
and the closed minds which undeniably drove Josephine to the
brink of the darkest depression was the absolute quality of her
own conviction of right.

To support her there was the unwavering loyalty and devotion of her friends – men for the most part, James Stuart,
Henry Wilson and the unfortunate Mr Bruce's Parliamentary
Secretary, Albert Rutson ('Dearest friend', or 'Darling Albert')
whom she loved, and who certainly loved her. And above all
else, there was the unstinting devotion and faith of her husband,
George:

He had great delicacy in dealing with the bitterness, or
petulance, of a soul in trouble. He had great faith in his fellow
creatures. And these, together with his unfailing love, like the
sun in the heavens surmounting the hours of cold and darkness, gradually overcame the mists which had wrapped them-

selves round the heart and obscured the spiritual vision of her for whom he had never ceased to pray.[6]

Today we are so unaccustomed to such language that the meaning of the words may seem to lose its force. It is necessary to understand the nature of the trouble, 'the hours of cold and darkness' in which Josephine's soul found itself. It was Evil which bore heavily upon her. The shock and repugnance at what she was forced to witness and to oppose was more dreadful than it would have been for a more prudish person. The prude has always the protection of his own smugness, and the expectation that what he will witness will be evil. Josephine was wholly a Christian, and to her, sexual activity was made holy by marriage. As a result she could not help but view promiscuous sex, and sex governed by a cash nexus, not as something 'dirty' or cloacal, but as a desecration of Divine and human love. She was appalled at the injustice of an age when books on etiquette for young wives assured their readers that it was perfectly acceptable for them to invite 'detrimentals' – i.e. young men who were known to lead sexually irregular lives – to their 'at homes' since such men were merely 'sowing their wild oats', while at the same time the novelist Charles Reade was banned from the same 'at homes' because he had once suggested that it would be no bad thing if girls were permitted to sow a few wild oats on their own account.

Prudishness combined with a complete disregard for any genuinely Christian view of sexuality confronted Josephine wherever she went. In 1878, she wrote to George from Oxford.

'Fancy Talbot [the Warden of Keble] saying to me, "But do you really think that sin is equal in men and women?" And an archdeacon said to Rawlinson, "But you know it is absurd to suppose that the seventh commandment is binding on men as it is on women." '[7]

Such an opinion to her was totally incomprehensible. Her reply was best formulated in answer to a question put to her in the Select Committee of 1882:

There is nothing in the physical being of a man answering to the sacredness of the maternal function of a woman, and that these functions and every organ connected with them ought to be held in reverence by man. Where this reverence ceases to be felt through the habitual outrage of any class of woman, however degraded that class may be, the demoralisation of society is sure to follow. I am not here to represent virtuous women: I plead for the rights of the most virtuous and the most vicious equally.

It was a sense of isolation, an inability to communicate the fundamental principles governing her attitude towards the Contagious Diseases Acts, combined with a terrible empathy for the exploited, the destitute, the outraged who, in being outraged and through no fault of their own, had been compelled to become the pariahs of 'decent' society, which drove Josephine to the very edge of despair – into the 'darkness' of the soul. And when that occurred it was to George and to George alone that she could turn. Only after he had died could she, in a profoundly moving book, pour out the words which expressed her feelings towards him: 'Where you stand now, beloved, I shall also stand one day – perhaps soon – on firm ground, and in the light of God.'[8]

When Josephine was away from home, and separated from George, as occurred more and more frequently during the 1870s, they wrote to each other almost daily. It is in these letters that the reader may appreciate the fact that they not only loved each other constantly, but were constantly in love with each other. It is clear that to both of them separation from one another was an unhappy duty imposed on them by providence. From Newcastle, one New Year's Eve, Josephine writes:

I feel so lonely here, listening to the bells clanging out the Old Year. My heart is with you. I will try and think of the great New Year of the Lord's glad appearing when this poor old world will be renewed in righteousness. I feel deeply how good it is of you, dearest, to lend me to this work. I think God will grant us some years of quiet happiness together after these calamities are overpast, and even in the summer of this year we will, please God, visit hills and green fields and quiet scenes together, and forget for a while the sins and toils of earth. We have not been much apart hitherto, beloved: and just now it is for love of those who are 'bound in the dark places of the earth wherein are the habitations of cruelty'. I am coming back soon, to you and to rest.[9]

As her domestic mainstay, George was tireless, waiting to meet her from her interminable journeys, at Liverpool's railway stations, at all hours and in all weathers, careful for her health and strength, anxious lest she overtax herself, and offering her continual assurance that, should she ever need him, he would immediately come to her. But he was also a very active participant in her campaigns when his academic and clerical duties allowed him sufficient leisure. In 1872, soon after the Pontefract Election, he addressed the Annual Church Congress at Nottingham on the subject of 'The Duty of The Church of England on Moral Questions', and, of course, one moral question in particular. The response to this was the sort of uproar with which Josephine was all too familiar. Sitting in the gallery, she was forced to watch passively, while her husband endured jeers and abuse from his fellow-clerics:

I recall vividly my husband's attitude while the tumult was prolonged. He continued to stand upright, his paper in his hand, and his expression was one of firmness and gentleness combined. Inwardly, I can imagine, he recognized the humorous aspect of this burst of wrath, for he was very quick in discerning any humorous element in the vagaries of human beings.[10]

Undoubtedly George's intransigence on his wife's behalf brought him into disfavour both with his ecclesiastical superiors and with the Government's Patronage Office. On more than one occasion he was informed that he could expect little preferment in the Church unless he took firm steps to curb his wife's activities. This, in all probability, concerned him little. Mrs Fawcett wrote of him, 'He remained to the end of his life essentially a layman and a scholar, rather than a cleric.'[11] He himself wrote to Josephine, reassuring her:

'You know I don't like parsons. I have a longing to be of use and I know of no line in which I can be more useful than the educational, my whole life having been turned more or less in that direction. It is a blessed office, that of teacher.'[12]

It was, perhaps, his ability to relax and to enjoy relaxation, the ability to throw off the quality of 'gravitas' appropriate to a Victorian headmaster without lapsing into the public school boisterousness and practical joking which so disfigured the masculine upper-middle-class idea of fun, which won him the friendship of so disparate a collection of personalities as Lord Coleridge, Sir James Stephens, Tennyson, Browning, Carlyle and J. A. Froude. Froude, indeed, was his closest friend. They spent every summer together, at Froude's cottage at Salcombe in Devon, or a small house rented by George in North Wales. They walked the Highlands and the Lake District together, and when George was compelled to visit London, which he detested, he stayed at Froude's town house in Onslow Gardens. Among the many distinguished visitors there was Carlyle:

> Froude and I were playing lawn tennis yesterday in the Square, when old Carlyle came round to take him for a drive in an omnibus, which he does about three times a week. Froude hid himself behind the bushes, and the old philosopher, unable to see him anywhere, retired, and we continued our game.[13]

Alone among Froude's friends, records the historian's first biographer, George Butler stood by him loyally during the ugly controversies which racked the latter part of his life.

Of George, Froude wrote, 'He possessed one of the highest characteristics which make friendship, namely the power of associating with a person without talking to him, or requiring to be talked to.'[14] George had, in fact, the quality of stillness which Josephine so conspicuously lacked, and it was this which made him so necessary to her.

'It is impossible', wrote James Stuart, 'to exaggerate the value of the support Canon Butler gave his wife.'[15] Yet their marriage presented a curious reversal of those roles expected within a Victorian married partnership. For it was George who provided the peace of mind and domestic tranquillity which it was the duty of an 'Angel in the House' to provide. Yet he did so without for one moment losing dignity, masculinity or his credit among his wide circle of male friends. Her contemporaries among women engaged in social work and the political campaigning that went with it – Mary Carpenter, Octavia Hill, Louisa Twining, Ellice Hopkins – all were spinsters. Josephine alone was a wife and a mother; a wife and mother who was held in deepest affection by both husband and children. She was a living denial of the role which middle-class urban society had imposed on its womenfolk.

## XV

IN October 1874, Josephine relinquished command of the Abolitionist cause in favour of Sir James Stansfeld, the statesman who was ultimately to succeed in obtaining the repeal of the Contagious Diseases Acts. Josephine herself had done as much as lay in her power to accomplish. In the broad spectrum of national politics, the Acts could never be more than a peripheral issue; Josephine, in common with other somewhat specialist reformers of more recent times, was to learn that whereas she could, with the assistance of her friends and colleagues, influence the course of a by-election, her views would have no impact whatever on voters engaged in a general election.

In the spring of 1874, the Liberal administration ended with a landslide defeat at the polls. Gladstone had succeeded in alienating, with his government's legislation restricting the sale of intoxicating liquor and a Criminal Law Amendment Act which was deemed to be an attack on the powers of strike action by the craft-unions, that very element in the electorate on which Josephine most heavily relied for support. Under the circumstances the Contagious Diseases Acts were simply not an issue. If any converts were to be won for the Abolitionist cause, they must surely be found among the Liberals. Yet Josephine's tactics had been to divide and weaken the Liberal vote and thus to favour the Tories, who would under no circumstances favour repeal of the Acts. She had led her followers into political confusion; the result of the election of 1874 depressed her deeply.

It was, of course, impossible for her to realise at the time that this apparent débâcle in her fortunes represented in fact a decisive advance in the Abolitionist cause. Freed from the responsibilities of office, a number of distinguished Liberals declared their support for a bill of repeal. Sir Harcourt Johnstone prepared such a bill to be presented in the House in early 1875, and again during each successive year of the Disraeli administration; Joseph Chamberlain, the rising star of the radical wing of the Party, inaugurated and presided over an

Abolitionist rally in his native Birmingham in the autumn of 1874; Samuel Morley, Whitbread and other distinguished radicals from the business world of the City of London declared their support for the Abolitionists. Even Gladstone voted for a second reading of Sir Harcourt Johnstone's bill of repeal in 1875.

The position of Gladstone with regard to the Contagious Diseases Acts was a cause of both bewilderment and bitterness among the more dedicated Abolitionists, and he has been treated with scant sympathy by historians of both Josephine and her cause. His well-known, not to say notorious, interest in prostitutes and their reclamation, led or misled those of his acquaintances who were opposed to the Contagious Diseases Acts to solicit his support, particularly when he was in office, for their repeal – with little success. The experience of James Stuart, who became a Member of Parliament in 1880, was fairly typical:

> George W. E. Russell and Scott Holland and I were staying at Hawarden together, and we resolved to speak to Mr Gladstone, and urge him to take more active steps with regard to the C.D. Acts. We went to his study, and had a formal interview. But he said he could not take up a new question at his time of life, and that was the difference between youth and age.[1]

George Butler knew Gladstone well, had entertained him as his guest on a number of occasions at Exeter College, Oxford, and had discussed with him a number of possible university reforms which were later, as Gladstone acknowledged in a graceful letter, embodied in Liberal legislation.

In the winter of 1872, Gladstone accepted an invitation from George to address the boys of Liverpool College and to spend a weekend with Josephine and himself. Josephine was pressed by her allies to take what seemed to them a golden opportunity to broach the subject of the Contagious Diseases Acts. 'This advice I did not follow, never having considered it a wise thing constantly to introduce "in season and out of season" any subject which may be near one's heart.'[2] It was a self-denying ordinance imposed on her, or so she believed, by the requirements of hospitality. Gladstone was agreeably surprised by, and grateful for, her reticence:

'I had a good deal of conversation with Mrs Butler,' he wrote to a mutual friend. 'Knowing her feelings about this special topic, I appreciated her perfect abstention.'[3]

Josephine, however, felt no obligation to abstain from her 'special topic' when she was a visitor at Downing Street. She did somewhat better than Stuart, Russell and Scott Holland – Gladstone had a penchant for attractive women – but not well enough. All she could persuade him to say was that he would always, as a private member of the House of Commons, support her views, but 'there is no use in an arrangement by which any leader of any movement warmly presses his views on any member of the Government, who is already well disposed towards that movement, unless he can, which I cannot, become a propagandist of it in the Cabinet.'[4]

Josephine was hard on him when she was engaged on writing her own account of the repeal movement after his death, and even harder on him in private:

> You know that, before he died [she wrote to her son a few months before her own death], he wrote a pamphlet which was a striking confession of blindness. He said, 'It has been my misfortune all my life not to see a question of principle until it is at the door – and then, sometimes too late!' I believe Mr Gladstone was a man of very pure private life, an old-fashioned family man. I'm sure of it. But O! how faulty in judgement. Stuart said to me one day that Gladstone could never see a question rightly until he was *kicked* into it.[5]

Josephine was far too 'thorough' in the Laudian sense to appreciate that the duty of a Prime Minister in a Parliamentary system based on a two-party democracy lies in ability to execute consensus opinion rather than in the promulgation of personal principles.

If all that was needed to combat the 'double standard' in sexual morality was 'one real lady who would dare to stoop', what was needed to secure the repeal of the Contagious Diseases Acts was one politician of Cabinet rank who would risk his career by adopting the Abolitionist cause in Parliament. On 15 October 1874, the Right Hon. Sir James Stansfeld, M.P. since

1859 for Halifax, addressed an Abolitionist rally at the Colston Hall, Bristol.

Stansfeld was no stranger to controversy. In his youth he had been a member of the group of Northern radicals who had sought, under the leadership of Joseph Sturge, to form an alliance between the Anti Corn Law League and the more moderate element among the Chartists. As a result he had been the object of a ferocious personal attack by Feargus O'Connor who – jealous of anyone who appeared to threaten his personal leadership of the Chartists – had described him as 'a capitalist wolf in sheep's clothing'. In 1849 he had become the leading supporter in England of Garibaldi and Mazzini's short-lived if heroic Roman Republic, and had become one of Mazzini's intimate friends after the latter had withdrawn from Italy into exile. After the *coup d'état* in Paris in 1852, he became an opponent of Napoleon III – which stood him in good stead with Palmerston – and he enthusiastically welcomed such self-appointed exiles from the Second Empire as Victor Hugo: to such an extent that Disraeli, after the abortive Tibaldi Plot against Napoleon III, accused him of 'being in correspondence with every assassin in Europe'.

However much Disraeli may have deplored his activities and sympathies, Stansfeld's forthright advocacy of liberal movements abroad won him considerable *réclame* among members of the emergent Liberal Party at home. When the Liberals came to power in 1868, there was little doubt that Stansfeld was destined for high office, ultimately perhaps the highest office. That year he was appointed a successor to Sir Edwin Chadwick as Chief Executive of the Poor Law Board; in 1871 he was created a Privy Councillor; in 1872 he achieved full Cabinet standing as Secretary to the Treasury.

He was not, of course, the only Liberal of distinction to support the Abolitionist cause once he was freed of the embarrassments of office. But none did so, so irrevocably:

> Full of a sense of special responsibility, I have dived down into the very depths of this question, and have impressed myself with the profound conviction that this system is immoral and unconstitutional, and calculated to degrade and debase the manhood and womanhood of the country . . . I have seen women with all their exquisite sensitiveness coming

before the public to plead the cause of virtue against that of legalised vice; and I have marked these women hounded down, hooted at with unseemly language, gestures, and even threats, and I know that, were not the spirit of the law of this country too strong, their lives and persons might have been exposed to danger and to outrage. I have marked these things. I have put my hand to the plough; I have cast in my lot with those men and women who hitherto have led a hope which too long has seemed a forlorn hope; and never will I desist, and never will they desist, from this sacred agitation, until these degrading laws are blotted out from the statute book forever.[6]

'It was like a trumpet-blast to call us afresh to battle, as well as the key-note of the future – full of courage and confidence,' a jubilant Josephine told George. 'Of course he has shut himself out from office for a long time, and checked his worldly career by this action, and he knows it; but he has cast his lot with us, and he will not draw back.'[7]

So excited was Josephine that she could not sleep the night following the meeting at the Colston Hall. At five o'clock in the morning she gave up trying, rose, dressed and crept out of the house at which she was staying in Bristol. Charles Butler was conveniently situated nearby, a pupil at Clifton College. As early as decency permitted she went there, extracted her delighted son from his classroom and took him for a picnic on the downs above the Avon Gorge. 'We had a delightful *tête-à-tête*. The trees are changing colour, and the woods are gorgeous.'[8]

But while Josephine rejoiced, the Press deplored. The *Pall Mall Gazette* and the *Saturday Review* tore into Stansfeld with a taunting savagery which, in the case of the *Pall Mall Gazette* reflected the distress of its editor, John Morley, at the spectacle of a valuable political asset throwing himself away on what was still to a great extent a disreputable and unpopular cause, and, in the case of the *Saturday Review*, was the predictable response from the entrenched redoubt of urban middle-class mores, and the literary shrine of that most guilt-ridden of all divorcées, Mrs Lynn Linton. More significant was the editorial comment of *The Times* on what it held to be Stansfeld's defection from the ranks of orthodox Liberalism:

'It is to be sincerely regretted that a statesman of Mr Stansfeld's eminence should identify himself with such an hysterical crusade, in which it is impossible to take part without herding with prurient and cynical fanatics.'[9]

Josephine had written that Stansfeld had 'shut himself out of office for a long time'. In fact, Disraeli had accomplished that – for the next six years, at least. It was not until 1880 that the full measure of his sacrifice was revealed. In that year Gladstone offered him the chance of accepting high office within the Cabinet always provided he would follow the Prime Minister's example and, while voting for repeal of the Acts, refrain from speaking on the subject. Stansfeld refused the invitation. In the early spring of 1886, when the Acts were finally and entirely repealed, Stansfeld was once again appointed by Gladstone to Cabinet office. But the Liberal Government, torn apart by the conflict over Irish Home Rule and still suffering the dissensions caused by Joseph Chamberlain's 'unauthorised programme', had little life left in it. For James Stansfeld, it was too late.

Twelve years were to pass before the cause was finally won, but Stansfeld's decision marks a turning-point in the struggle. The battle was shifted to the floor of the House of Commons, where it would be fought year after year with a slow but steady increase in the number of supporters of repeal. For a long time it may have seemed that the attempt to repeal the Acts was doomed to failure, but, equally, there was now little chance of extending the operation of the Acts either to further garrison areas or to the civil population. This, in itself, represented a signal victory. The case of Mrs Percy, occurring as it did less than five months after Stansfeld declared his support for the Abolitionists, combined the quality of a human-interest story of nation-wide appeal with confirmation of those fears which repealers had consistently expressed.

## XVI

WHEN the news of Mrs Percy's suicide broke, Josephine was torn between delight, that at last the Contagious Diseases Acts had caused a scandal sufficient to be discussed at length in newspapers not only in Britain itself, but also overseas, and

genuine compassion for the deceased, and more particularly for
Mrs Percy's sixteen-year-old daughter Jenny. This conflict was
clearly revealed in a letter to her niece Edith Leupold, who was
living in Switzerland:

> The suicide at Aldershot has created a great sensation. It is
> in every newspaper; already three London newspapers have
> leading articles strongly condemning the Acts. Every good
> cause requires martyrs, and this poor woman's death will,
> I believe, be a means in the hands of Providence, and of shak-
> ing the system more than anything we can do.[1]

She instructed her old friend, Henry Wilson, to go to Aldershot with a solicitor, Mr Eve, who was retained to look after the
interests of Jenny Percy and to arrange for her to be placed
under the Butlers' protection.

In the assembly room of the Military Hotel, Aldershot, where
the coroner was hearing the case of Mrs Percy, Josephine's
lawyer made little headway. The aim of the proceedings was
clearly to justify the police, and, if not to convince those present,
at least to have it read into the record, that Mrs Percy was a
known prostitute who had tumbled into the Basingstoke Canal
while very much the worse for drink. Witnesses, however, were
proving less than co-operative, and their testimony was being
recorded in shorthand for full verbatim reports in both the *Daily
Telegraph* and the *Daily News*, neither of which were renowned
for their opposition to the Contagious Diseases Acts.

Mrs Styan, wife of the landlord of the Artillery Arms, High
Street, Aldershot, was asked if Mrs Percy had not been seen
drunk in that public house on the night before she died. Mrs
Styan testified that Mrs Percy was sober, had only had a cup of
tea and some bread and butter for which she had paid twopence,
saying, 'This is all the money I have.' She added, according to
Mrs Styan, 'There has been a great scandal about me; did you
read the letter in the papers?' Mrs Styan replied that she had heard
about it but had not read it. 'She said she was not a bad character,' declared Mrs Styan, despite one or two attempts to invite her
to stand down, 'and before Monday come she would drown herself
if they wouldn't allow her to get an honest living in Aldershot. . . .
The thoughts of the hospital was preying on her mind.'

Mrs Styan was succeeded as witness by William Larkley, at

whose home Mrs Percy and Jenny had been lodging. On being asked whether it was not a fact that Mrs Percy was known for her sexual promiscuity, Mr Larkley replied that the opposite was the truth. 'She never missed coming home, and always kept good hours. She had an engagement at The Queen's Tap. She performed there every evening, and came home very regularly, and was always sober. She conducted herself with the propriety of a married woman.'

When William Larkley stood down, the jury consulted among themselves, and the foreman then declared that it was their opinion that the manager of 'The Queen's Tap' should be called to give evidence. The coroner, taken aback by this request, turned and, quite irregularly, consulted with a senior officer of the Aldershot police before refusing the jury's request.

The next witness was Mr Ritson, Mrs Percy's erstwhile stage partner, and the most troublesome of all the witnesses. On being asked whether he could give any reason why Mrs Percy should have committed suicide, he replied that he could give the precise reason. The coroner promptly ruled him out of order. Mr Ritson was not to be put down so easily. Any question was a good enough hook to hang on to it what he wanted to say, and against a rising crescendo of attempts to silence him, he gave his testimony. The senior inspector of the Aldershot morals police, Inspector Godfrey, had told Mrs Percy that she and her daughter were fit persons to be committed to a 'Lock' hospital – which meant, in case the coroner didn't understand the implication, that Inspector Godfrey claimed to know for a fact that both Mrs Percy and Jenny Percy were infected by venereal disease. The Inspector followed up this accusation by saying that the unpleasantness of a few months' incarceration in a 'Lock' hospital could be avoided if only Mrs Percy and her daughter would sign a piece of paper. The piece of paper was, of course, a form of 'voluntary submission', a formal request by the signatory that she should be registered as a common prostitute, in return for which she would promise to attend hospital each fortnight for instrumental examination. Mrs Percy's response was to throw the paper in Inspector Godfrey's face, whereupon the Inspector 'shook his fist in Mrs Percy's face and said he would bring her before a bench of magistrates'. At this point, the coroner succeeded in silencing Mr Ritson.

Josephine's lawyer then rose to his feet:

'There are other witnesses here,' he stated, 'who would give evidence as to the state of mind the deceased was in on this particular Saturday. Her daughter is here, and I should like her examined with reference to the signing of the paper.'

Again the coroner, taken by surprise, consulted with the police. He then told the lawyer that in his opinion 'it was not at all necessary to call the deceased's daughter'. The foreman of the jury rose and requested formally that Jenny Percy be examined. The coroner rebuked him saying that the matter had already been dealt with.

The attempt to demonstrate that Mrs Percy had been drowned while incapably drunk had met with dismal failure. The authorities, however, had one more trick to play. It came in the form of Mr J. C. Barr, the surgeon who would have examined Mrs Percy had she appeared for examination on the Monday following her death. The fact that Mr Barr did not, nor ever had, examined Mrs Percy was of no consequence. He was able to state, or so he affirmed, that she and her daughter were common prostitutes, and that her death was caused by falling into the Basingstoke Canal during an attack of delirium tremens, itself the result of venereal disease in an advanced stage. To support this conclusion he suggested that the unfortunate woman's belief that she was being persecuted by the police was yet another symptom of advanced syphilis.

The newspapers were far from happy with the result of the inquest. Typical of opinion generally held was a leading article in the *Daily News*, a journal which had always been hostile to the Abolitionists in general and to Josephine in particular:

> The inquest proves that the police who had endeavoured to drive Mrs Percy into prostitution, did also attempt to blacken her character by trying to make it appear that the unhappy woman whom they had hunted to death was drunk, so that it might be suspected that she had tumbled into the water.[2]

The same writer went on to deal with the views of Mr J. C. Barr. He pointed out that Mr Barr had given evidence before the Royal Commission of 1871 and had created a very unfavourable impression. He had been asked by the Commissioners whether he applied moral and religious influence to the minds of the women who were submitted to him for examination. He replied that he had welcomed the Acts almost solely because of the opportunity thus offered to him for morally influencing the girls brought before him. Four questions later he was asked how long he reckoned to take over examining each girl who came before him. Five minutes, he replied, during which time he taught them how to use certain measures 'as a prophylactic which they must use if they are to persist in prostitution'. He then went on to regale the Commissioners with the details of the prophylactic devices he recommended, until he was silenced by the Chairman.

As the uproar over the death of Mrs Percy grew, so did Josephine's belief that there was now a faint possibility of victory for the Abolitionists. She could hardly conceal her sense of triumph:

> Poor Miss Percy is coming to stay with us tomorrow or Monday to be safe and *comforted*, poor child. She is over-whelmed with grief. It was a noble act of her mother to drown herself rather than be forced into infamy. She has appealed against these wicked Acts to the All Merciful and All Just One. The hand of God is in all this also. Her dying appeal has sounded thro' England, and roused the country as no appeals of ours could do; every newspaper records it.

Josephine may well seem to have been callous with regard to Mrs Percy's suicide, and ruthless in her expedition in taking the helpless and destitute Jenny Percy under her protection. In some sense, she was both. On the other hand, Jenny was to live with the Butlers as their daughter – a surrogate Eva perhaps – until she reached her majority and was happily married. She, at any rate, never believed that her grief had been wrongly exploited, and, like so many others who had come under Josephine and George's protection, she felt nothing but love and admiration for them.

On 24 May 1875, the protest against the Aldershot coroner reached its climax. What Josephine described as 'a great indignation meeting'[3] was held in London under the presidency of Edward Backhouse, a rich and distinguished City banker, and an influential member of the Society of Friends. The principal speakers were Sir Harcourt Johnstone, Sir James Stansfeld and

Charles Birrell, but undoubtedly the speaker who drew most attention and interest from both the audience and the newspaper correspondents was George Butler, who read out Jenny Percy's account of the events leading up to her mother's death. She ended her statement with the following words:

What a law is this! I could never believe there was such a law. Since this law was made it is not considered respectable to speak to a soldier, nor have one in your house; but I can tell you that, though I have lived among soldiers ever since I was born, I never had a rough word or an insult from one in my life, and they were always respectful to my Mamma. I think you will find that all those who knew her spoke well of her.[4]

When George had finished reading the statement, he concluded by saying:

The fact of one victim having been done to death in England will be thrown away if we do not open our eyes to the danger to which some of the weakest and most defenceless of our countrywomen are exposed. The law virtually says to every woman of a humble class: 'If your conduct is in any way open to suspicion, you must henceforward submit to a course which will justify the very worst suspicions; you must sign your name upon this register, and enter upon a life over the portals of which might be written the fatal words: 'Lasciate ogni speranza, voi che entrate.'[5]

The result of the agitation over the case of Mrs Percy, like the accession of Stansfeld to the ranks of the Abolitionists, was not as spectacular as Josephine would have wished. Result there was, nonetheless. Lord Charles Beresford had placed a motion on the order paper of the House of Commons for the extension of the Contagious Diseases Acts to the major seaports. Richard Cross, Disraeli's reformist Home Secretary, quietly suggested to him that it was hardly a suitable moment for such a bill to be discussed in Parliament. The matter was dropped, once and for all.

# 4. The New Abolitionists

ONLY a few days after 'the great indignation meeting' over Mrs Percy, Henry Wilson sent a circular letter to leading members of the Repeal Association:

> Dear Friends – Our beloved and honoured leader, Mrs. Butler, is, as many of you are aware, compelled to rest for a time to recruit her strength which has been heavily taxed in her recent work both at home and abroad . . . and she hopes that while she is compulsorily withdrawn for a time from the heat of the battle, that we shall all be strong and of a good courage, knowing that the battle is not ours, but God's.[1]

Josephine was, in fact, on the verge of a complete breakdown. 'I feel', she wrote in a shaky hand to Wilson, 'as if I am doomed. I am filled night and day with terrors. . . . I wish so much to recover. I have worked hard since July 1869 – six years, and always till now I could put away thought of work, and *sleep*. Now, for the first time, I can neither get rid of anxious thoughts, nor sleep. I am full of hope. I can see "Satan fall like lightning from heaven" – but my brain is gone wrong. I am giddy and cannot see or hear at times, and my heart stops.'[2]

Josephine's collapse was hardly surprising. No sooner had the vice presidency of the Repeal Association been placed in the experienced and capable hands of Sir James Stansfeld, than Josephine had thrown herself into another and even more exacting sphere of activity: the fight against state-regulated vice on the Continent. Since 1825 various municipal authorities in France, Belgium and Switzerland, had been advocating some form of international regulation, some uniform scheme which would embrace all individual national systems. In 1867, the International Medical Congress had met in Paris, and had set up a commission under the chairmanship of Dr Jeannel, a world-authority on venereal disease and an enthusiastic advocate of Regulation, to draw up detailed plans for an international control of venereal disease through police measures.

The Regulationists had made such slow progress in drawing up a viable international plan for control that the Abolitionists had scarcely noticed what was afoot. In 1873, however, the report of the Jeannel Commission was submitted to the International Medical Congress meeting that year in Vienna. Partly as a result of this, and partly because the apparent success of the Contagious Diseases Acts led delegates into the belief that Britain was about to become Regulationist in line with the other European powers, the Vienna Congress demanded that there should be a prompt enactment of an international law regulating the practice of prostitution since, in the words of the Vienna declaration, 'from the moment when prostitution shall become a regular and recognized institution, admitted and regulated by states, its perfect organization will become possible'.[3] To Josephine it seemed that within only a short space of time Britain might be integrated into such a scheme, after which it would be impossible to obtain the repeal of any laws governing Regulation except through international agreement.

At a meeting in York, C. S. Collingwood, Rector of Southwick, near Sunderland, proposed the formation of an international abolitionist society capable of opposing the international medical congresses who upheld the principle of Regulation. His audience should remember, he added, that 'when Granville Sharp in 1772 obtained the famous decision that a slave is free as soon as he touches English territory, he did not think it one of the first steps toward the general abolition of the slave trade and slavery everywhere; but it was so.'[4] In the same way, the outcry of a few English men and women against state regulation of vice might carry across the world.

Acting on Collingwood's advice, the meeting at York decided that the Ladies' National Association, in the person of Josephine, should open a correspondence with known sympathisers abroad, and with anybody whose reputation for liberalism might lead them to suppose that he would prove sympathetic.

Soon after the York Conference, while she was collecting suitable names and addresses, she came across a small directory containing the names of people connected with various benevolent associations abroad. To all of these she sent a letter explaining the aims of the Repeal Association. One of these was addressed to a M. Humbert of Neuchâtel. An error on the part of a postman resulted in it passing into the hands of Aimé Humbert, who also happened to live in Neuchâtel. Aimé Humbert was one of the politicians who was responsible for the revolt of Neuchâtel against the government of Prussia, and had been responsible for its admission to the Swiss Confederation. For ten years he had held ministerial office in the Canton; he was a member of the Swiss Federal Assembly; and he had twice been elected president of the Federal Assembly.

Not realising that Josephine's letter was intended for other hands, he opened it. Noting her suggestion that she might travel abroad to meet and to discuss her views with anybody who was interested, he immediately replied:

I accept your communication as providential. I recall the vows and resolutions I made many years ago as to the formation of an International League against the scourge of this government-regulated evil. In my opinion, it is with much tact – I should even say, with a true divination of the mysterious depths of the question – that the English Abolitionists have decided to stretch forth their hands to those persons on the Continent who sympathise with their labours. England alone can take the initiative; but remaining alone, she would not arrive at a successful issue. Now she is able to give the signal, her appeal will be understood.[5]

This decided her. Despite the fact that it was already, in November, one of the severest winters in living memory, Josephine decided to visit France, Italy and Switzerland, believing correctly that her physical presence would accomplish more than any number of letters or pamphlets. The Society of Friends decided to contribute to the cost of her journey, and to provide her with letters of introduction to Friends living on the Continent. The Moderator of the Free Church of Scotland sent her a letter of support and further letters of introduction. Joseph Hornung, Professor of Jurisprudence at the University of Geneva, invited her to visit him, and sent her a list of acquaintances of his living in Paris, Rome and cities of northern Italy, who were men of influence and who would be sympathetic to her cause. Even Lord Derby, the Tory Foreign Secretary, was persuaded to provide her with a friendly letter of intro-duction to the British Ambassador in Paris asking him to give all possible assistance to Mrs Butler – Josephine never lacked influential support, even from the most unlikely sources.

In a gale certain to inflict the worst agonies of seasickness, to which she was peculiarly vulnerable, and calculated to bring on the symptoms of rheumatism which she already suspected, Josephine and her son Stanley set out on the first European campaign.

## XVIII

IN Paris, the Police des Mœurs was directed by its most per-suasive and articulate exponent, Lecour. Of him, Yves Guyot, who became a member of the Conseil Municipal at the age of thirty, and a senior member of the French government ten years later, has left a remarkably unflattering portrait:

He was a type. Son of an old prison warder, he had climbed all official grades by force of supple tenacity, and he had retained from his original condition a desire for all that appeared above him, and brutal scorn for all that was below him. He had the pedantry of ignorance, and the pride of office. Seated in his armchair behind his desk, with his great ill-furnished mouth open, and his lower lip hanging down, he talked of morality and public health, and showed his im-portance by a slimy phraseology which seemed to leave its track behind, like the foamy matter left in the track of slugs. He was not at bottom a bad man, but he was severe because he thought himself infallible. A defender of religion, church-warden of Belleville, attributing all evils to atheists and republicans, he thought he was doing God service by scrupu-lously seeing after the organisation of debauchery. By heredi-tary influences and first lessons, he came to the belief that certain men were born for the purpose of sending others to

prison. With such leanings he enjoyed his office like a virtuoso.[1]

Guyot was not an unbiased judge. An opponent of Lecour in
political matters no less than social – he was a radical and a
republican, whereas Lecour was a monarchist – he worked for,
and ultimately succeeded in obtaining, Lecour's dismissal. His
description, however, is borne out by Josephine herself, and
more significantly by Lecour's own recorded utterances. During
a sitting of a government committee appointed to inquire into
accusations of corruption against members of the Police des
Mœurs, he was asked if he had been responsible for the arrest
and detention during the course of one year of ten thousand
girls. Fifteen thousand, he replied. It was estimated that he
held sway over a minimum of thirty thousand girls registered at
his Préfecture as licensed prostitutes, many, perhaps a majority,
of whom had never practised as prostitutes but had been the
victims of the Police des Mœurs' undiscriminating round-ups.

Lecour's men, the *agents des mœurs*, were recruited from
demobilised soldiers who could not or would not find alternative
employment. Since they were plainclothes police, they lacked
even the vestigial discipline which a uniform might have in-
stilled into them, and their wage was approximately a pound
(twenty-four francs) a month, which, in the Paris of the 1870s,
was barely a subsistence level. The individual agent was faced,
therefore, with the necessity of accepting bribes and black-
mailing his potential victims, or with seeking promotion by an
excessive display of zeal, or both. Budgetary reports of the
Paris police confirmed that officers of the Sûreté who were
dismissed either for negligence or for dereliction of duty, were
automatically accepted into the Police des Mœurs; there was
one case reported of a high-ranking member of the Sûreté who
was cashiered for using his authority to terrorise girls into
having sexual relations with him, being seconded into the Police
des Mœurs, 'in order, no doubt,' wrote an outraged Deputy,
'that he might more freely give way to his inclinations.'[2]

The objective of the Police des Mœurs was to ensure that all
women plying the trade of prostitute were *en carte* – i.e. that
they held the equivalent of the English 'voluntary submission'.
They relied heavily on information received from street-girls

who were *en carte* and who resented intruders who *font la noce*, and from brothel-keepers who resented piratical inroads on their clientèle. The prostitute *en carte* was only slightly safer from the attentions of the Police des Mœurs than her unregistered sister. In France, Belgium and Italy, a street-girl was permitted to solicit custom only between the hours of seven and eleven in the evening. If for any reason she excited the displeasure of an *agent des mœurs*, she could be arrested simply on the grounds that she had been seen out of doors during daylight hours. One girl was arrested in Paris because she was seen shopping in Les Halles at nine o'clock in the morning, and was charged with speaking to a man (the stall-holder), and with being off the beat stipulated on her registration license. Another was arrested for looking out of her window one afternoon. A third was arrested when three *agents des mœurs* broke into her lodgings and found her with another girl; both were charged, despite the fact that they were both *en carte* and fully clothed, with lesbian prostitution out of hours.

The *agents des mœurs* had to fulfil a quota in order to qualify for their miserable wage. If on any evening they failed to arrest a sufficient number of girls they regaled the boulevardiers with the spectacle of a public round-up.

On one particular night there was a spectacular sweep at exactly eleven o'clock through the streets around the Place de la République, the Faubourg du Temple and the Boulevard Rochechouart. So many women were arrested that the police vans were still ferrying them to the prison of St Lazare at noon the following day. Later it was discovered that Lecour, on hearing that Borborukhin, the distinguished Paris correspondent of a leading St Petersburg newspaper, was writing a series of articles on the Paris Police des Mœurs, had instituted the sweep in order to demonstrate the efficiency of the forces under his control.

If a boulevard sweep failed to net a sufficient number of girls, attention was turned to girls living in furnished rooms and hotels. Agents, supported by uniformed police, would arrive between two and five o'clock in the morning. They were not of course looking for girls *en carte* but *insoumises* – girls without visible means of support; any girl who was not with her legal husband, whether she was alone or with a lover. Instructions were laid down as to the method by which the agent should establish that the girl was a prostitute: '*il devait regarder les draps, inspecter les serviettes et la cuvette*';[3] or, more simply, he must examine the girl's hands, and if they were soft he might legitimately arrest her. The number of innocent girls who were thus arrested must have numbered tens of thousands. On one occasion, a young seamstress whose hands would presumably have testified as to her innocence was so terrified when she heard the police smashing the lock of her door that she threw herself from her bedroom window and fell through a glass roof below, cutting herself badly and breaking both legs. One of the raiding party suggested that a cab should be called to take her to hospital. The Commissaire in charge of the raid replied that it was unnecessary since the girl would die anyway. She was taken to St Lazare in the police-van with the other women caught in the night's haul, where she died two days later. Lecour, when questioned about this incident, replied, 'When a woman is virtuous, she does not live in furnished rooms.'[4]

Girls *en carte* could evade the attentions of the Police des Mœurs by informing on *insoumises* or by bribery, but there was only one infallible method, and that was to become *en maison* – to obtain employment in a licensed brothel. Maupassant's Madame Tellier presents the portrait of a brothel-keeper as the client, either through guilt or wishful thinking, would have liked to have thought of her; brothel-keepers kept their girls as prisoners, deprived them of their outer clothing except during business hours, and retained legal ownership even of their underwear so that they might be apprehended for theft if they attempted to escape. Girls who ran away from state-registered brothels, if recaptured by the police, were given the choice of returning to the brothel or imprisonment in St Lazare. For reasons which will become evident, most girls preferred to return to the brothel.

The most obvious abuse of the system was the wholesale and indiscriminate arrest of *insoumises*. Guyot, in his attack on Lecour, cited dozens of cases of wrongful arrest – all well attested and typical of many thousands more. 'Agents have one rule,' he wrote; 'arrest poorly dressed girls, and do not arrest those who seem to be fashionably dressed.'[5] They must not, he added, arrest a well-dressed girl even if she was seen to be soliciting openly and in broad daylight on the Champs Élysées – she was almost certain to have rich and influential clients. This rule, however, was not universally adhered to. A banker's wife from Dijon was arrested as she stood on the pavement outside a Paris shop waiting for her husband. Lecour saw no reason for apologising to either of them: 'What sort of a husband is it that lets his wife wait for him on the street?' he asked.[6] In one case, a woman whose child was desperately ill went out to find a doctor and was picked up by the police. She was taken to St Lazare. Her child, left helpless and entirely alone, died in her absence. Another girl was arrested when, on returning home after a party, she went across the street to see if she could borrow a candle from a friend who had also been to the party. When Lecour's deputy, Coue, heard about this, he asked regarding the candle,

'*C'était pour vous la mettre dans le cul?*'

A Chef du Cabinet at the Sûreté, who overheard this ribald witticism, complained to Lecour about his deputy's behaviour. Lecour replied, 'If we can no longer say these sort of things, if we are now obliged to put on gloves to speak to these women, the Police des Mœurs is done for.[7]

Other forms of exploitation were all too familiar. Maids who refused to submit to their employers not only lost their positions but found themselves denounced to the Police des Mœurs. Girls who had been seduced and had become embarrassingly pregnant were denounced by their seducers, who wanted them removed from the neighbourhood. One such girl went mad in St Lazare, and delivered her child in the lunatic asylum of the Salpétrière.

Questioned about a suicide by a woman who had been black-mailed and later denounced to the Police des Mœurs, Lecour replied, 'We must tolerate an evil when we cannot suppress it without creating a greater one.'[8]

Josephine might well have said the same.

## XIX

JOSEPHINE and her son Stanley, whom she always referred to as the Cat, or Catty, arrived in Paris on a Saturday. The snow lay six inches deep on the pavements, and there was a dense fog. The following day she wisely decided to rest in her lodgings on the Boulevard Magenta. To George she wrote:

> We have three very little rooms, Cat and I, on one flat, and shut off from the rest of the house. We insist on having good fires, which French people don't seem to understand. Cat and I had our café-au-lait at 9 this morning in our room, and then we read and wrote till 1–30 . . . In the afternoon Madame Dumas called. She is very old, nearly 80. She is secretary of the Committee of St Lazare, where about 1000 poor women are imprisoned. I fear these French ladies are very unenlightened about some matters.[1]

In its initial stage, Josephine's mission to Paris was made somewhat easier than it might have been by the fact that the Protestant community had been notified of her arrival, and was prepared to welcome her, though it was pessimistic regarding her chances of launching a successful abolitionist campaign. She was better assisted in making influential contacts by Lord Lytton, First Secretary of the British Embassy, whose good offices, the result of her letter of introduction from Lord Derby, were the more necessary since she was dogged throughout the week by the Paris police. Through Lord Lytton, she obtained an interview with the aged Victor Hugo, who, enthroned amidst the wreckage of his own family life, was of little practical use, but whose name, like that of Mazzini or Garibaldi, carried great weight, a fact which Josephine was always ready to exploit.

A more effective ally was to be found in Jules Favre, to whom she also obtained an introduction. Favre had been foreign minister in the French government following the débâcle of Sedan, had been responsible for the attempt to negotiate peace with Bismarck following the battle (he had burst into tears when presented with the Prussian terms) and had been responsible for the decision to fight on and to confront the Prussian army with a *levée en masse* which, though not victorious, won, by its stubbornness and heroism, the grudging respect of the Prussians. Although he was old and sick he invited Josephine to meet him at his home. He assured her that he concurred entirely with her views, but doubted whether Regulation could be abolished in France. He pointed out to her that if she were to confine her activities to organising the Protestant community as her allies in France she would achieve nothing. A Catholic himself, he insisted that she should try to win over a few eminent Catholics since, following the suppression of the Commune, Catholics held all the important government posts in Paris. Finally he gave her a letter of introduction and a warm commendation to Jules Simon, the Minister of Public Works.

Josephine was sceptical at the idea of finding allies among Catholics. Regulation of vice was most strictly applied in Catholic countries. Ever since the Middle Ages the Church had admitted the impossibility of suppressing prostitution, and the corollary of such an admission was the regulation of vice. In the fourteenth century there were municipal brothels, notably in the Papal city of Avignon and in Toulouse, which were administered, supervised and inspected by the abbess and nuns from the nearest convent. St Thomas Aquinas had laid down the principle to which the Church subscribed: 'Prostitution in towns is like a cesspool in a palace; take away the cesspool and the palace will become an unclean and evil-smelling place.'[2] In Josephine's opinion, Catholics were so accustomed to blind obedience to authority, spiritual or secular, that they could never rise to fight a moral issue in a political arena: 'It is difficult for persons accustomed to be guided in all their actions by the Church to appreciate the necessity and worth of a personal initiative in any reform.'[3]

While there was an element of truth in such an estimation, it was too rigid. Within a year of her visit to Paris, Josephine was to find her cause warmly supported by both the Archbishop of Orleans and the Archbishop of Paris, while Cardinal Manning of Westminster was to become one of her most powerful allies.

During those first few days in Paris, however, she saw no reason to suppose she was wrong. Acting on Jules Favre's advice she decided to pay a call on a priest of some importance and influence – a Father Rogerson – who had been a near neighbour of hers at Dilston some twenty years earlier. He had been, she remembered, 'a jolly young Catholic priest, fond of fox-hunting, and not fit for the Church'. For all her hard opinion of him she drove in her carriage out through the snow beyond the suburbs of Paris:

I found [she wrote to Stansfeld] a middle-aged, well-dressed, cold, gentlemanly, rather fanatical man. . . . He is a worldly man I should think, but after a time became more genial and asked after Charles and all my people. He does not care even to speak of my mission. I saw that, so I merely asked him for the addresses of Catholic dignitaries. A man came in while we were talking with a grand gold goblet set with jewels for some church altar, and happened to say that Archbishop Manning was in Paris at the Hotel Windsor on his way from Rome to London.[4]

She took her leave of Father Rogerson as quickly as she could, and returned to Paris to try to see Archbishop Manning. When at last she managed to reach the Hotel Windsor through the driving snow, she found that he had been gone an hour. He had, however, heard of her presence in Paris, and had left her a letter together with a note addressed to all Catholic clergy with whom she might come into contact:

This lady has undertaken a needful and difficult mission. I beg you to give her such assistance and encouragement as you can in her work of charity, and to recommend her to persons who may have any influence in the matter of the reform she seeks to promote. No Catholic who fears God can refuse to give his allegiance to the sacred cause which she has espoused.[5]

They could, and did. For the most part, leading Catholics whom she attempted to contact on the strength of Manning's letter ignored her appeal, and for that reason and because her time in Paris was severely limited, she failed to appeal to the leaders of the Church hierarchy in France, some of whom would have been very ready to have helped her.

She had more success with the Minister of Public Works, Jules Simon. His attitude towards her was not unlike that of Gladstone, in that he was quick to point out that his public office forbade him from moving actively on her behalf. Unlike Gladstone, however, he was ready to go to some trouble to introduce her to politicians who were of an inclination and in a position to offer her assistance. Among these were Edmond de Pressense, a Senator, a notable orator and a distinguished Protestant theologian, who introduced her to the leading

Protestant preacher in Paris, Theodore Monod, who, in turn, was to galvanise the Protestant community into taking the sort of action she required of it; Yves Guyot, the volatile editor and Radical deputy, who was to become Lecour's most dangerous opponent, and who, after replacing Simon as Minister of Public Works in the Jules Ferry administration, was to achieve both the removal of Lecour from the Préfecture and the disbandment of the Police des Mœurs; and le Caze, the distinguished Catholic Senator, who was already engaged in a one-man crusade for the reform of the women's penitentiary of St Lazare. According to Josephine, le Caze was 'a true gentleman of the old school, full of goodness, like some of our old Northumbrian Roman Catholic gentlemen of the Liberal type'.[6]

To bring these people together, to encourage them into forming a united front against Regulation, required meetings, interviews, conferences, which occupied all of the day and most of the night. As a result, Josephine worried even more about Stanley:

> He is too young to work with me. He is very loving and companionable, but he has to go sightseeing without me, and when he comes in each day, he tells me he feels quite disgusted and that it is difficult to shake off the impressions of this wicked city. There are temptations presented in every kind of artistic and easy form at every corner. The guides had asked him if he would not go to a 'Bal de Nuit'. These are simply orgies where people dance *nude*. Rode says that many innocent young Englishmen follow the guides there, with the idea of seeing Paris. You enter these balls and there see at once the brilliant demi-monde lending itself to every kind of degradation. Then, when people come to see me about my work, it is a little awkward for Cat. But he is a dear Cat, and confides everything to me.[7]

On the morning of the day George was due to join her, she went to the Préfecture to meet Lecour. It was to her the most memorable incident of her visit to Paris; so memorable, in fact, that when she came to write her own account of her campaigns it was the only incident of her Paris trip she thought worth mentioning.

## XX

LECOUR, as well as being Chef de Bureau of the Paris Police des Mœurs, was an authority on the history and sociology of prostitution in France. For this reason alone Josephine was anxious to meet him.[1] But there was a more pressing, more immediate reason.

She had not needed to look far to find evidence of the activities of the Police des Mœurs:

> In this hotel there is a Russian officer [she wrote to Stansfeld]. The woman who keeps this house told me that he had seduced a poor good young Swiss girl, who was soon expecting a child, and that she had resisted many attempts to drag her up to the Bureau to be registered as a 'fille de joie'. I asked if I could see her and was directed to the place. Through wet and snowy streets we walked to some miserable side street into a poor courtyard, and up a flight of broken steps to where the girl lived with her widowed mother, a straw-hat maker. Oh, if you could have heard what I heard there!

The Swiss woman's room was kept under siege, and her daughter a prisoner since, if she were to step outside, the agents who lay in wait for her would seize her and drag her off to St Lazare. On one occasion, five or six agents had broken into the tenement and had dragged out the girl who was, by this time, in an advanced state of pregnancy. The neighbours, being aroused, had beaten off the raiding party and now kept permanent watch over the building.

The girl assured Josephine that under no circumstances would she allow the police to force her into a life of prostitution, and her mother maintained that 'We have defended our home, and we shall do it to the last.' It was a statement which met with raucous applause from the neighbours. Josephine promised to do all she could to help, promised that the girl should be sent to her home in Liverpool rather than be imprisoned in St Lazare, and that the younger child, a six-year-old girl, would be found a place in the Swiss Protestant School in Paris.

She then went straight to the arrondissement headquarters of the Police des Mœurs, where, with her usual determination and her fluent command of the French language, she insisted on an interview with its chief, a Commissaire Roux. The result of this encounter can be deduced from an outburst contained in a letter to Stansfeld:

M. Roux' view is, the girl has been *debauched*. In such cases it is well – it is indispensable – that these girls should be registered at once and without delay before they have time to pursue their career any farther, and become diseased and communicate the disease to *honest men* (I am quoting the very words spoken to me) *to honest men*! Yes, it is necessary to lose no time but at once to register and submit to medical surveillance a *debauched* girl. A girl young, perhaps, and ignorant, is seduced by a man of higher rank. Her fate trembles in the balance. But Lecour and his men say she must *at once* be inscribed in the Book of Hell, at once be made public property – a thing, not a woman! To think that I am a woman and that women are thus spoken of to my face!

The following day she went to the Préfecture, to the Bureau d'Arrestation des Femmes (Service des Mœurs), to meet Lecour in his citadel, which she described as 'the most impudent proclamation of the Father of Lies'.

Lecour rose to greet her but, since he was still engaged in hearing petitions, instructed the blue and silver liveried flunkey to assist her to a carved gilt chair by the huge open fire, and to provide her with newspapers to read until he had concluded his business. Josephine pretended to be immersed in the newspapers but listened carefully to the transactions around Lecour's Napoleonic, gold-encrusted desk. One of the petitioners was an elderly man leaning on an umbrella with both hands. She noticed with some dismay that he was in tears. 'There was a long altercation. On Lecour's side, flippancy, sentiment, many words, and an apparent desire to get rid of the man by a few promises, while working out a case against the woman for whom this man had come to plead.' In a choking voice the old man kept repeating the words, '*Mais vous l'avez accusée!*' while Lecour pointed out that, though the woman in question had not actually been found guilty of sexual immorality, she had been guilty of 'unpardonable levity' and, moreover, her antecedents were questionable. It was, therefore, a justifiable and socially hygienic precaution to have her placed *en carte*. Lecour concluded this interview by informing the old man that, under interrogation, the woman had shown signs of deep distress. 'I told her,' he said, 'if I saw signs of a real repentance persevered in, I should forgive her.'

I tried to judge him without prejudice [Josephine said later, though at this stage the effort must have been considerable]. He appears to me very shallow, vain, talkative; his arguments are of the weakest; he has a certain dramatic cleverness, and acts all he says with face, arms, and legs. His countenance is to me very repulsive, although his face, which is in the barber's block style, might be called handsome. He has a fixed smile – that of a hypocrite. He is simply a shallow actor, an acrobat, a clever stage-manager who is intoxicated with the sense of power, chattering and gesticulating like an ape. And such is the man who holds the keys of heaven and hell, the power of life and death, for the women of Paris.

She asked him if vice and the incidence of venereal disease were decreasing in Paris as a result of his endeavours. 'Oh, increasing!' he exclaimed, wafting the air with his hands in a theatrical gesture of despair; 'they continue to increase all the time!' She asked him to explain this strange phenomenon, in view of the thoroughness with which the regulations were applied. It was the result of the Commune, he explained; the Communards had closed the *maisons tolérées* and had disbanded the Police des Mœurs. It would take a long time to eradicate entirely the evil effects of Communard irresponsibility on the morality of the women of Paris. And then it was true, was it not, that there was an ever-increasing coquetry among attractive and fashionable women? At this, to Josephine's complete disgust, Lecour leered at her.

Josephine was in her mid-forties, but, according to her family, she continued to look absurdly young until she was well into her fifties. (Some four years after her meeting with Lecour, on arriving one evening at the railway station at Lausanne, she found herself being hustled away by a patrol of young women which had been organised to protect girls coming to the city from the attentions of brothel-procurers and Police des Mœurs alike. A few hours later she arrived at the home of the Humbert family, announcing happily that she had just been rescued from a life of shame.) She was not amused, however, by Lecour's heavy attempts at flirtatiousness.

Perhaps Lecour realised something of the nauseating effect he was creating. His attitude underwent a remarkable transformation. He placed his hand on her arm and said with an overpowering stare of sincerity, '*Madame, écoutez-moi je vous en prie! Moi, je suis religieux. Je suis religieux comme vous, Madame.*' To this, Josephine retorted sharply, 'That may be so, sir, but I did not come to speak to you about religion, but about justice.' In her letter to Stansfeld she added, 'Of course to me they are the same thing, but the religion he meant was merely a bit of sentiment not worthy of the name.'

Despite the ill-concealed anger in her replies to his remarks, Lecour was clearly taken by her beauty and her charm. He provided her with letters of permission to enter St Lazare and any 'houses' under government licence demanding that all officers of his department should offer every facility to 'this very honourable lady from England'. For the next ten years, and even after his dismissal, he continued to send her complimentary copies of his books, pamphlets and magazine-articles.

Before she took her leave, Josephine broached the matter uppermost in her mind, the case of the Swiss girl. 'He showed me what he *could* be,' wrote Josephine. 'Almost spitting like a cat, he said with sudden irritation, "*Mais quelles bêtises vous ont-elles dit?*" ' But quickly he recovered his composure, asked her solicitously to provide him with the name and address of the girl and assured her that he would intervene personally if he found that Commissaire Roux had been over-zealous in pursuing the matter. Finally he expressed the hope that on her next visit to Paris, Josephine would spend the entire morning with him and would honour him by being his guest at lunch.

It was an invitation she did not take up.


## XXI

EXACTLY ten days after her arrival in Paris, Josephine set off with George for Lyons, *en route* to the South. Because of the bitter weather – there was snow all the way, and even the

Rhône was frozen over – the train journey took eleven hours. For this she was very grateful:

'It was the first real warmth and rest I had had for eleven days – with the large rug wrapped round me from head to foot, foot warmers, and an easy smooth-running express, kind fellow-travellers, and no responsibility, I almost laughed to myself with joy! Like a schoolboy escaped from work.'[1]

The second day of their visit to Lyons, George and she took a carriage and drove through the snow to St Croix, the industrial suburb of the city. They were warmly welcomed by some of the silk manufacturers, who showed them round the mills, where Josephine talked to as many of the weavers, men and women, as she could. She had not realised it before she arrived, but Lyons provided the most suitable and fertile ground for her mission. Not only was there a sizeable population of skilled factory operatives of the type who had formed the backbone of her initial crusade in the North of England, but there was also a tradition of radical dissent among the factory-owners such as was commonplace in Manchester or Leeds, but rare in the industrial areas of France. It was, in fact, the employers who, in showing Josephine around their workshops, assured her that their operatives were 'intelligent and high-spirited, and that an appeal to them on our subject would not prove disappointing'.[2] It was not. 'They have a strong sense of fairness and justice,' she wrote to Joseph Edmondson. 'Moreover they combine more than in Paris, and there is more possibility in Lyons of expressing new and bold views in the newspapers.'

From Lyons they travelled on to Antibes where they spent Christmas.

'The weather was lovely, like the sunny, crisp weather of a fine September or October in England. On Christmas Eve we had a memorable picnic. We spent the whole day in the open air, sitting on banks of sweet myrtle, overlooking the wooded landscape and the sea.'[3]

It was the briefest of respites. Leaving her sons, George and Stanley, to spend the remainder of their holiday in the South of France, she travelled to Naples to pass a few days with Hattie, who had already formed a group of Abolitionists in that city.

Encouraged by Hattie and her friends, Josephine set off for Rome. Her task was less hard than in Paris, for the republican exiles to whom she had acted as hostess in Oxford days, notably Aurelio Saffi, were now men of importance in their own country. She had in her possession letters of commendation from Mazzini, who was held in greater honour now that he was dead and no longer a danger to the House of Savoy than he had ever been when he was alive, and from Garibaldi, who was paying one of his rare visits to Rome from his self-appointed exile on Caprera. Moreover, Regulation of Vice had never been readily accepted in Italy. When, just before his death, Cavour had extended Regulation from Sardinia-Piedmont to the territories newly acquired by the House of Savoy, he had been opposed not merely by the extreme radicals, but by representatives of the centre and the monarchist right wing.

A cold reception from Vigliani, the Minister of Justice, caused her to write: 'Poor Italy, beloved, beautiful Italy! The wicked system there has wrought a mass of corruption, and a *circle* of iniquity which is more strikingly unique in its moral and political ugliness than anything in France or other countries.' [4]

This was simply not true. What was unique about Regulation as applied in the Italian cities was its incompetence, which resulted in widespread graft on a petty level. Nowhere in Italy was there evidenced the ruthless cruelty of the Paris Bureau des Mœurs, or the total corruption which was manifest in Brussels. Josephine had harboured romantic illusions about Italy since the earliest days of the Risorgimento; what she knew of Italy was gained from her love of Italian art and literature, and listening to Hattie's stories of campaigning with Garibaldi's armies in the South.

Against the depression resulting from her interview with Vigliani she could set the friendly reception from various members of the Italian Senate and Lower Chamber. One politician in particular, Guiseppe Nathan, restored her faith in the Italian soul. He was aged thirty, handsome, charming, intelligent and artistic. From early adolescence he had been a dedicated admirer of Garibaldi, and had been a close friend of Mazzini despite the great difference in their ages. He was, as befitted a friend of Mazzini, an unbeliever, something Josephine was always ready to forgive provided unbelief was allied to a liberal and humane temperament and a proper attitude towards the rights of women in society (both Josephine and George were firmly convinced that John Stuart Mill had found his place in heaven). He had known, moreover, great personal sorrow, something which was calculated to endear him to Josephine; he had returned home one day to find that his beautiful young wife, who had been suffering a particularly difficult pregnancy, had died alone and unattended in giving birth to a still-born and premature baby. His terrible sense of bereavement was exacerbated by an even more intense sense of guilt. In Josephine, Guiseppe Nathan felt that he had met someone who could genuinely sympathise with his feelings. It would perhaps be too much to suggest that this alone accounted for his decision to dedicate himself to furthering Josephine's cause, but the fact remains that for the remaining six years of his tragically short life, he devoted himself exclusively to fighting Regulation, and that his death was at least in part due to his refusal to take the advice of his doctors and to rest.

While Josephine remained in Rome lobbying the Senate and the Chamber, Nathan went before her into the North. He organised meetings in Florence and Turin, and a rally in Milan, before her arrival. 'He succeeded', wrote Josephine, 'in rousing the working people throughout the length and breadth of Italy against Regulation, engaging the best men and women in the work, and the hearts of all to our cause.'[5] This optimism was short-lived: Josephine had not appreciated that there was a well-entrenched government which enjoyed little popular support, and that the Opposition saw in her attack on Regulation, supported as always by the working classes, a whip to beat that government. The Morals Police in Italy was not disbanded, despite the endeavours of 'the best men and women', until well after her death, and, even so, the government licensing of brothels continued throughout the Fascist era.


## XXII

SWITZERLAND was a country very dear to Josephine, not, as in the case of Italy, because of a romantic illusion born of vicarious experience, but through personal knowledge. Tell Meuricoffre, Hattie's husband, was Swiss, as was the husband of her favourite niece, Edith Leupold. Josephine and her family were frequent visitors to Switzerland, and they had made, in the words of her grandson, 'Grunewald, Zermatt, and the environs of Lake Geneva, the family recreation ground'.[1] Josephine herself admitted that she prefered the air and scenery of the Swiss Alps to any part of Britain save her beloved Cheviots, and she admired the spirit of independence and tolerance which informed its citizens, 'with their glorious traditions, their grand republican sympathies, with their theory of equal laws for all their people, their religious zeal and their open Bible'.[2] For these reasons, despite the confidence she reposed in Aimé Humbert, which was to ripen over the years into intimate friendship, she was unable to leave him in sole charge of the Abolitionist campaign in Switzerland as she was to entrust it in Italy to Guiseppe Nathan and in France to Yves Guyot and Edmond de Pressense. For the ensuing twenty years it was to be the scene of some of her most bitterly contested personal campaigns.

Switzerland was not a fully Regulationist nation. Government was, and is, primarily on a cantonal basis. Geneva was Regulationist; Berne operated one regulated street experimentally; elsewhere the decision to establish a Police des Mœurs and *maisons tolérées* rested, not with the Government of the Confederation at Berne, or even with the cantonal governments, but with municipal authorities. The difficulty confronting Josephine and Humbert in Switzerland was not the result, as in France and to some extent Italy, of a general apathy – on the contrary, Regulation was a hotly debated issue long before Josephine's arrival. It lay in the diversity of local administrations and the legislative powers they wielded.

Josephine travelled from Turin to Berne,where she held her first meeting. There she met with almost unanimous support, including a warm welcome from the Procureur Général of the Swiss Confederation – a refreshing change from her experiences with Lecour and Vigliani. Then she travelled on to Lausanne 'in one of those large, roomy railway-carriages, with chairs and tables and a fireplace piled up with logs'.[3] Josephine's mission, during which she crossed and recrossed the country, sometimes having to revert to sledges when severe snowfalls had blocked the railway, was physically as well as mentally and emotionally exhausting.

After a brief meeting with some of her supporters in Lausanne, she pressed on to Geneva, where she held a successful rally. The chair was to have been taken by Professor Hornung of Geneva University, who was to have addressed the meeting on the juridical aspects of Regulation. On arriving at the hall, Josephine was given a note informing her that he was taken ill. With considerable trepidation she opened the meeting herself.

As she was speaking, Professor Hornung arrived, wrapped in shawls, and looking very pale. When she had concluded, he asked for objections to be brought forward. Despite the fact that the hall was full, there were none. Afterwards, Josephine was approached by two men who were to play a leading part in her international campaigns. The first was Charles Loyson, better known as Père Hyacinthe. Loyson had been one of the most eloquent and fashionable preachers at Notre-Dame de Paris, until, following the declaration of Papal Infallibility, he had broken with the Church of Rome. Since then he had taken up residence in Switzerland, had married an American girl and was now a priest in the Old Catholic Church. Following the meeting he wrote to Josephine:

'One feels, dear Madame, that God is with you in your heroic crusade against what you have so well called "the typical crime, the gigantic iniquity". God is with you, Madame; it is necessary that men should be with you also. I beg that you will count entirely upon my weak but sincere services.' [4]

Josephine welcomed his assistance readily enough. His powers of oratory had not diminished, and over the next few years he was to address meetings on her behalf in Switzerland, France and Britain, with much success. The flamboyance of his style alienated some of her more discriminating friends, but Josephine warmly embraced the help of anybody who sincerely supported her views, and she was correct in supposing that Loyson would prove a valuable asset.

A far more noble and saintly figure was that of Pastor Borel, an old man who had dedicated his life in the Protestant ministry to helping and trying to save juveniles from prostitution. He described to her the conditions which prevailed in the *maisons tolérées*: the imprisonment without fresh air, daylight or proper clothes; young girls 'shut out from the world, without occupation, without interest in anything, cloistered in the twilight of

filthy and infected rooms, reduced to a social intercourse consisting only of quarrels, or obscene conversations; and at the
first appearance of revolt are beaten like slaves by the mistress
or her bully.'[5]

That she took no action on the basis of what Pastor Borel
told her is clearly accounted for by the fact that she was already
over-worked. In any case she believed that the whole problem of
juvenile prostitution and the traffic in children was an integral
part of the greater problem of Regulation and the corruption in
high places which was, to her at least, its inevitable concomitant.
Only the disbandment of a despotic Morals Police with its
unlimited and improperly supervised powers of arrest would
ensure that such atrocities would cease. Nevertheless it is clear
from her evidence before the Select Committee of 1882 that,
following her meeting with Borel, she began to collect information regarding such abuses.

In Geneva Josephine was confronted not only by the grim-
mest aspect of prostitution, but also the most stubborn form
of opposition she had to face. Since she had found that in France
and Italy her chief support lay in the Protestant communities,
she hardly expected to find on her arrival in the capital of the
Calvinist reformation an opposition based on Protestantism.
Such however was the case.

It was the view of many Genevans and their ministers that
any girl who had stumbled into prostitution, through her own
fault or the fault of others, was manifestly predestined to Hell;
that any girl who had suffered the misfortune to be seduced was
clearly not of the Elect; that the only obligation imposed on the
Christian was to see that such a lost soul did as little spiritual –
and of course physical – damage to others as possible. Pastor
Borel himself, wise and compassionate as he was, wrote of the
girl who had escaped the clutches of both brothel ruffian and
Morals Police in order to try to re-establish herself in society:
'Her vast experience of evil scatters the seeds of moral death
far and near.'[6]

In her disillusionment, Josephine could think only of the
lamentation of Christ over Jerusalem: ' "O Jerusalem, Jerusalem!" ' she quoted in a letter home, ' "if thou hadst known
in this thy day the things that belong unto thy peace; but now
they are hid from thine eyes." '[7]

After three days in Geneva, it was a relief to go to Neuchâtel to stay with the Humberts:

The tone was very different from that of Geneva. It was here that I first made the personal acquaintance of our beloved friends M. and Madame Humbert and their family. M. Humbert speedily called a conference, and it was on this occasion that I first gained a knowledge of his breadth of view and intellectual grasp. His long experience of political life and men had endowed him with a readiness and tact, and a power of controlling and guiding an assembly even of the most discordant elements, such as I have scarcely seen in any other man.[8]

During her stay at Neuchâtel, Josephine was particularly pleased when a committee of clock-makers from the industrial centre of Chaux-de-Fonds telegraphed to Neuchâtel, inviting her to address two meetings consisting of their fellow-operatives.

She remembered the journey to Chaux-de-Fonds for the rest of her life. When she was in her seventies and compelled into a physically inactive retirement, she described it:

The town stands high on the Jura. I was warned that the cold would be many degrees greater than at Neuchâtel; and indeed I found it to be so. Even the extraordinary beauty of the vast expanses of snow, the black forests of enormous pine trees, with their weights of heavy clinging snow, the glimpses of the distant Alps stretching from Mont Blanc to the Wetterhorn and Wellhorn, scarcely gave me courage enough to hold out against the cold as we ascended. Madame Humbert kindly accompanied me. As we came near the town however, I found that I had not come among cold hearts. Several venerable men met us a little way from the town, with fur wrappings about them and faces full of kindly welcome, and stood with heads uncovered until the sledges started again for the town. The deep snow made everything very silent; no rattle of wheels, only the soft sweeping sound of the sledges flying swiftly about, and the musical ringing of the horses' bells.[9]

Then, as if remembering what she was supposed to be writing about, she adds, 'We had two excellent meetings there.'

It was the climax and culmination of her visit to Switzerland. On 10 February 1875, she set off for home via Paris, where she had decided to stop off for several days to take advantage of the letters given her by Lecour allowing her to visit the institutions administered by the Bureau des Mœurs, an excursion for which she had lacked both time and inclination on her outward journey.

## XXIII

JOSEPHINE felt depressed about her second visit to Paris: 'I will not dwell upon the rather bitter experiences of this, my second visit,' she wrote twenty years later, 'which arose from the opposition and cynicism we encountered.'[1] She was affected by mental and physical exhaustion; in fact, the visit was as fruitful and effective as any during her six weeks' trip on the Continent.

Together with Humbert, who had joined her soon after her arrival, she went to the working-class districts of the eleventh arrondissement, the Faubourg St Antoine and Belle Ville. She was greeted with touching enthusiasm, particularly by the working girls of the district who had heard of her intervention in the case of the Swiss girl. She held two packed meetings in the area, at which she made no pretence of presenting an intellectual discussion of the subject but, sensing the mood of her audience, whose revolutionary traditions went back to the capture of the Bastille, and who were still ferociously embittered by the haphazard bloodletting perpetrated by the Army of Versailles during the suppression of the Commune, she indulged in that controlled sarcasm which was one of the features of her oratory. After commending, to the great satisfaction of her auditors, the Commune itself, and brushing aside all criticism of that somewhat incompetent attempt at revolutionary administration with the words: 'I do know that it abolished all houses of ill-fame, and that it also proclaimed the necessity of setting women free to earn their bread in industry and trades,'[2] she reached the climax of her peroration.

'If prostitution is an institution of public safety such as should be organised by Governments, even the Ministers, the

Prefect of Police, the high functionaries, and the doctors who defend it, fail in their duty if they do not consecrate to it their own daughters!'

According to Guyot, this was greeted with deafening applause, the audience rising to their feet to roar out their approval. An advocate from the Procureur's office who had, in all probability, been instructed to follow Josephine into the somewhat seditious climate of the eleventh arrondissement, was brave enough, or rash enough, to attempt to answer her. When he declared that prostitutes ' were the vilest of creatures, scarcely human, and justly expelled from and scorned by society', the women in the audience pushed him back into his seat and screamed at him, ' What about the men? What about the men? ' [3]

'I thanked God for this storm of righteous indignation,' Josephine wrote to George. But she was not entirely happy. Perhaps she remembered how these same women, or their friends, five years earlier, had pulled from his horse an officer of the Army of Versailles, had torn the unfortunate man to pieces, and had paraded his sexual organs aloft on a pike around Montmartre. Their shouts, she added, 'had a maledictory sound which reminded me of the deep and deadly wounds which had been inflicted on the population of Paris.' [4] For once, she was not merely thinking of the Police des Mœurs.

The weather on the day she went to the prison of St Lazare was not calculated to raise up her flagging spirits. It was raining, and the snow was turning to a grey slush. As she reached the huge stone portico of the prison, a prison-van arrived, black and windowless – she described it as being like an immense hearse – escorted by mounted gendarmes, their sabres drawn. The gates swung open, and she tried to follow the vehicle through, but they immediately clanged to in her face. She then asked the guards at the gateway how she should obtain admittance. They shrugged their shoulders, and one of them pointed with his thumb behind him at a postern-door and said, ' Vous pouvez battre, Madame.' [5] The door was made of solid wood, inches thick and studded with iron nails. Her gloved hand made no impression on it, and she saw that the guards were laughing at her. Angrily, she picked up a large stone and battered on the postern until, at last, it was opened. An aged porter emerged, and Josephine presented him with Lecour's letter. This produced an immediate

response. Smiling, he asked her to wait while he found one of the
nun-wardresses to act as her guide.

As they crossed the yard to the main buildings, Josephine
saw some of the younger inmates taking their hour of pre-
scribed recreation, walking in twos and threes in a wide circle,
shivering in their thin grey uniform-dresses, and up to their
ankles in mud and filth. The nun informed her that these girls
were by no means all French; there were Italians, Swiss,
Germans and English among them. Remembering what Pastor
Borel had told her of the international trade in women, Josephine wished to speak with some of them to find out their
histories, but she was sternly forbidden to do so; the regulations
demanded that the girls be kept in absolute silence:

> Never in my life [she wrote] did I so long to speak. They
> paused when they got near to me, with looks of kindness, or
> gentle curiosity. One knows enough of the heartless, artificial,
> or hardened women of Paris, but my memory recalls *these* who
> were the raw material, fresh from nature's hand out of which
> Babylon manufactures her soulless wild beasts who become a
> terror to their manufacturers.[6]

She was shown around the entire prison, as Lecour had instructed. That same evening, in her lodgings, she wrote to
Edmondson, 'I cannot recall the horrors I have seen today.'[7]
Yves Guyot, who, with de Pressense and le Caze, was serving on
a commission of inquiry into prisons administered by the
Service des Mœurs, has left a very full and detailed account of
what he found there, and his report explains Josephine's
reticence.[8]

Guyot's first impression of St Lazare was the smell of the
yards, which were used as a depository for every kind of slop, and
the way in which this stench penetrated every room of the
buildings to mingle with what he called the 'shut-up' smell
which was the result of the gross over-crowding in the wards.
He noticed that the girls' uniform-dresses were filthy, as were
the girls themselves. This was hardly surprising, since they
were permitted neither to wash their clothes nor their bodies –
the nuns insisting that they should never be permitted to
undress lest they commit an offence against modesty. The nuns,
however, did instruct their charges in the use of a syringe,

which, as Guyot pointed out, since it was never washed, probably accounted for the incidence of venereal disease among
Paris prostitutes.

The girls lived and slept in dormitories containing four rows
of beds crowded together in such a way as to provide exactly
half the space which government regulations laid down regarding ordinary prisons. Their working day began at 4.45 a.m.
when they were woken up to cries of *Vive Jésu!* By 5 a.m. they
had made their beds, completed the minimal toilet allowed to
them and were assembled in the workrooms for the Morning
Offering. There, they worked until 8.45 a.m. when they received
their first meal of the day, soup consisting of water-broth
containing a single carrot or leek. Afterwards they walked in the
yard until 9.45 a.m., when they returned to work. At noon they
had lunch consisting of bread which had been dipped in
vegetable soup (the soup itself being reserved for the staff),
after which, they worked again until 3 p.m., when they received
their last meal of the day, a plate of beans. They then had an
hour of recreation spent in walking silently around the yard,
worked until 7 p.m., had Night Prayer and went to bed.

Any breach in the regulations – failure, for instance to
genuflect when a nun passed by – meant removal to the punishment rooms, as did refusal to submit to being placed *en carte*.
These rooms consisted of windowless and airless garrets whose
sole furniture consisted of one tub for the performance of
natural functions, which was rarely emptied. In these garrets,
girls spent day and night, fed at irregular intervals on bread and
water which they had to consume without the use of their
hands, since they were bound in strait-jackets. Guyot inquired
of the Mother Superior in charge how long girls were confined
under such conditions. They remained there, answered the
Mother Superior, until they volunteered to be placed *on carte*,
or, in the case of those who had offended against the regulations,
until she – the Mother Superior – was satisfied that they were
sincerely contrite. There was a second alternative she might have
mentioned: until, in the permanent semi-darkness and am-
moniac dung-heap stench, they went insane – a condition
always put down by the medical officers as being the result of
advanced syphilis.

Finally Guyot visited the wing reserved for children suspected of having been engaged in prostitution. Their dormitory consisted of a darkened room, without windows or lights, and their beds were wooden cages. The reason offered for this was that these children must not pick up immodest habits by observing each other as they retired to bed, and the cages ensured against them instructing each other in lesbian practices in the darkness. He asked what happened to such children after they had been released. Lecour, who was with him during this visit, replied that the authorities wrote to the *mairie* of the district where they had been born, and if the officials of the *mairie* could not locate their parents or guardians, they were apprenticed to a licensed brothel.

That these were the horrors of which Josephine refused to speak or think so far as she could help is beyond doubt, and the impact of the experience upon her exhausted brain contributed to her breakdown during the following weeks. In a letter to Sir James Stansfeld she told all she chose to say of her visit:

M. Lecour (not present) got up a scene to impress me: a girl from England, I was shown, who had been brought in diseased to St Lazare, and was converted by reading a Bible given to her there by a deaconess. This deaconess called on me to admire, and said, 'Ah! M. Lecour is a man of good heart. He never gives a licence to a woman without a sigh or a tear.' She had been with Lecour—he flatters these good women, and now he believes I have seen the *religieuses* of his system. I told them (the nuns) I was horrified! That he should *ever give* a single licence to any woman, and that he dared to speak of his one wretched convert among 1000 hardened victims. I *feel* his influence wherever I go. I asked what the crime was for which the greater number were in prison, and was told it was for walking in streets which are forbidden, and at hours which are forbidden! I said, 'You falsify consciences.' I was shown a house full of some hundreds (400 I think) of little girls from 5 to 11 years old *who were prostitutes*, forced by bad men, victims, and my guides said, 'Now is not this good? All these, housed? You must not speak against M. Lecour.' I replied, 'I am horrified at the sight. By what process of corruption have your men come to that they victimise these infants?'[9]

To George she wrote, 'I have seen something of the true misery of Paris, but I dare not write of it. How can people say that London is worse! I know London.'[10] In Paris, she added, 'one perceives oneself in the midst of all the crowning abominations ever devised of human wickedness'. It was an exaggeration perhaps – she had yet to learn about Brussels, and, indeed, London – but exhausted, unhappy and homesick as she was, it was a pardonable one.

## XXIV

JOSEPHINE'S continental mission had lasted from the beginning of December 1874 to the end of February 1875. It had been a remarkably hectic undertaking, and, equally, it had been a remarkably successful one. As a result of her efforts, and the foreign guests whom she brought with her, 'The British and Continental Federation For The Abolition Of Government Regulation Of Prostitution' was founded. Stansfeld was elected President, Henry Wilson, Treasurer, and Josephine, Secretary. Within eighteen months the Federation had active branches in virtually every nation in Europe from Romania to Spain.

Josephine had to pay a high price for her success. Mind and body conspired together to force her determined will to allow them at least a partial rest from the apparently ceaseless activity she imposed on them. As she lay on her chaise-longue in her darkened drawing-room, with George sternly protecting her from all visitors, she was afflicted by a sense of guilt. To Joseph Edmondson she wrote telling of her misery at having imposed on him and Henry Wilson and others of her friends, the need to maintain and to persevere with the International Federation, and she left little room for doubt that it was her belief that without her constant personal involvement, it would probably wither and die before it had achieved anything.

Everything she had done up till now, everything she had accomplished, had been the result of her personal exertion, her will, her determination. It was difficult for her to realise that she had distinguished allies – Aimé Humbert, Yves Guyot, Edmond de Pressense, Guiseppe Nathan and Sir James Stansfeld – who were as anxious as herself to see through what she had begun, and who were, due to their rank or political experience, better equipped to do so. Although Josephine remained all her life the acknowledged and honoured leader of the Abolitionist movement, her sickness during the summer and autumn of 1875 taught her that she could no longer direct each and every battle in the struggle.

From the summer of 1875 to the spring of 1879, Josephine spent less time in active campaigning and more in writing – pamphlets, articles for the Press and appeals for funds to support the British and Continental Federation. During this time she wrote two books of major importance. *The Hour Before The Dawn* was published in 1876. In a magnificently sustained stream of eloquence, logic and compassion, it attacks the whole concept of the double standard in sexual morality:

> Come with me and look at the degraded woman in a corner of some hospital ward, consumed by disease and misery. What was her life, and what was yours? The abandonment of herself to a person beloved was perhaps her first step to ruin; and who shall say that that self-abandonment is altogether devoid of some trace of unselfishness? What is there in such a one which makes her a greater sinner than yourself? Be honest! She is lost to society; you are petted by society. She is killed by the poison she drank; you survive. She dies prematurely, and her place knows her no more. Your past life could reveal sins as great before God as hers have been; and you are – I will not say happy – but you are not in your coffin.[1]

The young man blackens the prostitute, 'speaks of her as beyond all hope of restoration' because 'it lessens the uneasy sense of guilt' which stirs within his breast. Does he know, then, how the prostitute thinks of him?

> They say: 'We are sinners indeed, but we are not hypocrites; we do not, after playing with impurity under cover of darkness, take our place smilingly in the daytime among pure men and women and go to church.' Now men who doubt the reclaimability of fallen women look upon unchastity as the one damning sin. The woman, on the other hand, looks on the hypocrisy as the one damning sin. Thus, while one

class of persons may be looking upon another class as utterly irreclaimable, the very class so judged may be holding the same view with regard to the judges.[2]

As she develops her argument, what begins as an attack on the double standard, and an impassioned appeal for charity towards the prostitute, becomes latterly her own apologia for Christian belief:

> I look back to the years when my soul was in darkness on account of sin. I could see no God, or such as I could see appeared to me to be an immoral God. Does he look down from His eternal order of heaven an indifferent spectator?[3]

Her answer to this problem would scarcely satisfy either theologian or unbeliever, for it is the answer of an honest Christian humanist. She can only say that when she looks upon the wretched, the destitute, the degraded and depraved, and feels the stirring of love and pity in her own heart, she recognises by that token the love and compassion of Christ. For why should she feel these stirrings except as the reflection of a greater love?

Joesphine's *Life of Catherine of Siena*, published in 1878, is perhaps her best book. She sent a copy to Gladstone, possibly because, in identifying herself with her subject, she had cast him in the role of Pope Gregory XI. Her aim in writing the book was to produce a sympathetic portrait of the saint as she had lived:

> It may truly be said that her biographers unconsciously represented Catherine in a form which as nearly resembled the real woman as the figures on the painted windows of old churches resemble the flesh and blood originals. To describe human enthusiasm in high and passionate action requires a gift which few writers have possessed. Instead of the high and beautiful humanity, the old biographers give us only a super-humanity which leaves us with an unsatisfied longing to possess the real portrait instead.[4]

Human enthusiasm in high and passionate action was something which Josephine well understood, and as Rembrandt employed himself as model for the portrait of an apostle, so she sat for her portrait of St Catherine:

> It is not difficult to understand what were the faults in

Catherine's character, and the natural tendencies against which she, most probably all her life, had to contend. Her zeal and fire would naturally carry on to impatience; and it must have been difficult for her to bear with equanimity the delays and checks induced by the stumblings and errors of others which so often postponed or injured the work she had at heart. It is evident also that her genius for command may have tempted her to exercise an imperious self-will, and to rule in too despotic a manner. Again, there is evidence that at times, when the strong claims of active duty were relaxed, she incurred a danger of being carried away by excess of feeling, in the exaltation of her spirit, and the intense communion of her soul with the unseen.[5]

During these years also she found time to take long-postponed holidays with George. In August 1876, they were in Switzerland together. Josephine had been engaged in making arrangements regarding the first conference of the International Federation which was to be held in Geneva the following year, and George had wandered off into the mountains by himself. Finding herself at leisure, Josephine procured a horse and rode off, quite alone, up from the Rhône Valley at Sierre to the Riffel, in the hope of finding him. There had been storms earlier; torrents, fallen trees and boulders blocked up the path. But Josephine, at forty-eight years old, had lost none of her skill or agility as a horsewoman:

> He was sketching. I shall never forget his face of joy when he recognised me coming up through the woods. I thought he would have broken his neck, bounding over the rocks to meet me.[6]

When she could be persuaded to take a holiday which was not in some way connected with her work for the British and Continental Federation, she and George would retreat into isolated companionship in a cottage in some wild part of the Peak District, or on to an island in Derwentwater. Occasionally Josephine would be firmly reminded of the duty of women by being employed as housekeeper in Froude's cottage near Salcombe on the Devon coast, while its owner went sea-fishing with George. In August 1878, during the third of these visits, Josephine wrote to her youngest son, Charles:

There has been a storm here, and the wind is high and the sea roaring. Father and Mr Froude have been out in a yacht all day, trawling. They caught a turbot, several mackerel, and many skates. They were burnt brown when they came in. Father says that Froude is quite at home in a storm, and laughs wildly, rather like a seagull! Father bathes every morning, and gets tossed about on the waves like a mad Mother Carey's chicken.[7]

In the meantime, the British and Continental Federation was expanding fast. In April 1876, Henry Wilson and the Rev. J. P. Gledstone set out from Liverpool for a mission to the United States.

The danger that a full system of regulation would be imposed on at least some of the states was much greater than in Britain. Slavery had resulted in a problem regarding prostitution, particularly in the Southern States and in the northern industrial towns, which was unique in that slave-prostitutes were regarded as chattels in a legal sense foreign even to the most stringent Bureau des Mœurs in Europe; and the Declaration of Emancipation following the battle of Antietam had worsened rather than eased the situation since Southern landowners could hardly afford to retain their armies of female slaves as paid labour. St Louis was, predictably, Regulationist, and Regulationist bills were under discussion in the city-halls of Philadelphia, Baltimore and Chicago, while a Federal system of Regulation was being mooted in Congress at Washington.

By drawing various small, ineffectual committees from various parts of the United States under the aegis of the British and Continental Federation, Wilson and Gledstone created a centralised American committee of the Federation. At the same time, they won the enthusiastic support and co-operation of the veteran anti-slave campaigner, William Lloyd Garrison, and his chief lieutenant, Wendell Phillips, the most eloquent orator of the anti-slavery cause. This was due in part to the interest taken by Josephine's father in the anti-slavery movement, but far more was it due to the fundamental interrelation between the institution of slavery and prostitution in the United States. The anti-slavery movement, the 'old' abolitionists, provided Josephine's representatives with a ready-made organisation, and a well-proven propaganda machine. Equally valuable in an immediate sense was the support of the chaplains of the Senate and the House of Representatives, through whom Gledstone and Wilson were able to form a Congressional lobby which blocked any attempt at Federal legislation aimed at producing a Regulationist system.

As Josephine had found in Europe, there was no lack of support for the Abolitionist cause once somebody emerged capable of providing a unifying centre and an organisation. Within a year of Wilson and Gledstone's visit, Regulation had been abolished in St Louis; Judge Snell, in a Washington District Court, had ruled that police were not entitled to compel a woman to go with them to a precinct station unless they had reasonable grounds for assuming that she had committed a statutory offence; the influential *Women's Journal* of Boston, which had received Gledstone and Wilson's visit with something less than enthusiasm, had set itself up as a watchdog, reporting any attempts at the imposition of Regulation by municipal authorities in the Eastern States.

While the American mission was in progress in the summer of 1876, Josephine remained with the Humberts and Giuseppe Nathan in Berne to set up a working-committee to organise the Geneva congress. There, once again, she proved her amazing capacity to win over and obtain the assistance of the right person, in this case Federal-Colonel Otto von Buren, the State President of Berne. In 1870, during the opening stages of the Franco-Prussian War when, prior to the Prussian breakthrough in Alsace, it seemed as though fighting might have been concentrated in the border regions of the Palatinate, as commander-in-chief of the Swiss army, he had led a small force to Strasbourg and had evacuated from it women and children, the old and the sick, and had brought them back into the safety of Switzerland. There he had supervised and administered their stay until it was safe for them to return to their city. This very considerable achievement had won him the respect, not merely of his own people, but also of both belligerents. When he joined the British and Continental Federation he brought with him three other Federal-Colonels of the Swiss army, ex-members of his staff who were understandably devoted to him, including Colonel Kaiser, the military commandant of the eastern region. The importance of these acquisitions to the cause cannot be over-emphasised. Everywhere, it seemed, military authorities formed the hard core of abolitionist support. The winning over of almost the entire upper echelon of the Swiss military establishment was a considerable victory.

The working-committee having been formed, Josephine travelled home through the Rhineland and Belgium on what was virtually an adjunct to her continental mission of the previous year. In Frankfurt, Cologne and Eberfeld she established Abolitionist committees to further the campaign against the Prussian Regulationist system she had so acutely analysed in her book *The New Era*. In Belgium she met Pastor Anet and the liberal leader Cor van Maaren, both of whom were to become dedicated allies of herself and her publisher, Alfred Dyer, when four years later they broke the vicious and corrupt hold of the Belgian police authorities over the Belgian *maisons tolérées*:

'It was during this visit to Belgium', Josephine wrote later, 'that I made my first acquaintance with the awful crimes and cruelties resulting from the system of Regulation long established there.'[8]

But in the autumn of 1876 she was distracted from investigating the Regulation system as practised in Belgium, by events taking place in Paris.


## XXV


IN the late summer of 1876, when he was visiting the Port of Brest for a yachting holiday, Yves Guyot read a newspaper article describing three arrests made by the Police des Mœurs in the municipality of Lyons.

In the first of these cases, a girl of about twenty who was alone waiting for a train at the station of Perrache, near Lyons, was accosted by three *agents des mœurs*. She refused to go with them and was dragged, screaming, out of the station. As the police-wagon was driven up, she broke free, and threw herself under its wheels, which crushed her legs. A crowd gathered, begging the police to leave her alone, or at least to carry her to a nearby hotel, there to await the arrival of a doctor. The police, however, insisted on dragging her along the street to a *poste de*

*Gendarmerie.* Members of the crowd managed to find a doctor and took him to the *poste* where he found the girl lying on the floor moaning in agony. After a furious argument, the doctor persuaded the police that he was a man with sufficient influence among the authorities to cause them trouble if they did not listen to him, and a cab was procured by which he might take the girl to hospital. Determined to accompany them, the police dragged the girl back across the pavement to the cab, threw her on to the floor and took the seats inside for themselves. They were just entering Lyons, passing along the Quai de la Charité beside the Rhône, when the girl managed to open the door of the cab, and threw herself out on to the street. Before either the police or the doctor could stop her, she had crawled on her hands and knees to the embankment and had thrown herself into the tidal currents of the river.

Three days after the death of this first girl, a squad of Police des Mœurs appeared at the kitchen door of the Hôtel du Guesclin in Lyons, and demanded that one of the maids be handed over to them. When the girl was informed of this by the hotel manager she threw herself from her third-floor bedroom window on to the paving-stones of the courtyard below.

Four days later, a girl already *en carte* was picked up by the Lyonnais Police des Mœurs for a minor infringement of the terms of her licence. Placed in a cell on the Rue Luizerne to await removal to the women's penitentiary of St Joseph, she tried to commit suicide by hanging herself in her apron, but was cut down in time. A little later she attempted to stab herself with the knife she had been given with her evening meal, but only succeeded in wounding herself. Despite the fact that she was still bleeding, and the wound had not been attended to, she was thrown into the punishment garret of the prison, a place similar to that in St Lazare.

Guyot was, at this time, editor of the radical journal the *Droits de l'Homme*. From Brest he drafted an article on the subject of these reports and cabled the dispatch to his editorial office. For the next few days he was happily engaged with his friend Captain Béléguic, the boat-designer, navigating a new yacht round La Chèvre and the Mer Sauvage, off the capes of Brittany, and it was not until he returned to Paris that he discovered that his hastily conceived article had started a

newspaper war in the capital. The line-up was predictable:
the *Droits de l'Homme* was supported by the radical and
socialist press, while the right-wing journals supported the
conservative-monarchist government of Marshal MacMahon
which had reintroduced the Police des Mœurs into Paris after
the Commune had been put down. The Centrist press tended to
rally to the side of the *Droits de l'Homme*, and participated in
the campaign by publishing their own accounts of women who
had been wrongfully arrested and detained.

The issues were felt more deeply in France than they were in
Belgium or Switzerland. There was a political emphasis on the
whole question more obvious than in other countries: the Police
des Mœurs were considered less as a national utility than as an
arm of a right-wing government which, after the honeymoon
period following the dark days of 1871 and 1872, was rapidly
losing support even in traditionally conservative rural France.
In Paris itself, by late 1876, fashionable boulevardiers, who had
tended to regard police round-ups as free evening diversions,
added to their evening recreation by attempting to prevent the
*agents des mœurs* from making arrests, and by rescuing girls from
police vans. As a result, wealthy and distinguished citizens
found themselves under arrest, which did little to enhance the
popularity of Lecour and the Bureau des Mœurs.

Aimé Humbert went to Paris to investigate for himself what
was happening. What he found pleased him mightily; it was
comparable, he wrote to Josephine, 'to a mine bursting under our
feet'.[1] He arranged meetings and rallies, and for once there was
little need for Abolitionist propaganda – petitions and memor-
anda were pouring into the offices of Senators and Deputies.

Yves Guyot, meanwhile, in his capacity as a municipal
councillor, was demanding that Lecour be made to answer for
cases of wrongful arrest. However, a few days later, it was
Guyot who was summoned before a *juge d'instruction* at the
Tribunal of the Sûreté National. There he was accused of
'having published in ill faith news which was false, and of a
nature to disturb public peace; and of having committed the
offence of abusing the depositaries or agents of public authority
for acts relating to their duty'.[2]

He was, in fact, fairly or unfairly trapped. A friend of his, a
young and celebrated actress, Mlle Rousseil, had been arrested in

full view of her public as she left the theatre in which she was playing. She had not, however, been taken either to the Préfecture or the St Lazare. Instead, she had slapped the face of the agent attempting to arrest her, and had then, in a most unlady-like fashion, kicked him in the groin, before flouncing off to her carriage leaving him doubled up with pain on the pavement. The next issue of the *Droits de l'Homme* fairly steamed with indignation; Lecour and his agents, Guyot declared, existed solely 'to provide for public harems guarantees to the customers of the good quality of the merchandise which they deliver to satisfy their appetites'.[3] It was the publication of this issue which had resulted in his being summoned before the Tribunal.

The principal witness for the prosecution was, of course, Lecour. He gave a performance which was latin rather than gallic in its unrestrained appeal to the emotions. It so happened, he announced, that by a lucky chance agents of the Bureau des Mœurs had apprehended the young man who had attempted to arrest Mlle Rousseil; he was never in the Service des Mœurs, but was merely 'a silly fellow who had done this for his own amusement'.[4] Lecour knew Mlle Rousseil to be a young lady of irreproachable reputation, and regretted what had happened as deeply as anybody. At this point, he burst into tears – how could an honest servant of the state bear with equanimity the abuse, the slanders, which had been heaped upon his head and upon the honest heads of the honest men who had the privilege of serving society under him? As he was led, still weeping copiously, from the podium, the 'silly fellow' was brought before the Tribunal. The man testified to the accuracy of the Prefect's statement. No attempt was made to discover the witness's real occupation, and he was summarily sentenced to imprisonment for several days. Guyot, on the other hand, was fined three thousand francs with costs – a total of five thousand, five hundred francs in all, a sum which, since he was far from wealthy, was a heavy burden to bear – and three months im-prisonment. Josephine, when she heard the verdict, raised as much money as she could from the British and Continental Federation – the best part of five thousand francs – and dis-patched James Stuart with it to Paris. Guyot was set at liberty while lodging an appeal (ultimately unsuccessful) with the Court of Cassation.

Josephine and George arrived in Paris to testify before a Commission set up by the Conseil Municipal. They then attended a meeting at the Salles des Écoles in the Rue d'Arras. Thousands of people, working class for the most part, came to listen to speeches by de Pressense, le Caze and other distinguished members of the National Assembly who advocated the Abolitionist cause. But it was George's speech which was the climax of the evening.

'It was touching and strange to me', Josephine wrote to Hattie, 'to look at his calm face as he stood and spoke words of gentle force to a great French republican crowd.'[5]

He spoke quietly in the idiomatic French over which both he and Josephine had fluent command, to the irritation of their opponents in Paris who looked for any excuse to mock at them. Taking as his text the words of Voltaire,

> Si l'homme est crée libre, il doit se gouverner;
> Si l'homme a des tyrans, il les doit détrôner;
> On ne sait que trop ces tyrans sont les vices;[6]

he succeeded, without raising his voice, in bringing his audience to its feet again and again.

After George had returned to Liverpool, and Guyot, whose appeal had been dismissed by the Court of Cassation, had surrendered himself to prison, Josephine remained for a time in Paris. She sent a copy of George's speech to Hattie in Naples. Hattie wrote back directly to him:

> My dear George – I have just been reading your speech at Paris, so logical, generous, and courteous. I am so glad you were able to be at Paris: it was such a precious support for Josie. She feels so much strength and rest in your presence; but it must have cost you something to leave her behind. If other people will not be husbands and wives in the future life, I am sure you two will. All these generous sacrifices and separations will be rendered back to you in some delightful union, more than to other people.[7]

He had done much; enough in fact to bring down on his head a scathing attack from elements in the British press, notably the *Standard* and the *Liverpool Mercury*. Did the governing body of Liverpool College know that their headmaster had been addressing left-wing mobs in the working-class faubourgs of Paris, and that his wife, even now, was stirring discontent against a friendly government? What business, asked another paper, has a clergyman of the Church of England to be addressing republican crowds in Paris? One might as well expect the Archbishop of Orleans to address an army of Communards.

Since Josephine had the support of Archbishop Dupanloup, the simile was ill-chosen. 'It is not those who point out the flaws in our social system', George continued in his temperate reply to his assailants, 'and endeavour to indicate the best methods of dealing with them who deserve reproach, but those who wilfully shut their eyes to the evils around them, and assail with invective the pioneers in the way towards constitutional liberty and equal justice to men and women.'[8] In a brief moment of acerbity, he pointed out that it was not altogether surprising that in a republic he should have addressed himself to a republican crowd.

In the meantime, Josephine remained in Paris holding meetings and talking to the stream of working-class girls who passed through her hotel rooms to the undisguised worry of the proprietor. Lecour was said to have stated privately that 'the régime of the Service des Mœurs was lost, and that certain changes or ameliorations' would have to be introduced. He was right. Largely thanks to Guyot, who persisted in his attacks on Lecour despite his imprisonment, the Bureau des Mœurs was closed in 1878 and eighteen months later the entire apparatus of the Police des Mœurs was dismantled. Guyot himself generously ascribed the victory to Josephine.

## XXVI

THE International Congress assembled in Geneva in September 1877. There were over five hundred delegates, coming from the United States, Russia, Britain, Belgium, Holland, Germany, Denmark, Italy, France and Spain, the Spanish delegation being led by the President of the Cortes. In order to ensure the smooth running of the Congress, Stansfeld went to Switzerland some weeks ahead of Josephine and the other leaders.

He had not been in Geneva a matter of days before he sent an alarming report back to Josephine. He had discovered that a large number of the delegates, notably de la Harpe, the Swiss delegate whom both Humbert and Hornung had proposed as President of the Congress, were of the opinion that the first aim of the Congress should be to advocate a full Prohibitionist policy. This was an ideal which had been frequently suggested to Josephine and consistently rejected by her. It meant, in effect, that the struggle to abolish the Police des Mœurs, the licensing of prostitutes, and *maisons tolérées* should be dropped, and instead there should be a campaign to make prostitution an illegal offence subject to severe penalties. Such an aim, if declared, would carry certain obvious advantages. It would remove once and for all the accusation so frequently hurled at Josephine that her attitude towards prostitutes was so permissive that she seemed little better than a prostitute herself. It would undoubtedly win the support of the more Calvinistic communities, such as the Genevans; and it would prove that the Regulationists were no less serious regarding the hygienic aspects of sexual promiscuity than their opponents. Josephine's objection to the Prohibitionist view was threefold. First, the making of prostitution a criminal offence would be a direct affront to the concept of individual liberty; secondly, it would make rescue work well-nigh impossible, and would prevent girls from seeking help, since an appeal to would-be rescuers would be a confession of criminality; thirdly, it would mean the abolition of one set of arbitrary police powers to make way for another. Prohibition was, she declared in a letter to her British colleagues, worse than 'Mr Bruce's Bill'.

In order to overcome the threat of such a proposal being implemented by the Congress, she decided, with a fine disregard for normal democratic processes, to enlarge the British delegation by recruiting a regiment of ladies under the captaincy of a Mrs Bright Lucas, with which to pack the Legislative and Hygienic sections of the Congress – the sections in which, according to Stansfeld, the danger was most likely to arise. With this small army, and her eldest son, George, who was now an examiner with the Civil Service Commission, and who was deputed to act as her personal press officer, she proceeded to Geneva, where she was met by Aimé Humbert, who provided her with a professional shorthand writer. This last acquisition hugely pleased her. She wrote to George senior:

> I am sure you are working *hard*, dear one. Only don't work *too* hard. How delightful it would be if we could work together, and I would lend you my short-hand writer an hour a day. It is such a help. I just say straight off all the letters I want written and he takes them down in short-hand as fast as I speak, and then he writes them all out in his own home and posts them without my *ever seeing them* any more! I will send you a letter through him some day to show you. He is a young man, a thorough automaton. I often have to dictate strange or terrible things to him. He is a very nice fellow; but he does his part so well that if I were to write to you by him saying I had bought a horse with a pig's head and a cow's tail, he would put it down and make no remark.[1]

Her prediction regarding trouble spots in the Congress was correct. The Legislative section met in the Hall of the Reformation, which was densely crowded by sightseers from the city. Voting on the propositions raised by section delegates took three hours of almost continual uproar. Professor Hornung, who presided over the section, demanded that a vote be taken on a list which contained no mention of the Prohibitionist attitude, but an Italian delegate rose and declared that there had been a lack of proper discussion on most of the points. It was late in the evening, and many delegates were both hungry and thirsty. The German delegation, apparently hungrier than their colleagues, bolted in desperation for the doors at the back of the hall. Afraid that this would leave a majority in favour of the Prohibitionist attitude, Josephine jumped up from her seat, slammed the doors shut and placed her back against them, shouting in German that nobody was going to get any food until they had voted. The Germans sheepishly returned to their seats, but after a noisy half-hour, it was apparent that no voting was going to take place. Professor Hornung, therefore, with malice aforethought, decreed that delegates would assemble for voting at half-past six the following morning.

As dawn crept up over the Swiss Alps, Mrs Bright Lucas and her company of English ladies swamped the voting in the Legislative section, and then, after a short break for breakfast, marched over to the Hygienic section, there to perform the same task. This time, arguments over voting procedure lasted until midnight. At eleven o'clock, Josephine's son, who was keeping watch for her, ran back to her hotel to tell her that the English ladies in the back rows had all fallen asleep. Josephine went over to the hall to find that Mrs Bright Lucas, 'her eyes shining like bright coals' with the effort of keeping herself awake, was shaking and pushing each of the ladies into a state of consciousness every time a clause was presented for a vote to be taken.

At the end of the Congress Josephine had every reason to be pleased. The resolutions passed by the general meeting, which were communicated by her son to the Press of every nation represented, corresponded largely with her own eight-point declaration of 1870. There were, however, two significant additions, both the work of Pastor Borel, who had presided over the section dealing with Preventative and Reformatory work: firstly, that homes for fallen women 'should be as little as possible of a penitential character, in as much as sympathy and Christian love are the only efficacious means of rescuing and reforming young women'; and secondly, that there should be set up a system of intercommunication between the national branches of the British, Continental and General Federation 'to prevent the trading in women and young girls for immoral purposes'.

'This Congress', wrote Josephine to her friends at home, 'has been a wonderful event. The anxiety which we could not but feel, went on augmenting until Friday. On Friday, we began to see daylight, and all has ended well. Many of us are tired and stupified for want of sleep, but at the same time inwardly giving thanks to God.'[2]


## XXVII

DURING the months following the successful outcome of the Geneva Congress, Josephine had a new worry to contend with. Despite her advice, George was over-working. For twelve years he had been headmaster of Liverpool College, and a conscientious one; he had engaged himself fully in Josephine's work;

now, on top of this, he was playing a leading part in the establishment of the University College of Liverpool – the future Liverpool University – which was involving him in a massive and ever-increasing volume of correspondence, administration and lecturing. He was working at his desk every night until long after midnight, and Josephine would creep into his study in the early hours of the morning to find him asleep, his head on his desk, papers clutched in his hand. During the season of school examinations, when his work-load was particularly heavy, he complained that he had not enough time even to say his prayers, and took to writing what he described as 'letters to God' since the act of writing, so he said, forced him to remain awake. A letter written by Josephine, when she had succeeded in sending him away for a short holiday, reveals her concern for him at this time:

> My own darling – How are you? Every day my heart is aching to write to you. I long so to see your face. . . . I wish I could go somewhere to be near enough to you to see you whenever you called me to your side. I never knew *quite* till this winter how much you are to me. . . . I dread to think what the blank would be to me if you were gone. . . . Others are very kind, but they do not know by instinct all that passes in my soul, as you do.'[1]

There had always been disapproval of George's support for Josephine's activities in certain political and ecclesiastical circles, and now this disapproval began to take a more vicious form than previously. It was rumoured that numbers at Liverpool College were rapidly falling off, that academic standards at the school were in decline and that both these factors were due to the headmaster's neglect of his work in favour of more unsavoury activities. It was rumoured also that the Board of Governors was considering demanding of him his resignation.

There was no truth in such stories – in fact, the esteem in which the school and its headmaster was held in the great universities had never been higher. But the circulation of such rumours could make them come true, and of this, George was all too well aware. By 1880 he was profoundly depressed and spoke seriously to Josephine about resigning before his existence at the school became a liability. For both of them the position was extremely grave. Josephine had always tended to be slightly extravagant for herself, particularly in dress, but a great deal more so on behalf of others: her personal income had long since been exhausted in maintaining her refuges, complete with staff and small luxuries and comforts for the girls she had taken under her protection. George's family, though successful in their chosen fields – his brother, Montagu Butler, was now Master of Trinity, Cambridge – had never been wealthy. If George was to be forced into retirement, they were faced with poverty – genteel poverty, perhaps, but poverty nonetheless.

Henry Wilson was sufficiently close to Josephine to appreciate the situation. He wrote therefore to a friend, Robert Martineau, a Birmingham businessman, suggesting that a subscription fund be opened to provide the Butlers with an annuity of three thousand pounds, yielding an income of not less than two hundred pounds a year. Robert Martineau undertook to organise this without the Butlers' knowledge, and opened a list headed by himself, Wilson and Stansfeld, and three other Members of Parliament, all contributing a hundred pounds each. Within a matter of six weeks the money was raised and invested, and the news conveyed by Robert Martineau to the Butlers. Josephine replied:

> I must tell you that we sat in the garden, under the shade of the trees yesterday and read your letter and talked it over, and that our hearts were filled to overflowing with wonder and gratitude. I assure you, I could hardly believe it when I read it. I thought my eyes deceived me (and indeed they were dimmed with tears) . . . You should know that a weight is taken off our minds. We feel now so free. We need not fret or hurry to obtain some new post or income. We are only two of us and our wants are not many. You know that I love my work, painful as parts of it are; and my husband loves it, and continues to aid and to second me. But I want him to take six months or even a year of comparative rest. Your kindness, you see, makes it easy to carry out my heart's desire of a few months of rest for my dear old companion.[2]

As if wishing to dissociate himself from the rumours, Gladstone, himself a vice-president of Liverpool College, wrote a letter of Christmas greetings to George, in which he warmly congratulated him on the school's academic prowess during the year, which 'affords a striking testimonial to your powers and to your successes',[3] and offered the hope that George would remain in office for many years to come. George, however, had made up his mind. In the spring of 1882 he wrote a dignified formal letter to the Board of Governors tending his resignation, while seizing the opportunity to point out to them the extent to which the school had expanded and had proved academically successful – 'few schools can boast of a better average of honours in the Universities'.[4]

He had, in fact, built up the reputation of the school from very little, and now that he proposed to quit, even those governors who seemed to have endorsed the rumours began to realise what sort of a man it was that they were losing. Governors, staff and leading citizens of Liverpool all expressed more than formal regret at his departure, and many sought to change his mind. But George, now he was financially secure, genuinely desired to yield to the temptation offered by the thought of rest.

He was overjoyed, however, when he received a letter from Gladstone informing him that he had been appointed to a canonry in Winchester Cathedral. 'How faithfully God answers prayer!' he wrote to Josephine. 'This certainly came at the last rather unexpectedly to me, perhaps not so to you, as the answer to prayers offered up by you, as I know, for so long.'[5]

In the autumn of 1882 they took up residence in their new home in the Cathedral Close, Winchester:

> How can I describe the charm which that new home had for us? [wrote Josephine in her memoir of her husband] the beautiful old house with its thick walls, its picturesque gables, its antiquity (dating from the time of St Swithin, Chancellor to Alfred the Great), and its surroundings of fine ancestral trees and flowering shrubs. The well-fed thrush's song, the gentle breeze among the trees, and the periodical sleepy chimes of the cathedral clock, or of the bells calling to prayer, were often the only sounds to be heard in the stillness. The quietness in the evenings after the gates of the Close

were shut was very soothing. In the closing years of a busy
life, nothing could have been sweeter.[6]


## XXVIII

EIGHT months after George's retirement to Winchester came
the moment of Josephine's most complete triumph. It had been
long in coming. Year after year, Stansfeld and his colleagues had
called for the repeal of the Contagious Diseases Acts in the
House of Commons, and year after year the proposal had been
defeated. The House, moreover, was becoming increasingly
bored with the subject, and as there was no danger, since 1875
and the Percy case, of the Acts being extended to cover the
whole Kingdom, it was difficult to assure popular indignation.
'Each time I address myself to speak upon this subject', Stansfeld wrote wearily, 'I lift a heavier weight.'[1] In 1879 he tried a
new tactic. Instead of launching a frontal attack on the Acts, he
complained about the expense on the public purse of maintaining a morals police in the thirteen regulated areas, suggesting,
in effect, that this practice of Regulation should be retained, but
should be implemented by the ordinary police apparatus, a
precedent for which was already being set in France. Behind this
was the belief that with the abolition of the plainclothes morals
police, police round-ups followed by compulsory medical
examination would become impracticable. For once he was
heard sympathetically by a House always willing to listen to
proposals aimed at reducing national expenditure. On the
strength of the ensuing debate the Home Secretary decided to
set up a Select Committee of the House of Commons to examine
the expense, and the efficiency, of the Acts.

In 1880 the Conservative government fell, and the Liberals
once more took office, with the result that the composition of the
Select Committee was more sympathetic to the Repealists (it
included Stansfeld himself) than they had dared to hope. It took
its time, sitting for sixty-eight days and examining seventy-one
witnesses. It did not commence its transactions until the summer
of 1881, and did not complete its hearing of evidence until the
summer of the following year. Much of the evidence was little
more than a repetition of the Royal Commission of 1871. Once

again there were the opposing processions of priests and ministers who were prepared to swear that the Acts provided an opportunity for the conversion of fallen women – three Irish priests maintained that any girl who failed to be converted to a Christian way of life in a hospital was so depraved as to be beyond redemption – and those who maintained that compulsory inspection and confinement made the task of the missionary that much more difficult.

On 15 May 1882 Josephine was called to give evidence. On this occasion she prepared her brief thoroughly:

'My dear beloved,' she wrote to George, 'I find it *very* hard work learning all the details I have to answer tomorrow; they say it looks bad to read from a paper. When you get this (if you come home to lunch), I shall be in the 'lion's den'. The examination will last from about 12 to 6 p.m. 7 *hours*. You will be praying for me, *I know*.'[2]

She had little need to worry. Even if a majority of the Committee did not agree with her views entirely, she had long since won the respect of the individual members for her courage and her integrity. She was given every opportunity of stating her case without interruption. She herself, though she remained 'fierce', had mellowed over the years, and was less inclined to find obduracy and hostility where none existed. Her interrogators, on the other hand, were consistently courteous and considerate.

In the Committee rooms she encountered members of the Salvation Army who had been called to give evidence. It was the first time she had come into contact with the Army and she readily accepted an invitation to one of their meetings at the Queen Victoria Street Citadel.

'It was *lovely*,' she wrote to George. 'No peeresses there,' [she had been engaged on a particularly tiresome round of social calls in London] 'but the humble people with faces radiant with happiness. I never saw *spiritual joy* like it. A good many clergymen were there, as listeners, and looking much impressed. What a blessed work that *Army* is doing! The joy and peace are infectious. I felt so happy at night I could not sleep.'[3]

This was a view of the Salvation Army not universally held by ladies of Josephine's social standing, even those who generally shared her opinions. The peculiar form of evangelical enthusiasm which motivated the Booths was redolent more of the radical dissenters of the late eighteenth century – Dan Taylor or Jeremy Brandreth – than of the more compromising noncon- formity of the late nineteenth century. Commandant of the Queen Victoria Street Citadel was Bramwell Booth, the General's son and Chief of Staff. Aged twenty-eight, he was quiet and introspective through force of circumstances – he was so deaf he relied entirely on an accousticon hearing device – and compassionate to the point of sentimentality (he treasured a uniform button all his life because his wife Florence had fondled it when they were courting). He was, nevertheless, well washed in the Blood of the Lamb, and as enthusiastic as his father.

'We were pelted in the open air with cabbages and turnip tops,' he reported to that patriarch on one occasion, 'and one woman came and smashed one of the brethren full on the face. He bore it. I had a good time. The Holy Spirit was at work!'[4]

To his fellow-Salvationists, assembled in the Citadel, he would suddenly yell out in his queer, high-pitched voice:

'Are you persecuted enough?'

They were. The same year that Josephine encountered them for the first time they were enduring the worst period of persecution in the history of the Army. Wherever they preached in public they were threatened with, or were forced to endure, violence. Mobs of Irish labourers stoned them for their extreme Protestantism; brothel-keepers and their hired gangs – with which Josephine was all too familiar – broke up their meetings on account of their rescue work; above all, the rival Skeleton Army, raised and paid by brewers and publicans, attacked Citadels up and down the country on account of their temperance campaigns.

Together with her sister-in-law, Kate Booth, Florence Booth had campaigned in Paris among the working classes, and had learnt, like Josephine, of the squalor and horror of prostitution in that city, and also of the traffic in young girls. On her return to England she had opened and encouraged followers to open refuges for prostitutes who sought to escape both their way of life and the brothel-keepers who held them to it. Her father-in- law, General Booth, was none too happy at this new line of action:

'We must have some more *spiritual* work up and down the

country,' he wrote to his son. 'I cannot go in for any more campaigns against *evils*. Reformers of Society have no sympathy with the Salvation Army, nor with Salvation from *Worldliness* or *Sin*.'[5]

Josephine, however was an exception. Undoubtedly a Reformer of Society, she was profoundly concerned with Salvation from Worldliness and Sin, and she was deeply impressed by what she saw of the work of Bramwell and Florence Booth. To Bramwell's mother, Mrs Catherine Booth, she wrote:

> I ought not, perhaps, to give you the trouble of reading a letter from me in the midst of your arduous and blessed work: but I cannot any longer refrain from writing you a line to express, first, my joy in the advances being made by the Salvation Army, and secondly, my sympathy with you in the numberless criticisms and strictures forced upon you, your teaching and your practice. The attack of enemies are [sic] comparatively easy to bear, but the fault-findings and misunderstandings of Christian people, these are what hurt and grieve. I do so feel for you, and with you. My own duties, domestic and public, keep me from being among you as often as I would wish, but I doubt if there is anyone living who is more with you in spirit.[6]

From that time on, Josephine was to help the Salvation Army whenever she could, and to seek its help. It was to become, together with the Society of Friends, her chief ally.

While she was visiting the Queen Victoria Street Citadel, her most dangerous opponent was giving evidence before the Committee. Chief Inspector Annis of the Devonport Police had been an enthusiastic upholder and administrator of the Acts for many years. He had testified before both the Select Committee of 1868 and the Royal Commission of 1871, and his evidence had carried great weight. It was to do so again. He maintained that over the years the Acts had greatly diminished the number of prostitutes in his area, and that his Morals Police were ardent part-time welfare workers who had reclaimed hundreds, if not thousands of girls. He maintained that juvenile prostitution had been completely eliminated in Devonport without the cost being incurred of taking brothel-keepers to court, and that, in his view, there was no need to seek legislation raising the age of

consent, which Josephine had been consistently urging, provided
the Acts were properly enforced; there were, he maintained, no
girls practising prostitution under the age of fifteen in Devonport. He held to these statements despite Stansfeld's shrewd
questioning regarding the statistics he had produced.

For all the courtesy, consideration and tact the Committee,
when finally it issued its report, did little more than amplify the
views of Chief Inspector Annis. The Acts, it maintained, served
the purpose for which they had been established, and there was
no evidence to suggest that they actively encouraged 'safe'
prostitution. The Acts diminished the incidence of child prostitution – a startling statement in view of the findings of a House
of Lords Committee sitting only a few doors away. It also
pointed out that police witnesses were far more familiar with
Regulated areas than were the Repealists. For these reasons the
Committee could not recommend the repeal of the Acts; on the
contrary, but for public hostility to the idea they would
have liked to see them extended to cover the whole United
Kingdom.

It was this latter statement which Josephine seized on. The
newspaper-reading public was bored by the campaign for repeal
of Acts which affected only thirteen towns. With the threat of
extension there was a way of revitalising interest. Once again
she set herself to turning out statements for the Press, pamphlets and letters addressed to churches, working-men's associations and philanthropic associations. Above all she would pray
the Acts off the Statute Book; through the good offices of the
Society of Friends and the Salvation Army, mass prayer-meetings would be held up and down the country.

In the meantime Sir James Stansfeld, Professor Stuart and
Henry Wilson, all now Liberal members of Parliament, assisted
in the preparation of a Minority Report. Based firmly on
verifiable statistics – whereas the Majority Report was based on
hearsay and supposition – it demonstrated that the health of
troops in Regulated areas was no better or worse than that of
troops in unregulated areas; that the percentage ratio of disease
among prostitutes had shown a marked increase in Regulated
areas; and that where there was a reduction in child prostitution,
the police had engaged in welfare and rescue work outside the
duties laid upon them in the Acts. The Minority Report, backed

by Josephine's renewed campaign, made a considerable impact on the House of Commons.

At this point, in March 1883, Stansfeld decided that the moment had come to strike. Once again he proposed to demand the repeal of the Second Contagious Disease Act only, suggesting to Josephine that with the abolition of the Morals Police and an end to compulsory examination and 'voluntary submissions', the other two Acts would fall into desuetude. Josephine accepted his view, and the motion for repeal was presented to the House, while she exerted all the influence she could command. In this, her success astounded many Members.

'The amount of pressure brought to bear on Members', one M.P. told her, whom she met one afternoon in Stuart's garden in Cambridge, 'is unprecedented in the history of any agitation.'[7] And it was true, that from towns, and even remote villages, petitions were pouring in, including those from individuals, notably Cardinal Manning and the Moderator of the Free Church of Scotland. Hopwood, one of Stansfeld's most loyal supporters in the House, told her that Members who had been hostile to The Cause had promised their support. Josephine herself was in the lobby of the House two days before the bill was due to be read and saw, to her excitement, an M.P. carrying a petition for repeal marked 'from 1,553 inhabitants of West Ham'.[8]

At four o'clock in the afternoon of the day the Bill was read, 20 April, George and she returned to the lobby of the House of Commons to meet the crowd of her supporters who were waiting there. Outside a dense fog – a 'London particular' – hung over the river filtering through into the halls and passages to hang damply in the air where her friends stood tense and expectant. Mr Whitwell, one of the oldest Liberal members, came over, took her by the hand and drew her into a corner, 'as if he had taken me under his protection'. He asked her: 'Has it ever struck you that there is no one thing in the whole of Christ's discourses to which he has given such emphasis as that of the certainty of prayer being answered? Now, you may be sure that your persevering prayers will be answered in this matter.'[9]

Mr Williamson, member for East Fife, told her – and the news moved her deeply – that Stanley, her beloved Catty, now a lecturer at St Andrews University, had sent a petition by telegram, signed by himself and his colleagues. 'Tell your son', said

Mr Williamson, 'that I will support the prayer of it with all my heart.'[10]

As the lobby cleared and members filed into the Chamber, one figure remained, 'a tall, frail figure in a clerical frock coat, a rim of vermilion beneath the high Roman collar'. Although ill, Cardinal Manning had come to exert what influence he could over Parnell's powerful Irish block-vote. Josephine went to him. 'I think you are going to win,' he said, and for about a quarter of an hour Josephine and the spider-thin, ascetic-faced and shrewd Prince of the Church stood side by side talking quietly together.[11]

Then she and George went through the fog, across Parliament Square, to the Westminster Palace Hotel. They had taken the assembly room for a prayer-meeting of women which would go on as long as the debate continued. All through the late afternoon and evening the peeresses and women of rank, who formed the nucleus of the gathering, were joined by working women, shop girls, domestic servants and even prostitutes ('outcast girls from the streets'), until the hall and the corridors around it were packed to capacity, and all 'directing a beam of prayer upon the House of Commons'. As the night wore on, overspill groups met in the houses of repealist M.P.s and in churches and chapels around Westminster.

At midnight a messenger came to tell Josephine that the debate was reaching its climax. Leaving George, who was leading the meeting, she returned to the House. As she wearily mounted the stairs to the Ladies' Gallery, the Gallery steward, Mr Gerard, whispered to her, echoing the words of Cardinal Manning, 'I think you are going to win!'

She was surprised by the uniform quality of the debate, and even found it in her heart to praise her opponents for their seriousness of purpose and their spirituality. There was one resounding exception to this general charity. Cavendish Bentinck, who consistently opposed every attempt to protect children from white slavery or to raise the age of consent, and who, on the whole, thoroughly deserved Josephine's savage denunciation of him as 'the brothel-keepers' parliamentary representative', insisted, as he always did when such matters were before the House, on treating the chamber as if it was the extension of a public-school junior common room. (He had called on the sergeant-at-arms to 'debag' Charles Bradlaugh on one of these occasions, when the latter demanded the right, as a Secularist, to affirm rather than to take the oath.) This time, he announced happily that he could not speak 'as a moral man', a statement which was no more than the plain truth, but which set the tone of his speech and caused Gladstone pointedly to rise and leave, and to return, equally pointedly, as soon as he had finished.

The atmosphere created by Cavendish Bentinck was dispelled when Sir James Stansfeld rose to move the division of the House in what was probably the finest speech of his career. The wait while members on a free vote filed into the lobbies seemed 'very long, and we could hear each others' breathing, so deep was the silence'. As the M.P.s streamed back, Josephine looked into their faces, and knew that she did not have to wait for the tellers to announce the result. Stansfeld and Hopwood, who led the procession back out of the division lobby, were severely restrained. It was the face of Mr Fowler, the same William Fowler who, virtually alone, had denounced the Acts thirteen years before, which told Josephine the good news. 'It was beaming with joy and a kind of humble triumph.' In her mind she heard the words 'Say unto Jerusalem that her warfare is accomplished', then she jumped up, and ran down the stairs to the lobby to greet her friends as they came streaming out of the chamber. She was openly weeping with joy.

The repeal of the Contagious Diseases Act (1866) had been carried by 182 votes to 110. 'Regulation', as Josephine observed later, 'had received its death-blow in Britain.' It was half-past one in the morning. A few of her closest friends, Stuart, Stansfeld, Wilson, Fowler, took her out on to the terrace of the House of Commons. 'The fog had cleared away, and it was very calm under the starlit sky. All the bustle of the city was stilled, and the only sound was that of the dark water lapping against the buttresses of the broad stone terrace. ... I felt at that silent hour in the morning, the spirit of the psalmist who said, "When the Lord turned the captivity of Zion we were like unto them that dream." It almost seemed like a dream.'

# 5. The Maiden Tribute

## XXIX

I N the late autumn of 1879, the British, Continental and General Federation held its second great International Congress, this time in Liège. It was an occasion which caused Josephine unqualified joy. Not only were there none of the disputations regarding the aims of the Federation which had occupied so much time and energy in Geneva, two years before, but the gathering seemed less inhibited, less concerned with religious differences (one of the causes of the debates in Geneva had been the desire to gratify Calvinistic Protestantism) and more democratic. Josephine particularly rejoiced at the spectacle of working men and women mixing freely and discussing questions openly with people she, like any upper-class lady of her day, considered to be their betters.

That euphoric sense of triumph, so clearly revealed in a long and enthusiastic letter (it filled a large exercise-book) which she wrote to her friends at home, was rudely shattered by the arrival of Alfred Dyer, her young Quaker publisher. Dyer had specialised in the publishing of books and pamphlets on social questions, and, as a close friend of the aged Benjamin Waugh, the founder of the N.S.P.C.C., had become interested in the question of child prostitution in Britain and the campaign for the raising of the age of consent to sixteen. A few evenings before there had occurred the event which inspired his sudden trip to meet Josephine in Belgium. He had been attending his usual Sunday Meeting of the Society of Friends at Clerkenwell when another Friend had asked to speak to him on a confidential matter of some delicacy. Dyer had invited the man home, and was told how an English businessman on a trip to Brussels had visited a brothel. The businessman had been allocated a nineteen-year-old English girl, who, when they were in the privacy of her room, had burst into tears, had literally thrown herself on her knees before him and begged him to help her to escape. She had described how she had been in service in London in a respectable house where she had met a Belgian gentleman who evinced every sign of having fallen in love with her, but, unlike most of his kind, had made no attempt to take advantage of his social position to seduce her. Instead he had asked her to marry him and had invited her to come with him to his house in Brussels. She agreed, but on their arrival in Calais, the gentleman discovered that he had left all his money in his hotel in London. Fortunately he had a friend in Calais who was prepared to take the girl on to Brussels and to lodge her in a hotel while he returned to London to collect his money. The hotel in Brussels was, of course, a brothel, and the girl had been a prisoner there ever since.

The businessman believed this story, but, being unwilling to compromise himself, had taken no action. His conscience, however, had continued to trouble him, and, at last, he had confided in Dyer's acquaintance. Dyer himself found the story no more than a confirmation of what he already suspected – that there was a considerable traffic in young English girls intended for brothels on the Continent. He interviewed the girl's parents, the businessman concerned and the girl's previous employers, and on the evidence thus collated he believed the girl's story to be substantially correct. He had therefore come to Belgium to seek Josephine's help in finding her.

There was little at the time that Josephine could do. As always, she was involved in rather more work than she should have taken on, most of it a result of the Liège Congress. She introduced Dyer to two of her Belgian colleagues, Pastor Léonard Anet and a lawyer, Alexis Splingard, who undertook to locate the girl. Whether or not they would have succeeded had she remained in the brothel is a matter for doubt. This was hardly surprising since Splingard was notorious among brothel-keepers for his prosecutions of their kind in the courts of Brussels. The girl, however, was found in a hospital where she was being treated for syphilis preparatory to being returned to the brothel from which she had sought to escape. At this point Pastor Anet befriended her and arranged for her return to England.

Splingard, during the course of his investigation, had discovered further facts regarding the brothel which was in the Rue St Jean Népomucène. He had called on the landlady of a respectable tavern nearby who told him that a gentleman had confided in her, after visiting the brothel, that he had been offered a twelve-year-old English girl. He had gone up to the cell in which she was kept, and, after the brothel-keeper had left them together, the girl had thrown herself into his arms 'in an agony of crying and weeping, and asked his help to get away. She said she was never allowed out of that room – never, never. The child was so small and so full of distress that the man was touched, and told the landlady of the tavern that if he were not a married man, and afraid to compromise his family, he would lodge a complaint against the brothel-keeper with the Procureur du Roi or take the child out by force.'[1] Splingard reported the story to a Juge d'Instruction, but, in consideration of the wealth and influence of the clientèle of the brothel, the latter took no action. Splingard then sent his report to Josephine and Alfred Dyer.

Dyer, in the meantime, was receiving reports of other cases in which English girls had been inveigled into Belgian brothels in the belief that they were taking up respectable positions. He communicated the information he had received to the *Daily News*, the *Standard* and the *Daily Chronicle*. He stated that, in conjunction with Benjamin Scott, Chamberlain of the City of London, and Benjamin Waugh of the N.S.P.C.C., he proposed the formation of a Committee for the Exposure and Suppression of the Traffic in English Girls for Purposes of Continental Prostitution, and appealed for funds to enable him to procure the rescue of girls from Belgian brothels:

> My object in communicating these sad facts [he wrote] is to put parents on their guard, and to ask sympathy for the poor young woman who has been rescued, whose parents are very poor, and sympathy for the effort which is about to be set on foot by a few gentlemen to recover other victims of this diabolical slave traffic.[2]

There was some need for warning the middle-class parents who made up the readership of the *News*, *Standard* and *Chronicle*. Abduction was not confined to girls of the labouring or servant classes. The Belgian and English merchants who, under the protection of Lenaers, the unspeakable Brussels chief of police, and his agents acted as middle-men in the supplying of women to brothels, employed faultlessly trained governesses among their decoys. These might well stay with a family for three to six months, or even a year, before committing the abduction, earning their employers' friendship and trust, and placing themselves above suspicion. In one such case the governess had been with the family for well over a year, and had won its complete confidence, when, after the children – a brother and sister – had been afflicted with measles, she was instructed to take them to convalesce in a hotel at Bognor Regis. After they had been there for a few days the governess told the children that she had received a telegram from their parents instructing her to take them to Southampton to visit friends of the family. On arriving at Southampton, they went to a hotel, the governess informing them that the friends would come to collect them the following morning. That same evening the brother was sent to bed early for some imaginary offence, but the sister was invited to go with the governess to the harbour to see the ships. Governess and sister were never seen again. The police, when summoned by the distressed and astounded family, manifested no surprise at what had happened; such stories were not unfamiliar to them.

An equally unpleasant case was on the files of the Salvation Army. This concerned a prosperous tradesman in a north country industrial town who asked a local brothel-keeper to procure for him a young girl of twelve years old or so. The following Sunday afternoon he received a message telling him that the 'goods had arrived'. On arriving at the brothel and having been taken to an upstairs room, he found his own daughter, whom he had sent off to Sunday school earlier, lying on the bed, stripped, bound and gagged. His horror at this experience was sufficient to drive him into the arms of the Salvationists.

The response to Dyer's communications to the Press was negligible, and where it existed, it was hostile. One letter, supposedly from the Honorary Secretary of the British Charitable Fund in Brussels, was fraudulent. It praised the efforts made by English residents to protect their compatriots who were in trouble, declared that brothels were constantly visited by English chaplains and that the Fund already was used for placing girls who wished to leave brothels, and that there was no need of another Committee and another fund. The British Pro-consul in Brussels, Thomas Jeffs, wrote suggesting that Dyer's information was inaccurate, and that in any case, the Consulate was in a better position to help British subjects in Belgium than a society based on London.

The most important letter, according to Dyer, was one received by the *Standard* from Lenaers:

> No woman [he wrote] can be admitted to a licensed house of prostitution before she has formally declared to a police officer appointed for that purpose that she enters of her own free will, and that in cases of strangers the interrogationing is always in their own language, and never in the presence of the keeper of the place into which the girl asks to be received. This latter precaution is taken for the purpose of securing to the girl interested in the matter the full exercise of her personal liberty and freedom of action. . . . You see, Sir, that the story of your correspondent is as erroneous as it possibly can be. I admit that he has allowed himself to be carried away by a very laudable feeling, but before publishing such a serious allega-tion he ought to have verified the facts he was about to pub-lish. After having duly weighed the above statements you will no doubt warn your readers against the call for money on behalf of the girls in question, which looks very like a new form of speculation. I do hope, Sir, that the English papers that have published the letter of Mr Dyer will kindly publish mine.[3]

The refutation of Dyer's charges, coming from various respec-table and responsible sources, seemed final, but at the very time this correspondence was appearing in the English press, a French lawyer wrote to Josephine, giving an account of a case in which he had been involved, in which two men, Jean Sallecartes and Jean Deroo, both Belgians and known to the London police as pimps and procurers, had been convicted of repeatedly luring English girls into Belgian brothels against their will. Josephine communicated this fresh evidence to Dyer, who, while believing that Lenaers, in writing to the *Standard*, had acted in good faith, nevertheless was of the opinion that the procedure he had described 'although it might exist in theory, was not carried out in practice '. He decided to undertake a full-scale investigation in Brussels for himself.

He spent a week with the Brussels Police des Mœurs, in whose integrity he still had some confidence, examining the official system as practised in Belgium. He then proceeded to a fashionable brothel despite being warned by friends that to attempt to aid an English girl to escape from a brothel might well result in his being murdered by the ex-convicts whom every prosperous brothel-keeper retained as bodyguards. There he encountered an English girl almost immediately who, when they were alone, begged him to obtain her release. She declared that she had been lured to the address, which was advertised as a hotel, in the belief that she was to be employed as a domestic servant. When she arrived she was asked by the *patronne* if she had registered with the police in order to obtain an employment permit, and on replying that she had not, was told that it was necessary to take her birth-certificate to the police in order to register. The girl answered that she did not have her birth-certificate with her. The *patronne* assured her that it was the merest formality, and offered to provide her with a false one. The girl foolishly accepted it. This being a criminal offence, the brothel-keeper was in a position to blackmail her; at the same time, by registering under a false name, the girl had made certain, now she was a prisoner, that the British authorities would be unable to trace her whereabouts.

Dyer promptly went to Lenaers' office. Lenaers was absent, but he obtained an interview with his deputy, Lemoine. To his astonishment, Lemoine behaved as if he himself was a brothel-owner, and Dyer was a rival attempting to steal his girls. Then, when Lemoine realised the ghastly mistake he had made, he became flustered, got up, ran from the room and did not return. It was this that first caused Dyer to suspect that the Belgian police were involved in this trade in women. When he at last encountered Lenaers, his view was confirmed: Lenaers was polite but bland, repeating merely what he had said in his letter to the *Standard*. Dyer asked him to accompany him to the brothel, but Lenaers refused; it had already been inspected, he said, and there was no point in repeating the inspection.

Dyer, accompanied by Alexis Splingard, Josephine's friend, returned to the brothel without the police. He was met at the door by the brothel-keeper who, white with rage, advised him for his own good never to return. The threat was made more explicit when he and Splingard, after the door had been slammed behind them, found themselves face to face with a gang of 'brutal looking fellows',[4] who told them that if they were seen in the vicinity again their heads would be smashed in.

Dyer then attempted to interest the British Consular officials in the fate of the girl, with no success. Thomas Jeffs appeared both then and later to be a personal friend of Lenaers. Dyer then proceeded to visit other brothels in Brussels, and on almost every occasion encountered English girls, some of them children, who begged him to obtain their release. Armed with the case-list he had thus assembled, he returned to England, when he communicated his information to the Press. Only one small-circulation newspaper, the *Christian*, published it. This was enough, however, to inspire the Foreign Office to instruct Thomas Jeffs to visit the first of the brothels concerned. That worthy reported back that the girl was no longer working for the brothel – she had left *clandestinement*, and no trace of her could be found. He added, for good measure, that Mr Dyer had been making a great deal of fuss over nothing.

Mr Dyer, however, was convinced that the girl had been murdered. He decided to make use of his own business as publisher to make the facts more widely known, and printed at his own expense a short booklet, *The European Slave Trade in English Girls*, supporting it with an English translation by Joseph Edmondson of Pastor Borel's *The White Slavery of Europe*. These works may not have reached a wide public, as Dyer hoped, but they did reach the Belgian Embassy. As a result the Procureur du Roi took the unprecedented step of inviting British senior police officers to investigate for themselves conditions obtaining in Belgian brothels. Inspectors Greenham and Williams were sent to Brussels by Scotland Yard, and spent three weeks on a conducted tour. Since their conductors were Lenaers, Schroeder and Lemoine, it is hardly surprising that they found nothing to cause them the least concern.

Within a matter of days of the return to London of Greenham and Williams, Josephine, who was attending a conference in Paris, was approached by a Belgian detective, a member of the

Police des Mœurs. He had been a member of the group of Belgian Police who had escorted Greenham and Williams round the brothels in Brussels, but had become so uneasy in his conscience at the corruption of his superiors that, discovering Josephine to be in Paris, and knowing her by reputation, he had decided to make the journey to speak to her. Josephine, with unaccustomed caution, asked if he was prepared to state what he was about to confide to her in the form of a sworn deposition. With an initial, and understandable reluctance, the detective agreed.

He told her that the day before the Procureur du Roi, an honest man, invited the British to send over police representatives to Brussels, he sent to Lenaers and Schroeder and informing them of what he was about to do asked them, 'You have no minors in these houses, have you?' Schroeder replied, 'Not one, not one, and for the rest, there is not one word of truth in all that Messrs Dyer and Splingard have said.' The Procureur du Roi accepted Schroeder's word and retired. As soon as he had gone, Lenaers 'became of a livid paleness' and fell back, fainting, into his chair.[5] When he came to he gave orders that Schroeder and Lemoine were to go round the brothels and collect all the English children they could find so that he could have them sent into the country and even abroad if need be – one or two had in fact been lodged and concealed as far afield as Rouen and Limoges. In the meantime all brothel-keepers were warned of the approaching visit. In the case of one girl whom Dyer had mentioned by name, the brothel-keeper assured Lenaers that she would deny what she had said since she had been well and truly beaten and knew what would happen to her if she repeated what she had said to Dyer.

The detective also told Josephine that the police had themselves circulated the brothels ordering that on no account were Splingard and Dyer to be admitted to them, and, if the brothel-keepers deemed it necessary to kill them, the police would be none too thorough in their investigations. He concluded by explaining how Lemoine was himself the owner of two brothels worth a hundred thousand francs each, how Lenaers's son was the superintendent-in-chief of immigration, and was in a position to ensure that girls were safely, and surreptitiously, imported and how Lenaers *père et fils* were the proprietors of a wine-retailing business and held a monopoly in supplying brothels.

'Now', wrote Josephine, in a letter home, 'how astonished Lenaers and Schroeder will be when they find in print the minute account, which I shall give. Splingard has carefully verified all the statements of the detective and finds them corroborated on all points.'[6]

## XXX

JOSEPHINE decided to intervene personally in the campaign launched by Dyer, Benjamin Scott and Benjamin Waugh, because following her interview with the Belgian detective and with his sworn testimony in her possession, she realised that she was in a better position to create an effect on public opinion than they were. In order to avoid charges of sensationalism she did not attempt to communicate her information to the national press in Britain, but confined herself to writing a letter to the weekly journal of the British, Continental and General Federation, the *Shield*, knowing that it would be distributed to her friends and allies abroad, would be taken up by continental newspapers and would thus come to the attention of the British press.

This letter, later expanded into a pamphlet, *A Letter to The Mothers of England*, did not merely seek to draw the public's attention to what was going on in the Belgian *maisons tolérées*, but also examined the factors which made such abuses possible. Josephine's frankness in dealing with such matters, her habit of referring to prostitutes as prostitutes and brothels as brothels rather than as 'unfortunates', and 'certain houses', her attack on Society for its tolerance of these abuses, went much further than Alfred Dyer had done. She dared to point out, and it was the first time anyone had done so, in print, the strange Victorian taste for deflowering virgins, preferably children (explicable perhaps in terms of a squalid and pathetic act of defiance against, or revenge for, oppressive maternal prudery). She emphasised the twin factors that made the international trade in young girls possible: the Regulationist System controlled by a corrupt police force abroad, and the defective laws regarding the protection of children in England.

In most of the countries of western Europe the age of consent stood at eighteen. Offences against minors were severely punished, and laws concerning abduction severely upheld. The system, therefore, presided over by venal or ruthless Commissaires des Mœurs was ideal for the practice of juvenile prostitution, but made recruitment of children for such purposes extremely hazardous. In Britain the opposite held true; the age of consent was twelve, and the laws regarding abduction, since they were framed entirely with a view to protecting the property of heiresses, were easily voided. On the other hand, the British police were relatively uncorrupt – senior officials of Scotland Yard were to provide the most conclusive evidence of the trade in women and children – the costs of exploiting child prostitutes were high, and procurers found that there was a greater profit margin in selling their victims on a foreign market where the police were less disposed to pry into the goods offered in brothels. Josephine was thus prepared to attack on two fronts: to oppose regulation abroad, and to advocate the raising of the age of consent at home.

Her friends strongly advised her not to have her letter published even in a periodical as small in circulation as the *Shield*. By her own account a number of them told her that so appalling was her recital of actual cases that 'all sensible persons would say of the writer, "She is mad." '[1] Others, quite correctly, warned her that she might find herself accused of the same crime committed by Yves Guyot in Paris in 1876, and that there was a treaty of extradition between Britain and Belgium. Josephine was not, however, averse to the idea of temporary martyrdom; it was the speed with which the Belgian authorities reacted which took her by surprise.

Her letter was, as she expected, scarcely noticed in Britain. On the Continent, however, where Guyot and Humbert were prepared to draw the attention of newspaper editors to it, it was widely reprinted, inspiring a storm of controversy. Within a matter of weeks a 'Juge d'Instruction' in Brussels was in contact with the British Home Secretary, demanding that Josephine either withdraw her allegations publicly, or, under the terms of the extradition treaty, make a deposition on oath before a magistrate,thus laying her open either to a charge of perjury, or, in the case of her refusal, to libel action. Once again her friends begged her not to proceed, Benjamin Scott going to the extent of sending a special messenger by train to Liverpool to beg her to withdraw her allegations despite his own knowledge that they were true. Josephine was, however, in no mood for retreat; apart from the fact that it was not in her nature to do so, some new and even more terrible evidence had come to her notice.

A Mrs Steward, a member of the British, Continental and General Federation, had gone to Brussels to escort home an English prostitute who was being discharged from prison under a deportation order for having registered as a prostitute under a false name and having at the same time misrepresented her age:

> Mrs Steward, [wrote Josephine in a letter to Dr Carter, her medical adviser] found her like a crushed woman, hopeless, sullen, and at times quite wandering in mind. Thank God she is recovering. I had a beautiful letter today from the poor child from her own village home (her sister's house, her father is dead). She says she hopes we will publish her story for the sake of other poor tortured girls whose sufferings she saw.[2]

Adeline Tanner was very prepared to tell her story, on oath if need be, and her testimony was hard – her body bore the scars of the tortures and perversions that had been practised on her. She was aged sixteen, well-educated and highly articulate. She was also undeveloped physically with the appearance of a pretty eleven-year-old. Her father had been a successful commercial traveller, and she had been brought up in comparative luxury. He died when she was fifteen, and, his income having died with him, she was forced to come to London to find employment as a superior domestic servant. One evening, when it was raining heavily, she was at Tulse Hill Railway Station after visiting a friend, and was drying her coat in front of the waiting-room fire, when she fell into conversation with a Mr Roche who claimed to be a visitor from Paris and was, in fact, a Brussels brothel owner engaged in recruiting children for his fashionable clientèle. Adeline Tanner was struck by his air of *politesse*, and, no doubt, glad to be talking once again on equal terms with a gentleman. A few days later she met him accidentally – or so she thought – in Tottenham Court Road, and he invited her to go to a restaurant with him. Everything that happened after that, until she arrived in Brussels, she remembered only through a drugged haze. She came to her full senses in a place which she

dimly remembered being told was a customs house, to find herself in possession of a birth certificate ascribed to an Ellen
Cordon, aged twenty-one, and being subjected to a medical
examination. From then on she endured a crescendo of horror.
The examining doctor found what her own doctor already knew,
that, according to Josephine, 'she was unable to be a prostitute
owing to the smallness of her person and to some defect in her
private parts'.[3] This same doctor visited her in the brothel to
which she was consigned by Mr Roche, and there he found, wrote
Adeline in the statement which was later presented to the
Foreign Secretary, 'he did not and could not examine me with
the instruments as he did the other girls; and although he knew
and said I was a virgin, and knew also that I was incapable of
sexual intercourse, the cruel villain let me remain in this den of
infamy.'[4]

She might not be capable of normal sexual congress; she was,
however, forced to practise perversions, and, on one occasion,
having been made drunk by a titled client, was so assaulted
(Dyer, who published her statement, noted that the details were
beyond description) that she suffered 'undescribable torture
both of body and mind; I thought I should have died under it'.[5]
The result of this client's choice of love-making was that she had
to be sent to a hospital for prostitutes, which was, of course,
under Lenaers's jurisdiction. There, it was decided to make her
fit for normal sexual intercourse:

> They attempted to examine my person with an instrument
> which put me to terrible pain, and seemed to chill my blood;
> and I was seriously ill in consequence. I was detained there
> for six months, and during the first half of that time, I was
> treated for the illness caused by the cruel examinations and
> yet more cruel lust of which I had been the victim. When I
> began to recover from that illness fresh horrors were in store
> for me, and they commenced to operate on me for the purpose
> of making me capable of prostitution. They did not even give
> me chloroform, but the students held my hands and feet,
> whilst the operator seemed to cut and tear away my living
> flesh. This was repeated at intervals about seven times, and
> during the operations my screams and appeals to my tormen-
> tors for mercy were heard, as the other patients told me, over

the whole building, and the other girls who were there used to cry at the sight of my sufferings. The principal doctor seemed to hate me, and take a pleasure in prolonging my torments. He would delay the operation and stop to explain to the surrounding students what he was doing.[6]

Adeline Tanner was saved by the arrival of Alfred Dyer. Dyer did not know her, nor she him, and they did not speak to one another; he was, in fact, engaged in another case altogether. His appearance in the hospital, however, accompanied by the troublesome Alexis Splingard, frightened the authorities, and they decided to rid themselves of possible embarrassment by deporting Adeline.

Adeline Tanner's statement was sent to Lord Granville, the Foreign Secretary, who sent it on to the Home Office where it was referred to Inspector Greenham. Greenham recommended that no action be taken, and that he saw no reason to alter the findings of his own, earlier, inquiry in Belgium. The Foreign Office was less sanguine, perhaps because Lord Granville knew and admired Josephine. Certainly Lord Tenterden, Under Secretary of State for Foreign Affairs, was instructed to start negotiations with the Home Office with a view to setting up an independent inquiry.

In the meantime, Josephine appeared before the Stipendiary Magistrate of the City of Liverpool, Mr Thomas Stamford Raffles, to swear her affidavit. Ignoring the advice of her friends, she submitted case after case, citing names and addresses of brothel-keepers and holding nothing back. When she began to charge Lenaers and Schroeder with complicity, Stamford Raffles advised her not to continue. When she went on to describe how Lenaers had personally ordered the concealment of minors in Belgian brothels, he refused to allow her to go on, for her own sake. In doing so, he underestimated Josephine's determination. She went home and wrote an extension of her deposition in the form of a statement, signed and witnessed, and sent it, together with a copy of the Belgian detective's statement, to the Home Secretary, Sir William Harcourt. Sir William, like Lord Granville, knew and respected Josephine. Regardless of any action the Belgian judiciary might choose to take, within days of receiving her letter, he commissioned a London barrister, Mr

T. W. Snagge, to go to Brussels to make an inquiry into the facts relating to young English girls persuaded, induced or abducted into prostitution in Belgium. At the same time, a Treasury solicitor was dispatched to look after the interests of such girls in the case of legal action taken by the Belgian authorities. A copy of Josephine's deposition and statement was sent to the Hôtel de Ville in Brussels where, whether by accident or design, it was leaked to the Belgian press, and was reproduced in full by the leading Brussels daily, *Le National*. As a result, Lenaers was forced to sue the newspaper for libel. This was the opportunity for which Splingard, long experienced in such cases, was waiting. Under his devastating cross-examination, Lenaers broke down. The Procureur du Roi, who felt that the police-chiefs had personally betrayed him, was in no mood to be merciful. Schroeder and Lemoine followed their superior into the dock, and following them eleven of the most celebrated and prosperous brothel-owners of Brussels.

## XXXI

THOMAS WILLIAM SNAGGE was as thorough in his investigations as Josephine and her friends could have wished. His report entirely justified their views regarding the gravity of the situation. In his preamble, answering the specific questions contained in his brief, he stated:

(1) The exportation of English girls to Belgium, France, and Holland for purposes of prostitution has been carried on systematically as a trade or traffic.

(2) English girls have been induced by mis-representation and false pretences to leave England, and to become inmates of houses of prostitution in foreign towns, and this is a frequent occurrence.

(3) It is a fact established by satisfactory evidence that English girls who have, willingly or unwillingly, become inmates, have been detained by duress or subjected to cruelty in such houses, and forced against their will to lead a life of prostitution.[1]

In addition to the thirty-four English girls released in Brussels as a result of the prosecution of brothel-keepers, Snagge cited the cases of thirty-three children imported into the Low Countries which he had discovered for himself. The victims, he declared, were invariably respectable girls, since the procurers were looking for girls who were 'clean' and still, for the most part, virgins. They were advertised to brothel-keepers as *colis* (parcels) together with descriptions of physical features, real age, plus the age which could be credibly given to a client seeking a child, colouring and so on. False birth certificates were easily obtainable at Somerset House, where they were issued to anybody on request; they were, however, hardly necessary, since the Belgian police were well aware of such practices, and the Metropolitan Police knew of twenty-three foreign procurers in London, none of whom were ever brought to trial.

Visits to *maisons tolérées* caused him to conclude that the life of girls in such houses was virtually one of slavery even when Belgian law had not been violated. Street doors in such houses could only be opened *from within* by a key retained by the proprietor, this being officially countenanced in order to prevent girls from soliciting on the open street. Police regulations demanded that girls be clothed at the proprietor's expense, who invariably provided them with garments too indecent for wear in public. The girls were never allowed out alone, and only in a carriage lest they solicit in the open street. The girls were debited for bed and board and, in the case of girls purchased from agents, for their purchase money, and were thus kept permanently in debt, the law forbidding them to quit the premises prior to payment of this debt.

Mr Snagge's report ended with three proposals. Firstly, that there should be a statutory definition of the term 'common prostitute' so that the courts could take more effective action to protect girls who had been abducted for purposes of prostitution. Secondly, that restrictions should be imposed on the issue of birth certificates from Somerset House. Thirdly, that upon the application of any English girl to be registered as the inmate of a brothel in a foreign town, immediate notice of the fact should be forwarded to the nearest British consulate, together with a copy of the girl's birth certificate. Particulars of the case should then be sent to the C.I.D., Metropolitan Police, for investigation.

This last, apparently blameless and potentially effective, suggestion met with Josephine's intense indignation. In a letter to the Bishop of London, she wrote: 'Such a remedy is *morally* inadmissible. It is impossible that a Christian government can consistently take part in any plan for permitting women to take upon themselves the trade of prostitution.'[2]

Such a response was, of course, at one with her absolute rejection of any form of Regulation and, as was not always the case when she rejected apparent advantages in favour of principle, her colleagues and supporters in and out of Parliament agreed with her.

Her more positive reaction to the Snagge Report was to draw up a petition to Lord Granville, signed by a thousand ladies, 'many of them of the highest rank,' submitting 'that such changes ought to be made in the English laws as shall make it impossible for any young girl or child in our country to be deprived of her liberty by fraud or force, and to be kept in a foreign city in bondage for the basest purposes'.[3] To this end, she suggested, not for the first time, that the age of consent should be raised. Lord Granville was sympathetic to this proposal, and in response to the petition, his friend and colleague Lord Dalhousie moved on 30 May 1881 in the House of Lords, 'for the appointment of a Select Committee to inquire into the law for the protection of young girls from artifices to induce them to lead a corrupt life, and into the means of amending the same'.[4] He was supported by the veteran Lord Shaftesbury, who had by now become an almost legendary figure and whose words commanded infinite respect.

On 28 June 1881, the Select Committee, which included Lord Salisbury, Lord Dalhousie, the Bishop of London and Josephine's old friend Lord Mount-Temple (Cowper-Temple), met to consider the Snagge Report and to take evidence. The first witnesses included Benjamin Scott and Benjamin Waugh, both of whom urged the raising of the age of consent to eighteen. They pointed out that all over the Continent, regardless of variations in the age of consent, girls were protected from abduction and inducement into prostitution at least until the age of twenty-one, and that the discrepancy between British and continental practice accounted for the trade in English girls. They presented actual cases of abduction to the Continent and accused the Metropolitan Police of being less than zealous in their investigation into them. This latter part of their testimony was expunged from the minutes of the Committee.

Despite such evidence, the Snagge Report, and the trials of brothel-keepers in Belgium, British consular officials brought home to appear before the Committee continued to express their incredulity. Confronted with Mr Snagge's evidence that he had discovered five cases of English children held in Calais, Mr Treitt, legal adviser to the British Embassy in Paris, replied, 'It is not possible for girls to be kept in brothels against their will because of the care exercised by the police.'[5] The redoubtable Thomas Jeffs maintained the same to be true in Belgium despite the downfall of Lenaers, Schroeder and Lemoine, and the release of thirty-four English girls as a result of Snagge's investigation. Lord Mount-Temple asked him, with reference to the case of Adeline Tanner, 'Do you say there is no case of an innocent girl being procured?' To which he replied:

'There is one girl about whom there seems to be some doubt. But I believe it is impossible for a virtuous girl to be admitted into one of these houses. I do not believe it for a moment.'[6]

Undoubtedly the witnesses who created the greatest impact on the Committee were Sir Charles Howard Vincent, the director of the C.I.D., Scotland Yard, and Superintendent Dunlap of C Division, Metropolitan Police. Howard Vincent had previously described the accounts of the traffic in women published by Dyer, Scott and Josephine as the work 'of enthusiasts more zealous than accurate',[7] and in giving evidence before their Lordships was clearly intent on protecting the reputations of those of his officers, Inspectors Greenham and Williams, who had found nothing to complain of in the administration of Belgian brothels. Because of this commentators on the Select Committee have tended to disparage or even to condemn outright the part played by Sir Charles Howard Vincent. A reading of the Report of the Lords' Committee (1881) shows, however, that his evidence was decisive.

Howard Vincent believed that the efforts of Josephine and her Abolitionist friends were misdirected. The trade in women for exploitation overseas had to be examined within the context of juvenile prostitution indigenous to Britain; such was his opinion. To support this he pointed out that by far the majority of children abducted for purposes of prostitution were intended for the domestic market.

'Juvenile prostitution in London prevails down to the statutory limit, in no European city to so large an extent.'[8]

This statement ran clean contrary to the views expressed by Dyer, Scott and Waugh in their evidence and by Josephine in her published statement. The immediate reaction of the Abolitionists was to express the belief that Howard Vincent was attempting to account for his own inadequacy in failing to suppress the export of girls. In this, motivated perhaps by their mistrust of police authorities, they were less than just. Both Howard Vincent and Superintendent Dunlap obviously felt frustrated in their inability under existing laws to suppress the traffic in girls. This was emphasised by Superintendent Dunlap in his testimony. He complained that in the Tower Hamlets area, he and his colleagues had discovered old gentlemen actually in bed with girls of twelve and thirteen, and had been unable to take any action even when the girls sought police protection. For such girls to obtain redress at law it was necessary for them to produce medical evidence confirming that they had been physically violated against their will. Such evidence is notoriously hard to produce, even today, and since frequently the victim had been chloroformed or drugged prior to being violated, virtually impossible then. Children of eleven and under were scarcely better protected. Often sold by irresponsible and inadequate parents to procurers – under-age children commanded high prices – they could not be rescued until the police obtained a writ of Habeas Corpus against the brothel-keeper for a specifically named child. The only charge which could be laid, even in such circumstances, was that of abduction, and then only if the father of the child was prepared to prefer such a charge. Since mothers could not, in law, prefer charges of abduction, fatherless children who had no legal guardian, children of widows, children whose fathers had deserted the family, illegitimate children, were completely unprotected. Finally in the rare cases where a brothel-keeper was actually brought before a court on abduction charges, it was necessary that the child-victim should give evidence on oath. To do this she had to prove that she understood the meaning of the oath, an absurdly difficult test for a working-class girl of those days, and impossible for a young child. Prosecutions virtually never proceeded beyond the oath-taking.

On 10 July 1882 the Lords' Committee published its findings. While it offended Dyer, Josephine and their friends by suggesting that most girls entrapped into foreign brothels were probably not averse to the idea of prostituting themselves, but were distressed by the conditions in which that prostitution was carried out, its recommendations were all that the reformers could have hoped for. It recommended that attempts to solicit or to procure English girls to leave their homes in order to enter foreign brothels (regardless of whether the girls be willing or not) should be treated as a serious misdemeanour; that the age of consent should be raised to sixteen; that the age up to which it was unlawful to abduct for purposes of carnal knowledge should be raised to twenty-one; that it should be illegal for anyone to receive into their home a girl under the age of sixteen for the purpose of her having sexual intercourse with any particular man, or generally; that a police magistrate should be empowered to issue a warrant of entry to a police officer for purposes of searching a house where the police officer had reason to believe a girl under sixteen years of age was being harboured for the purposes of sexual intercourse.

Ten months later, on 31 May 1883, Lord Rosebery, who was then Under-Secretary of State at the Home Office, presented 'A Criminal Law Amendment Bill (to make further provision for the protection of women and girls, for the suppression of brothels, and other purposes)'. This embodied the recommendations of the Lords' Committee. It passed through the Lords, but was shelved in the House of Commons *sine die*. The official report gave as the reason for this 'the congested state of public business'; a more accurate reason was the complete indifference both among Members of Parliament and members of the public.

The reason for this indifference is easily explained. An atrocity on a massive scale (it is worth mentioning here that a hundred young girls a year were sold to one client, King Leopold of the Belgians, and a similar number to a wealthy Harley Street physician, to arrive at some idea of the numbers involved) redounds on the human condition in general, demanding the admission that humanity rather than an individual villain is capable of such viciousness, that Society itself is in some way deficient. The upper classes in the age of the Forsytes, with their essentially Liberal belief in the perfectibility of Society through scientific progress, Free Trade and laissez-faire, were peculiarly unready to be convinced regarding the atrocities committed within the very heart of their capital city. Even Josephine, possessed as she was of a unique knowledge and understanding of the problem and anxious that the age of con-sent should be raised to eighteen, nevertheless held that the chief villain was the Regulationist system abroad rather than the 'deficiency of the law' at home.

Josephine can be forgiven for her unusually tame reaction to the findings of the Lords' Committee. She herself was deeply involved in the Select Committee of the House of Commons on the Contagious Diseases Acts and Stansfeld's successful motion for repeal of the Contagious Diseases Act (1866) which was the result of that Committee. She was, at much the same time, dis-tracted by her concern over George's health, his retirement, their removal to Winchester and the need to ensure the continuance of her homes of refuge in Liverpool, and the need to establish such houses in Winchester.

Her work in the latter field attracted the attention of the more pious ladies of that city, which was, of course, a garrison town, who had organised themselves into a Vigilance Society for the suppression of vice. These ladies asked her to join them in petitioning for the closure of a theatre which was notorious as a place of assignation frequented by professional and part-time prostitutes. To their astonishment Josephine rejected this firmly:

'My principle has always been to let individuals alone, not to pursue them with any outward punishment, nor drive them *out of any place* so long as they behave decently, but to attack *organized prostitution*, that is when a third party, actuated by the desire of making money, sets up a house in which women are sold to men.'[9]

This – to the ladies of Winchester – staggering declaration of permissiveness did nothing to win their friendship, but Jose-phine, profoundly involved in her work as she was, and pro-tected by a wide circle of devoted and distinguished friends, was no longer the vulnerable young woman who had found social ostracism in Cheltenham so difficult to endure.

George was supremely contented with his new position. He loved the cathedral which 'grew gradually to be to him as a friend',[10] and was fortunate in his close friendship with, and deep affection for, the Dean, Dr Kitchin. As his health gradually but perceptibly deteriorated, the cathedral services 'seemed to withdraw him from the anxieties of the world, to lift him in some measure even above bodily pain and weariness, and to enable him simply to contemplate the eternal realities and the "rest which remaineth for the people of God"'.[11]

They celebrated the repeal of the second Contagious Diseases Act by going to stay in Switzerland with the Humberts. It was to prove a stormy holiday in every sense. George and Josephine decided, one Thursday afternoon, to row across Lake Bienne with Aimé Humbert's two daughters to St Pierre to visit the house where Jean-Jacques Rousseau had written the *Contrat Social*. They were returning across the lake at six o'clock in the evening when they were caught in a sudden thunderstorm. Despite the pleas of Amélie Humbert and her sister, George and Josephine elected to row on. Soon they found themselves 'swept up in a horrid darkness, and we were in a cloud in the midst of a howling wind so strong that no boat could have stood it. Lightning hissed into the lake like sticks and bars of fire, and the water which had been so calm before was torn up into furious waves with foaming crests. I never saw anything so sudden. Everything was soon blotted out of sight except a piece of wet rock jutting out, where we wished to land.'[12] They all 'jumped into the foaming water, and scrambled up to the top of the rock as best we could, but even when we landed, we could hardly stand'. Their boat 'whirled round and round before the blast', tossed about like a withered leaf in autumn'. Finally it filled with water and sank, and, when the squall passed, George, Josephine and the Humbert girls were forced to climb the precipitous rocks above them. At the top they were fortunate enough to find they were close to a railway-track along which they walked until they reached a station, 'very wet, of course, but glad to be alive'.

The tranquillity of the summer holiday was even more rudely shattered by the arrival in Neuchâtel of Kate Booth, Bramwell Booth's sister. Kate had been assisting Florence, her sister-in-law, at the Paris citadel, and had decided to extend the scope of the Salvation Army by 'invading' Switzerland. Following riots in Geneva, Kate Booth and her chief-of-staff, the giant Major Arthur Clibborn, were arraigned before the Grand Council charged with a technical offence – that they had been soliciting contributions of money without a licence from the municipality. Kate's appearance did nothing to appease the indignation of the city fathers, as she stood before them in the Hôtel de Ville. To the more easy-going British the uniform of the Salvation Army was discretion itself; to the Calvinist Swiss Kate's uncovered golden curls and her close-fitting jacket – she was a handsome girl – were scandalous. When she attempted to justify her actions she was checked abruptly.

'You are a young woman; it is not in accordance with our ideas and customs that young women should appear in public. We find it offensive.'¹³

Reduced to silence, she was forced to listen to evidence that she had bribed poor men with four francs apiece to come forward as converts, and that she with Major Clibborn had drowned out the voice of a drunkard in the street by singing hymns. The Grand Council decreed that it was an offence to wear Salvation Army uniform in Geneva, and to conduct Salvationist services. As a result, Kate removed herself to Neuchâtel, while Major Clibborn went to Berne.

In Neuchâtel, Kate was made welcome by some members of the community. Soon after arriving she held a meeting for the faithful in the early morning to avoid intervention by trouble-makers. Opposition had, however, pursued her from Geneva. Like Josephine, Kate had not realised the extent to which the raw Calvinism of Switzerland differed from the evangelicism of the Army. The doctrine of pre-election did not allow for sudden, life-changing encounters with Christ, and found little room for the Salvationists' perverse concern for alcoholics, prostitutes and the human debris of society. Despite the fact that it was barely dawn when Kate's little group of supporters met in a church hall some distance from the town, lent to them by a sympathetic pastor, the door was smashed in and a gang of men entered armed with pitchforks and scythes. When Kate came down the aisle to confront them personally, one of these men shouted out, 'It's our money you're after!' At this, she lost her temper, shouted, 'Say that again! You say that again!'¹⁴ Then she grabbed the unfortunate by the scruff of the neck, threw him on to his knees on the penitential kneeling-stool and prayed over him loud and long. So taken aback were the gate-crashers, or perhaps fearful that the same condign fate might overwhelm them, that they retreated and fled into the morning mists.

The Neuchâtel Grand Council were made of sterner stuff. Forewarned by what had happened in Geneva, they were not to encourage similar breaches of the peace. Once again, Kate was arraigned before them and forbidden to hold meetings in the Canton. She was, moreover, virtually expelled.

A worse reception was accorded to Arthur Clibborn in Berne, where he had gone to petition the President of the Confedera-tion that the Genevan ban might be overruled. For five hours his lodgings were under siege, his window being smashed with rocks 'upwards of five pounds'; tradesmen banded together to ensure that he could not buy food; while Suzanne Küpjer, a young, pretty girl, whom he had recently rescued from a life euphemistically described as that of a chambermaid, remem-bered all her life the sound of the men baying round the house, 'Crucify him! Crucify him!'[15]

Josephine could hardly help but hear of the adventures of the Salvationists so near to her holiday resort. As soon as she heard that Kate Booth had been arraigned before the Grand Council of Neuchâtel she set off for Berne to demand an interview with the Chancellor of the Confederation. The Chancellor told her that he was not empowered to interfere in the judicial processes of the cantonal authorities, and that, in any case, he had absolute confidence in the integrity of those authorities. Josephine and he parted on terms of mutual irritation. She returned to Neuchâtel to find that the Humberts' home had been attacked and broken into by gangs of ruffians who had learnt of the sympathy of Aimé Humbert's guests with the 'Salutistes'.

Kate, meanwhile, had joined her five hundred followers in the mountain pine-forest overlooking Lake Neuchâtel. The Prefect of Police, Charles Gerster, was also present, accompanied by a troop of gendarmerie. As Kate raised her voice in prayer, Gerster and his men silently emerged from the shadows of the trees, and the Prefect came and stood beside her. For two hours of hymn-singing and Salvationist witness he remained with her, courteously silent. Even when one of the 'Salutistes' turned on him in the middle of testifying to Grace Abounding and shouted at him, 'That policeman knows me, but I am a changed man!' Gerster did not lose his composure. Only when the service was finished did he turn to Kate and hand her the warrant for her arrest.

'This is a magnificent work,' he told her quietly. 'In my opinion, you do nothing but good. I beseech you not to hold me responsible for this act.'[16]

The President of the Council, Robert Comtesse, who had issued the warrant, was equally reluctant to execute it. He allowed Kate immediate bail, with George Butler, who was by this time a personal friend of Comtesse, standing surety.

A few days later, at the instigation and in the company of Josephine, who was stretching her influence over the leaders of the community of Neuchâtel to the limit, Kate broke her bail and went to Geneva. The cause was the funeral of a Swiss 'Salutiste', and at the head of the cortège, which filed through the streets packed with hostile demonstrators, Josephine and Kate walked arm-in-arm. The Mayor of Geneva and a police escort were waiting at the grave-side. As soon as the interment was over he politely requested that Kate should accompany him in his carriage to the Hôtel de Ville where the Grand Council was already assembled. Kate's reply on being asked why she had broken the expulsion order issued by the cantonal authorities of Geneva has an unmistakably Butlerian ring:

> She stated first, that her expulsion was illegal, she not having been guilty of any offence which could justify it; secondly that it was a breach of the Treaty of Friendship, Commerce, and Establishment between Britain and Switzerland; and thirdly, that the Chief of the Department of Justice and Police had falsified a Cantonal police regulation in order to furnish an excuse for expelling her.[17]

For a time the Councillors scarcely knew how to reply in their turn, and Kate, taken aback at the silence, ran to the door at the back of the court, put her head through and whispered to Josephine out in the passage, 'What had I better say next?' To which Josephine replied, 'Go and say the same words over again.'

Mercifully this was not necessary. Either because of the strength of Kate's defence, or as a result of Josephine's known friendship with the Federal Procureur Général, Kate was set free upon condition she did not return to Geneva. As soon as she recrossed the cantonal boundary, however, she was arrested by the Neuchâtel police for breaking bail, and was taken to the ancient prison of Chillon which had been made famous by Lord Byron in his poem 'The Prisoner of Chillon', there to await trial. Josephine was quick to recognise the emotive advantages thus offered: the newspaper-reading public could not help but be moved by the image of an English girl held in durance where Byron's hero had suffered. Josephine immediately wrote a long letter to the *Standard*, and drafted a long article for the *Daily News* in which she gave a graphic description of the persecution of the Salvation Army in Switzerland and an even more graphic picture of the gothic horror of Swiss prison conditions.

Both letter and article were duly published, and were supported by sympathetic editorial comment. Other newspapers, both British and continental, took up the demand for the release of Kate Booth, and her parents were gratified by the publicity thus gained for the Salvation Army.

'I am delighted dear Mrs Butler is with you,' Mrs William Booth wrote to her daughter, 'though I dare say the Swiss authorities hate her as much as they hate us.'[18]

In fact, the authorities in Neuchâtel did not hate Josephine. If anything, they had come to consider themselves rather as being persecuted by her than as persecutors of her, and were, no doubt, greatly relieved when she was compelled to leave Kate awaiting trial in Chillon in order to preside over her third great Abolitionist International Congress, which was due to open in The Hague in September 1883.


# XXXII


OF her first afternoon in The Hague, Josephine wrote:

The town was very gay, for the King had opened Parliament in this hall on the morning of the opening meeting. As soon as this ceremony was over, we entered amidst decorations of flowers and banners, and with the sound of retiring military bands in our ears. It is pleasant when we think how any allusion to our work is still avoided and disliked in England, to find such a cordial welcome here, and so much kindness from members of the legislature and of the King's household, as well as from the people generally.[1]

Josephine enjoyed herself in The Hague. She was not averse to flattering attention provided it embraced her views as well as her person, and she received it in full measure from the Dutch court. It is, perhaps, more a comment on the innate courtesy of the Dutch than a criticism of Josephine, to remark that, whereas there have never been *maisons tolérées* in England save in a few restricted areas, and that, with the exception of Geneva, they were abolished within her own lifetime in Switzerland, they persisted in the Netherlands and continue to do so, providing one of the main tourist attractions in Amsterdam and other major cities. Nor, despite the warm welcome afforded to the abolitionists, did the Dutch make any serious attempt to abolish them. Perhaps Josephine was unconcerned by this apparent irony. The existence of the 'houses' with their ground-floor, picture-frame windows, was unaccompanied by the barbarities of the Police des Mœurs as practised in France and Belgium, or, at their worst, in Romania and Russia. The Dutch, as ever, lived and let live, maintaining, as they have throughout their history, the delicate balance between earnest piety and the frailties of the human condition, a *modus vivendi* which outsiders too often have interpreted as hypocrisy. Josephine herself was always less concerned with purity for its own sake than with man's inhumanity to woman.

On returning to London Josephine threw herself into a campaign to procure the release of Kate Booth – unnecessarily as it turned out, since the cantonal authorities of Neuchâtel were already trying to arrange her release with minimum embarrassment to themselves. Within a few days of her arrival back in England, Josephine was addressing a mass meeting at Exeter Hall on behalf of the Salvation Army. Present at the meeting was W. T. Stead,who, though he had never met Josephine, had taken an interest in her career and had propagandised against the Contagious Diseases Acts for the past eight or nine years.

He reported, in the *Pall Mall Gazette*, that he was not much impressed by the 'somewhat boisterous petitions addressed to the Deity' by Josephine's Salvationist colleagues on the platform. No such qualification was attached to his reception of Josephine's address. He was, in fact, profoundly impressed: 'She has a voice of great charm and softness, and intense but subdued earnestness, and perfect simplicity in her style of speaking such as only the most accomplished orator possesses.'[2]

As the audience spilled out into the night, Stead waited behind in order to meet her face to face for the first time.

William Thomas Stead was, and has remained, the subject of controversy – exciting unqualified admiration from those sympathetic to his views for the courage with which he propagated them and maintained them, and in equal measure, scorn and even contempt for his addiction to sensationalism. Beyond dispute, however, is the fact that he was the most powerful and influential, and one of the most readable, journalists in the history of the British press. At the time he met Josephine he was at the peak of his extraordinary career.

Stead came of Yorkshire yeoman stock on both his parents' sides. His father was a Congregationalist minister who, though very poor, was determined to give his son a good education and, since he could not afford to send him to a good school, kept him at home and educated him himself. From his father, Stead inherited that strong evangelical piety yet broad humanity and compassion which were to govern his actions throughout his life.

In 1863 he left home to become an apprenticed office-boy in the counting-house of a Congregationalist merchant in Newcastle upon Tyne. In 1870, as the result of the publication of an essay on Oliver Cromwell, he was invited to submit articles to the *Northern Echo*, a radical daily whose editorial views on social and moral questions were similar to those of his father and employer. Stead's natural ability in reportage was such that in 1871, barely eighteen months after his first article had been published in the paper, he was invited to become its editor. He was twenty years of age, and had never set foot in a newspaper office.

From then on, success came to him with extraordinary ease. The circulation of the *Northern Echo* increased rapidly. Within five years 'that little yellow halfpenny paper', as members of the Conservative Party contemptuously referred to it, had become the authentic voice of the radical, industrial North. It was read carefully by both the Government and the Opposition. Gladstone publicly commended Stead's editorial policy, as well he might, while Carlyle endorsed it in the famous words, 'Tell that good man Stead to go on with his work.'[3]

In 1877 Stead was offered the post of assistant editor on the *Pall Mall Gazette*, an evening paper which, under John Morley, was struggling to increase its dangerously small circulation. Between 1877 and 1883, Morley and Stead worked together with some success, but it was not until Morley retired from the editorship to be succeeded by Stead that the *Gazette* began its meteoric career. With Alfred Milner as his assistant, he made it the most significant paper in London, wielding an influence over events unequalled in the history of modern journalism. Two examples of this must suffice. In 1884 Gordon was dispatched on his disastrous if legend-building expedition to Khartoum as the direct result of Stead's intervention with Gladstone; while, in that same year, Lord Northbrooke, First Lord of the Admiralty, was forced to raise a supplementary grant of three-and-a-half millions to re-equip the Royal Navy, as a result of a series of articles written by Stead accusing the Admiralty of neglecting Britain's maritime defence.

Stead's attention was drawn to the appalling conditions obtaining in London's East End in part due to his friendship with Annie Besant, then just beginning her career as a Socialist agitator, but more because of a series of articles by the popular versifier and social investigator, George R. Sims, in a rival journal, the *Pictorial News*. Convinced that nobody was better equipped to undertake such a task than himself, he produced a series of highly-coloured and tendentious reports (most of his reportage was highly coloured and tendentious since, if he was pressed for time, he was inclined to write it without leaving his cramped little editorial office in Northumberland Street), which, under the general title 'The Bitter Cry of Outcast London', brought him into contact with Bramwell Booth, and through him, with Josephine.

Stead was not unaware of Josephine's past activities. In 1876 he had written editorials in the *Northern Echo* supporting her attacks on the Contagious Diseases Acts:

'Mrs Butler', he had written on one occasion, 'is not a thunder-trump, but her still, small voice has aroused the slumbering conscience of Central Europe to a recognition of its duty to morality and to women. As yet, however, we see but the beginnings. What will the end be?'[4]

Josephine had thanked him with a personal letter in which she described the more fashionable brothels in Paris patronised by members of English Society, notably members of the diplomatic corps, and urged him to take up the cause of 'the tormented creatures which God created and cares for'. Stead replied, in his turn, with the fairly unhelpful suggestion that Josephine should write a fictional exposé of enforced prostitution on similar lines to *Uncle Tom's Cabin* regarding Negro slavery. Josephine, who had never attempted fiction except for a few juvenile attempts at narrative verse, wisely ignored the suggestion.

According to members of her family, Josephine was not particularly attracted to Stead, and did not give him her entire confidence. In this she was far from unique. Although he was well-nigh worshipped by members of his own staff (and by his children, a significant point in the estimation of any character), his fellow journalists would have as little to do with him as possible. This may be put down in part to professional jealousy; but his belief that his power and influence had been vouchsafed to him from on high – a responsibility he was far from loath to accept, and which rid him of the finicky necessity to observe factual accuracy if it did not suit him – was scarcely calculated to endear him to colleagues less favoured in the eyes of the Deity. Certainly his behaviour on occasion appears to have manifested symptoms of a mild paranoia; on the other hand, his fundamental integrity cannot seriously be called into question. When he indulged in journalistic crusades, it was because he believed wholeheartedly in their validity. Nor can he possibly be accused of any lack of moral and physical courage, both of which he displayed in full measure when, finally, he was persuaded to launch the *Pall Mall Gazette* into the campaign for the passing of the Criminal Law Amendment Bill.

Since the failure to implement the findings of the Lords' Committee on the Protection of Young Girls in the form of a Criminal Law Amendment Bill in 1883, Josephine and her friends were becoming more and more frustrated in their attempts to expose the traffic in juvenile prostitutes. The Bill was placed before the Commons at regular intervals, only to be suppressed or thrown out, or shelved due to the pressure of parliamentary business. The trouble was that neither Josephine, nor Bramwell Booth, had any real idea of the scope of the abuse as practised in London itself, and were entirely preoccupied by an international traffic which however Stead might deplore it (and he did, in the *Gazette*) still seemed somewhat limited.

Of the group which formed the leadership of the Society for the Suppression of the White Slave Traffic, Benjamin Waugh, the founder of the N.S.P.C.C., and his old friend, Benjamin Scott, alone had any inkling of the extent of juvenile prostitution in the Metropolis. Waugh was continually coming across cases of young girls, often no more than seven or eight years of age, and sometimes much younger, who had been raped and tortured in some brothel, and had then been thrown out into the street to fend for themselves. He attempted to prosecute their assailants under existing laws relating to assault. The result was a series of failures, the reason for which is summed up in the report on one such case published in *The Times*:

> The Counsel defending objected to the child's evidence being taken, on the ground that she was 'too young to understand the nature of the oath'. Thereupon, the judge asked her to come closer to him, which she did with great reluctance. She was put on the table just beneath him. Then from above, he said in his kindest voice, 'What do you know, my child, about the Supreme Being?' The child looked for a moment at the most terrible-looking man she had ever seen in her short life, hesitated, and then, perhaps naturally, began to cry. 'I don't think I can take this evidence,' said the judge.[5]

Josephine was inspired to take an active part in this sterile campaign, when a letter was passed to her from a Miss Mary Jeffries of Chelsea. This letter, which had been delivered to Miss Jeffries in error, was in fact addressed to her close neighbour, Mrs Mary Jeffries. Mrs Jeffries was the most notorious, and the most prosperous, of the fashionable brothel-keepers in London. Her chain of establishments included four in Chelsea alone (Nos 125, 127, 129 and 155, Church Street); Rose Cottage in Hampstead, a house specialising in flagellation which was patronised by Swinburne, or so legend would have it; a house in Grays Inn Road dedicated to the sodomising of under-age girls; and a large, walled-in country house at Kew which was used as a clearing-house for virgins intended for the continental market. The letter consisted of a request, sent from Italy and written in Italian, for 'a lively young girl of sixteen years, nice complexion, with pretty throat, to live with me as my mistress',[6] and gave, as the author's referee, the name of King Leopold of the Belgians.

This hard evidence was reinforced by rumours which were spreading through the servants' quarters of Chelsea and Knightsbridge. One of Mrs Jeffries's maids, a Maria Watts, had been so appalled at the spectacle of a young child being flogged nigh to death with a wire whip for the delectation of a wealthy client, that she had made her escape (it would have been less than wise to have offered a more formal notice of her intention to quit Mrs Jeffries's employment). Before disappearing into safe obscurity, Maria had confided her appalling testimony to some of her friends and colleagues in the neighbourhood. The ensuing scandal had resulted in Mrs Jeffries's dismissal of her lieutenant and immediate accessory, Mrs Travers, the lady primarily responsible for the procuring of a steady stream of hitherto unblemished children. Not that Mrs Travers had much cause to worry about her loss of occupation. She was a regular churchgoer who was particularly noted for organising amateur theatricals in private houses for charity, was accepted as a guest in the most fashionable society and had saved enough money from her partnership with Mrs Jeffries to send her sons to Eton.

While Josephine tried to raise money from her various organisations to initiate a prosecution of Mrs Jeffries, Waugh and Scott retained the services of a retired member of the C.I.D., ex-Inspector Minahan, to make further investigations in the Chelsea area. Almost immediately this initiative ran into difficulties. Minahan presented his erstwhile superiors at the Yard with a formidable and foolproof dossier of Mrs Jeffries's activities, only to be told that his own action in compiling it had been 'most improper', and that under no circumstances would the evidence thus compiled be forwarded to the Director of Public Prosecutions. Minahan then presented the dossier to the Westminster magistrates, who, on seeing the list of Mrs

Jeffries's most distinguished clients, refused to issue a warrant.

Scott, Waugh and Josephine then decided to take the only course which remained to them if they were to proceed. Under the statute 25 George II they obtained a writ against Mrs Jeffries on the grounds that she was keeping a disorderly house. The trial was a farce. Mrs Jeffries arrived at the court in a carriage lent to her for the occasion by a member of the House of Lords, and was escorted by a miniature army of young guards officers. As she dismounted she proclaimed her guilt to her assembled supporters and the waiting crowds, declaring that nobody would dare to imprison her as she counted among her clients the very highest in the land. She was cheered loudly from the public gallery as she entered the dock, and no attempt was made by officials of the court to suppress either that or ensuing demonstrations of sympathy. Counsel for the defence pleaded guilty on behalf of his client, to a charge which was, he submitted, purely technical. He asked the court to take into account the respect in which Mrs Jeffries was held in Chelsea, and the evident malice of those who sought to prosecute her. He pleaded her age, which he exaggerated by a full twenty years, and her infirmity of health, which was openly belied by her handsome and robust appearance in the dock. The judge, however, took all these mitigating factors into account; he had been provided with a list of the names of her clients, an example of pressure on the judiciary scarcely equalled since the prosecution of Raleigh by Sir Edward Coke. Mrs Jeffries was fined two hundred pounds, which was paid into court by her admirers, and was bound over on a recognisance of a further two hundred pounds, which was guaranteed by her well-wishers among her guardee escort. Amidst scenes of jubilation she was restored to her carriage, which was then drawn through the streets by yelping guards officers. Because of her plea of guilty, no evidence had been presented against her; she was free to torture, maim and, no doubt, to murder further children. Yet Vice was not entirely triumphant. As a result of Stead's revelations a few months later, in which he denounced her by name, her clients decided to keep well clear of Church Street, Chelsea, and her trade dwindled almost to nothing. At the same time her military guarantors withdrew their recognisances on orders from their commanding officers. She was effectively ruined, being, it would seem, less provident than her colleague, Mrs Travers. In the meantime, however, her prosecutors were conscious of nothing save the wrath born of impotence. It was an impotence and wrath made more bitter by the fact that, yet again, the attempt to pass a Criminal Law Amendment Bill for the protection of children had met with failure.


## XXXIII

At the same time as the Lords' Bill was being moved, and defeated, in Parliament, both Bramwell Booth and Josephine were beginning to appreciate the nature of fashionable vice as practised, not in Brussels, Paris or Geneva, but on their own doorsteps. One early morning, towards the end of May 1885, a Major William Fenny opened the main doors of the Queen Victoria Street Citadel to find a girl sitting on the step. Her trade was indicated all too clearly by the short, red silk dress and coloured silk stockings which she was wearing, but in her hand was a Salvation Army songbook. She asked Major Fenny if she might see the General, but, since General Booth was absent, Major Fenny roused Bramwell Booth, who came down immediately. Over a much-needed breakfast (it was a principle of the Army that the Devil could not be cast out from an empty stomach), the girl recounted her story.

Her name was Annie Swan, and she was aged seventeen. The previous day she had travelled up from her home in Shoreham, Sussex, to apply for a post as general maid which had been advertised in a local paper. On arriving at the stipulated address, a house in Gloucester Street, Pimlico, her day-dress was taken from her, and in exchange she was given the red silk dress and the silk stockings. Annie was sufficiently acquainted with the ways of the world to realise immediately that she had been lured into a brothel. Finding that the front door was locked, she bolted down a flight of steps to the basement, and barricaded herself in the cellar. For some hours she endured the cajolerie, abuse and threats which were shouted at her from the other side of the door. At four o'clock in the morning, when her besiegers had grown tired of bawling abuse at her, she dismantled her barricade, crept up the steps and succeeded in letting herself out through a side-door reserved for distinguished visitors to the house who did not wish to be seen entering through the front door. She then managed to walk the three miles across London to the Queen Victoria Street Citadel, having found the address in the Salvation Army songbook she kept in the pocket of her petticoat.

Bramwell Booth verified her story by the simple expedient of going to the house and demanding the return of her day-dress. The proprietors were already profoundly disturbed by the escape of Annie, and, wishing to excite as little disturbance as possible, handed over the dress. Bramwell then drove straight on to the house of Benjamin Scott and recounted Annie's story to him. Scott recommended that he should go to see W. T. Stead at the editorial offices of the *Pall Mall Gazette*, which Bramwell did. A few days were wanting, however, before Stead was prepared to take seriously such a story.

In the meantime, Josephine was being acquainted with the realities of metropolitan prostitution through the unprepossessing lips of a reclaimed procuress, sent to her by Florence Booth in the hope that the Butlers would offer her refuge, and thus give her an opportunity of resisting the temptation to return to her old haunts.

The Butler residence had opened its doors to many strange guests, but to few as repulsive as Rebecca Jarrett. She was grossly fat, with the bloated, blotched features of the chronic alcoholic. She was also filthy in body and in speech, lame to the point of deformity, and was embittered by the fact that the one woman she had come to trust had dispatched her in almost indecent haste miles out into the provinces.

For twenty years she had dedicated her life not merely to prostituting her own body, but also to procuring children for purposes of prostitution. She had commenced her career as a prostitute in 1860, at the age of eleven. At fifteen she was managing her own house, and recruiting working-class children, largely from the notorious Cremorne Gardens and from Marylebone. At thirty-three, ruined in health, a confirmed drunkard who had been crippled in an accident while incapable with drink, she was taken into the protection of the Hanbury Street refuge, which was superintended by Florence Booth. Despite feverish bouts of penitence, dramatic rather than sincere, and vague resolutions to win back her health through sobriety (probably in order to pursue her chosen profession), she would abscond to the gay houses of the West End, where her old colleagues would stand her drinks for friendship's sake. Again and again, Florence Booth would rescue her (in the most literal sense), and take her back to Whitechapel, to the Hanbury Street refuge.

On the last of these occasions, Florence Booth had come to collect her from the London Hospital, where Rebecca Jarrett had been taken by the police to 'dry out'. Florence told her that she intended to send her to Josephine, in Winchester; to Rebecca this seemed like rejection and betrayal. But Josephine and George welcomed her, as they welcomed all their strange guests. At the end of her life Rebecca would still remember how, after she had gone to bed each night, 'Mrs Butler and the dear old Canon' would look into her room to say goodnight. She had repented for the last time, and was to maintain that it was because of the Butlers that she was truly turned to God. Of the day she met Josephine on the station at Winchester, she wrote, 'I felt as if that day, I had truly met with Jesus.'[1]

She still had thirty gold sovereigns saved from her immoral earnings, and these she offered to Josephine, asking that they should be used to help her in her rescue work. Josephine declined them; she had just acquired a cottage in the cathedral precinct for use as a refuge, and she suggested that Rebecca should use her money to furnish and decorate it, with a view to her taking up residence in it as housekeeper-matron. Rebecca grasped at this opportunity to be of use, and assumed full responsibility for the administration of the cottage.

She now entered on the happiest period of her life. Not only did she succeed in making the refuge as attractive and as comfortable for its inhabitants as her savings would permit, but she exploited her experience as a procuress by going out at night into the streets of Winchester, and persuading the young, homeless girls she encountered soliciting to return to the cottage with her. She succeeded in rescuing more than a hundred children during this brief period of her life, removing them from the streets and brothels of Winchester and Portsmouth, and returning them either to the care of their parents, or taking them to

the cottage and keeping them there until they could be found
places as domestic servants in homes which could be trusted to
treat them well. At the same time, again according to Josephine,
the attractiveness, vivacity and charm which had made her so
successful as a prostitute in her early youth were returned to
her. She was, after all, only in her mid-thirties, and she had
fifty years of life ahead of her.

This heroic episode in Rebecca's career was of very short
duration. Her worst trial was still to come, and, bearing in mind
that an alcoholic is never truly cured, and that a woman reclaimed from the streets must learn to overcome the fecklessness
and irresponsibility ingrained into her in the course of such a
life, it was a miracle that she survived spiritually and physically
the burden which her friends imposed upon her. For imposed it
was, and largely by Josephine.

W. T. Stead had by now been persuaded to look at the Jeffries
dossier. Initially he had not wanted to involve himself: far from
embracing the idea of a series of sensational disclosures regarding prostitution in London's West End, he knew perfectly well
that such a campaign would, in the long run, irretrievably
damage the middle-class family circulation he had so carefully
built up over the past three years. It would almost certainly
bring him into conflict with his proprietors.

When Benjamin Scott presented him with the dossier, he
asked Stead if he knew 'that Mrs Jeffries sends round circulars
to Members, advertising "new attractions"?'

Stead was astounded at this allegation. He now realised why
the Criminal Law Amendment Bill had met with so little success
in the Commons, and that its failure had little to do with
Members' 'loquacity'. He glanced through the dossier, then,
within two hours of Scott's departure, he was with Sir Charles
Howard Vincent, who was now retired from the C.I.D.

Howard Vincent fully endorsed the findings of ex-Inspector
Minahan, and added information of his own regarding the
treatment of children in London brothels.

'But do you think these things are going on now?' asked
Stead.

'Yes, now – every night,' answered Howard Vincent.

'Vincent! It's enough to raise Hell!' Stead exclaimed.

'It doesn't even raise the neighbours,' replied Howard Vincent.

At this point Stead made his decision.

'I'll make it raise England!' he told Howard Vincent.[2]

Even so, he would have been very ready to have shrugged off the responsibility he had thus placed on himself. He went straight from Howard Vincent's home to that of the President of the Council for the Protection of Women and Children, hoping that he might be able to leave with him the Mrs Jeffries dossier for the Council to take appropriate action on it. The President of the Council, however, would not so much as look at it, and was, indeed, very reluctant to receive Stead at all when he discovered the nature of his business.

Stead then went on to Scotland Yard, where he was strongly advised to forget the whole matter. The following morning, Scotland Yard reported his visit to the Home Office, and was instructed that under no circumstances should they co-operate with him or with representatives of his paper. Stead, in the meantime, had retired to the one place where he could be sure of an enthusiastic welcome – to visit Benjamin Waugh at the headquarters of the N.S.P.C.C.

Stead asked Waugh if he might be allowed to interview some of the children in the Society's care who had been victims of Mrs Jeffries and her kind. Waugh took him round to one of the Society's shelters, where he was shown two little girls recently picked up by the Inspectors of the N.S.P.C.C. One of them, seven years of age, had been abducted to and raped in a fashionable brothel; her persecutors could not be brought to justice, since no magistrate would accept her statement on oath. The second girl, who was aged four-and-a-half, had been lured into a brothel one evening and had been raped twelve times in succession. Her assailants, though brought to court, had been discharged absolutely.

On seeing the huge, bearded figure of Stead approaching her, this second child began to scream hysterically, imploring him not to hurt her, and calling out one phrase again and again which he could never bring himself to repeat. Arrogant, flamboyant and sensationalist he may have been, but his compassion, and his love for children, were genuine enough. He broke down.

'I'll turn my paper into a tub!' he roared through his tears.
'I'll turn stump orator! I'll damn, and damn, and damn!'[3]

For those, like Waugh and Scott, who were familiar with
Stead's journalistic methods, it was scarcely a propitious
beginning. Waugh, an old Evangelical reformer in the noblest
Victorian tradition, rebuked him for his emotionalism, reminding him sternly that people such as Bramwell Booth and himself encountered such victims almost daily and did the Lord's
work without so indulging their feelings. The rebuke may have
been deserved, but, as a newspaper editor, Stead knew better
than to overstate his case. When his articles finally appeared,
they were written as a cold and dreadful recital of fact.

## XXXIV

On Whit Monday, 25 May 1885, two days after Scott had visited
him in his office, Stead assembled those members of his reporting staff, officers of the Salvation Army, and the handful of
friends whom he had selected to form his 'Secret Commission'
on prostitution in the West End. It was a brave undertaking
on the part of the individuals concerned; they were threatened by the social and political influence of powerful *habitués*
of London brothels, such as Cavendish Bentinck and Lord
Euston, while reporters who proposed to infiltrate the actual
brothels were, of course, risking physical violence, if not their
lives. Two girls, one a member of the *Pall Mall Gazette* staff, and
Jenny Turner, a Salvation Army officer, both undertook to
enter brothels as prostitutes bound for the continental market.
Jenny Turner was to be rescued from Mrs Jeffries's clearing-
house at Kew by her Salvationist fiancé, only just in time to
save her from being murdered (and, miraculously, with her
virginity intact).

Contrary to what has previously been believed, Josephine,
together with George, her eldest son, was an active member of
the Commission. It was not a subject she cared to enlarge on –
not unnaturally in view of the nature of its findings – but, in a
letter to an unnamed friend, she wrote:

I have been for ten days in London helping several friends

in a most terrible investigation concerning the crimes (vice is too pale a word) of the aristocracy. It seems that all that goes on in Brussels and Paris goes on also in London. .... I have been about the streets all day, and sometimes late at night. O! What horrors we have seen. .... All this is not concerned with the vices of the poor, but of the rich, and there are guilty men on the Treasury Bench who now begin to be most uneasy. My dear son has volunteered to go in disguise into one of the high class dens where there are *padded rooms*. We have had to assume disguises.[1]

The horrors they had seen were enough to bring Stead to the point of nervous breakdown. Josephine recounted to Bramwell Booth how, one night, she had 'entered his office after a day of hand-to-hand wrestling with the powers of Hell', to find Stead alone, and the lights off. 'I scarcely recognised the haggard face before me. . . . He threw himself across the desk with a cry . . . and sobbed out the words, "Oh, Mrs. Butler, let me weep, let me weep or my heart will break!"'[2] Bramwell, fearing that if Stead were to fall sick the whole enterprise would be lost, hurried round to Northumberland Street to find him stretched out on the floor in a state of collapse.

Bramwell's own reaction to the horrors he was unearthing was as typical of the man as it was admirable. He saw in them the obverse of positive sexual love, and it seemed to strengthen the joy he found in his own happy, Christian marriage:

I believe I can see in a way I have not seen it before, that a man and a woman who love God, and love each other, can and do glorify Him in the happiness of that very closest union and oneness of flesh and spirit. I think I see it now – how it is pure love that makes all pure and beautiful and lovely before Him and to each other.[3]

Bramwell shared with Josephine a vision, rare for their generation, of the integrity of sexual congress within a context of love. Thus, despite the considerable spiritual agony inflicted upon them as a result of the appalling discoveries they were making, they retained a sense of proportion. Stead, on the other hand, for all his experience as a newspaper man, had led a life far more sheltered than those of his two leading partners in the investigation.

Nevertheless all three were shocked with the shock which comes of the unexpected. The reality was so much worse than the hearsay. For Josephine, nothing if not a patriot, who had confidently asserted when quarrelling with Sir Charles Howard Vincent over the findings of the Lords' Committee that London was nothing like as bad as Paris or Milan, the discovery that it was if anything rather worse than either was particularly hard to swallow. Towards the end of her life she was to write to her friend Miss Forsaith, regarding this episode, 'There is no need for anyone to press upon me the reality of *Hell*, as the Calvinists did with stony hearts. For I have *been* in Hell.'[4]

Even today, after the publication of countless exposés of the darker side of Victorian sexuality, the Commission's findings as published in the *Pall Mall Gazette* retain something of their original power to horrify and to excite indignation. They are contained in four special issues, the first of which bore the headline which was to give the entire campaign its name, 'The Maiden Tribute of Modern Babylon'. Under this somewhat colourful title, the actual material was presented with a blunt unelaboration which must be unique in nineteenth-century journalism.

In the fashionable brothels of London, according to the *Pall Mall Gazette*, the profit derived from conventional prostitution was minimal to the point of loss-leading. The real profits were to be found in the exploitation of 'fresh girls' up from the country. West End club-men would pay anything up to twenty-five guineas for a teenage virgin, and up to a hundred for the privilege of raping or tormenting a young child. One house, in Half Moon Street – and it is difficult to imagine a more fashionable area – specialised in the flagellation and rape of young children imprisoned in sound-proofed rooms. In Panton Street and Jermyn Street, which had been sanctuaries for affluent vice since the 1830s, no such precautions were deemed necessary, and the air was rent with the screams of the victims.

In such establishments, girls who attempted to defend themselves were strait-jacketed, strapped to their beds or simply held down by servants of the house. When fastidious clients wished to take their pleasure undisturbed by screams, the chil-

dren – mostly between the ages of ten and sixteen but not in-
frequently much younger – were chloroformed, or drugged with
'drowsers' (a medicated snuff), or, most frequently of all, were
gagged with the leather thong which was employed in the armed
services for those undergoing field punishment by flogging.
Young girls frequently died from the combined effects of shock,
mental and physical, and suffocation from the gag and the
pressure of their assailant's body lying on top of them. In the
more expensive establishments a permanent medical staff was
retained to repair the lacerations caused by the violation of
young teenagers. This was not the product of an improbable
compassion, but was due to the fact that these girls could still
command a high price provided their vaginas were not grown
slack: there was, indeed, a considerable trade in 'second-hand
virgins'. Needless to say, there was little benefit to be derived
from patching up the sexual parts of infants: they were thrown,
bleeding, out on to the street. Virginity, and pre-pubescent
virginity in particular, was the intrinsic specie of West End
brothels – all else was but a poor substitute.

Methods of recruitment varied. The most usual was the outright purchase of children from drunken or feckless parents,
though kidnapping was far from unusual. Unwanted babies were
acquired, often from day-nurses in slum areas, and from baby-
farmers. They were kept until they were old enough to practise
fellatio; at four or five they were deemed to be sufficiently
developed for penetration, after which they were discarded,
brutalised and tormented beyond the capacity of sanity to
endure. Stead, himself, encountered one of these miserable little
survivors; a little girl in a rescue home who would scream and
grow violent whenever anyone went near her, and who, remembering some fragment of scripture imparted to her by a kindly
intentioned brothel-servant, believed she was possessed by
devils.

Older girls were lured into brothels by the same means as in the
case of Annie Swan; by procuresses dressed as nuns, or 'ladies'
who maintained they represented charitable welfare services; or
by charwomen who said that they could recommend positions
where pay was high and no 'character' was needed. Girls, even
of the more prosperous classes of society – particularly from the
class of skilled artisans, whose families had pretentions to

gentility – were peculiarly vulnerable since, as Stead emphasised, far from being on their guard against plausible abductors, they had absolutely no knowledge of sex, let alone of prostitution.

On 10 July 1885, the series was concluded with an account of the trade in English girls on the Continent, and a savage denunciation of the C.I.D. and the Metropolitan Police. The police, declared the *Pall Mall Gazette*, was riddled with corruption. The fashionable brothels paid a fixed annual sum into police funds – Mrs Jeffries paid five hundred pounds per annum – while London's most notorious procuresses, notably Mrs Travers, were active in assisting police charities. Fathers whose daughters had been abducted, whose daughters had crawled home maimed and bleeding from houses whose purposes were well known to the police, were unable to obtain any redress. This was not entirely due to bribery and graft; there was also the power and influence exercised by Josephine's 'guilty men on the Treasury Bench' to be taken into account, and it would have been a brave police-inspector who would have dared to interfere with Lord Euston's pleasures. Friends of the brothel-keepers were to be found in Government, on the Queen's Bench and in the higher echelons of the Established Church; a senior cleric, a member of the 'familia' of the Archbishop of Canterbury at Lambeth Palace, believing that one of Stead's reporters was anxious to dispose of a troublesome mistress, offered to have her abducted and incarcerated in a Belgian brothel for the sum of ten pounds.

To Stead, there seemed to be one thing lacking in all the evidence which he had collated: incontrovertible proof that a child could actually be bought as a slave might be bought, for purposes of prostitution. In his opinion this was the only way in which the argument that children entered into prostitution willingly, however much they might later regret it, could be refuted. To this end he wrote to Archbishop Benson of Canterbury, Dr Temple, Bishop of London, and Cardinal-Archbishop Manning disclosing the evidence he had amassed, and stating his intention of forcing a *cause célèbre* which would provide the ultimate proof of his allegations.

Archbishop Benson was appalled, and said so. Cardinal Manning and Dr Temple were equally shocked but, having thought the matter over, agreed that it was the only way in which no doubt could be left in the readers' minds as to the accuracy of his allegations.

'In order to demonstrate that a vicious man can have a girl of thirteen procured for him for vicious purposes,' Stead had written to these eminent divines, 'I will personate such a man, playing the part in every detail short of actually consummating the crime.'[5]

The difficulty lay in finding somebody who would actually effect the initial purchase of the victim. Attempts by female members of Stead's staff to impersonate procuresses failed miserably, even farcically. It was easy enough to procure a child for one night's use; Stead, however, wished to prove the possibility of buying a child outright – the existence of slavery in every real sense. For this a professional procuress was necessary, and only one such was known to the members of the 'Secret Commission'. Very reluctantly, Josephine was persuaded to recruit Rebecca Jarrett to this end.

Using her old contacts to obtain introductions to likely victims, Rebecca finally lighted on an Eliza Armstrong, a thirteen-year-old living in a Marylebone slum. At first Mrs Armstrong refused to consider selling her daughter like 'a sack of potatoes'. Rebecca shrewdly assessed that this reluctance was due to fear of the neighbours' comments, and, recognising that Mrs Armstrong was both an alcoholic and in need of money, decided to return after dark with an improved offer from Stead. On being presented that night with five sovereigns in gold, Mrs Armstrong's maternal instinct was miraculously blunted, and Eliza was sent off with Rebecca to a destination of which the drink-sodden mother knew nothing, and cared less. In fact, Rebecca took her to the house of one of her erstwhile colleagues, a Madame Mourez.

In court, six months later, Madame Mourez claimed to be a trained midwife. It is possible that this claim was true; certainly she was a brothel-keeper and an abortionist. She was not the best sort of witness for Stead to obtain, but was probably the only person he could obtain to play the role he required. Madame Mourez examined Eliza and proclaimed her *virgo intacta*. Eliza endorsed this verdict by crying loudly, and protesting that the woman 'had done something dirty' to her. The poor girl's protests and terror greatly increased when she was taken to one of Madame Mourez's cell-like bedrooms, where Rebecca attempted and failed to administer a 'drowser' to her. By the time Stead appeared in the bedroom, dressed and made-up as an elderly roué, Eliza was, not unsurprisingly, beside herself with fear.

While it can be argued that the apparent ruthlessness with which Stead treated Eliza Armstrong was necessary for the safeguarding in the future of many thousands of her kind, his personal performance in this incident is less supportable. It is difficult to perceive the necessity for him to render himself hideous with such stage-props as flour-water and rouge, and then to burst in on the terrified child in such a disguise. One can only surmise that there was something in Stead's personality which required that he should experience the role of the girl's client for himself. Certainly, he backed out of the cell horrified at the effect he had had on Eliza, and it is true also that, when she learnt the reasons why she was being thus used, the girl became one of his most devoted admirers.

After Stead had beaten his retreat from the room, a female Salvation Army officer took charge of Eliza and escorted her to a private nursing home, where a gynaecologist of unimpeachable character examined her, and certified her as still being a virgin. She was then returned to Rebecca, who took her with her back to Josephine at Winchester, where she remained for a few happy weeks.

The morning following the publication of the first issue in the 'Maiden Tribute' series, Stead's offices were virtually in a state of siege. Northumberland Street was 'blocked by a dense crowd of men and boys fighting promiscuously in their eagerness to get near enough to the office to buy the paper, and the faces of the group round each door were positively purple from the pressure in which they were standing'.[6]

The Government was not anxious to open a prosecution of Stead, and hoped that the crowds seething in Northumberland Street would either sack the offices of the *Pall Mall Gazette*, or would effectually obstruct by their presence the second issue of the series. For this reason, all police were quietly removed from the vicinity, and the plan succeeded to such an extent as to become self-defeating. As the second evening drew on and no fresh issue of the paper emerged, the crowds grew bored and began to drift away. In the early hours before the dawn, the delivery-vans tore out of the dispatch-gate; the *Gazette* was on the breakfast-tables of its subscribers.

The provincial press was almost unanimous in its support for Stead. Not so the London dailies.

'There will scarcely be a boy or girl in England,' thundered *The Times,* 'whose ignorance will not be tainted by the disgusting pabulum with which they have been so plentifully supplied.'[7]

Sir Richard Cross, the Home Secretary, was in an extremely difficult position. The entire House of Commons, like London society in general, was waiting for the awful moment when the *Pall Mall Gazette* would begin to recite the names of their most distinguished associates who were participants in the abominations which it was recounting. Stead was, moreover, the friend, in some cases the intimate friend, of the leaders of the Opposition, Gladstone, Morley, Bright, to name but three. He had the declared   public sympathy of the Bishop of London and the Cardinal-Archbishop of Westminster. At the same time, the position of the Government, thanks to the furore over the Irish Question, was far from secure, and an appeal to the nonconformist and Roman Catholic vote based on the evidence of dissolute and vicious behaviour among the wealthy, apparently endorsed by a Tory government, would certainly result in its downfall.

For this reason, Sir Richard, after a few weeks of irresolution and flustered inactivity, decided to push through the Criminal Law Amendment Bill, together with a clause raising the age of consent to sixteen, with almost indecent haste. In an interview at the Home Office, Stead had hinted that, should he do so, the *Pall Mall Gazette* would not name  names – an easy promise since he had no intention of doing so in any case. Sir Richard moved the final reading of the Bill in a speech which was designed to convince those members of the electorate whose daughters had been most at risk, that nobody was a more convinced adherent of Stead's cause than himself:

This is a question which has stirred England from one end to the other. There is nothing more sacred to the English people, and there is nothing they are so determined to maintain as the purity of their own households. The feeling has gone abroad that the purity of their households and the honour of their daughters has been, and is liable to be, violated, and they have made up their minds that this shall no longer be the case.[8]

Attempts by Cavendish Bentinck to laugh the Bill out of Parliament were rendered inaudible by colleagues who, anxious to convince the electorate of their own simon-purity in sexual matters, jeered, 'Fornicator! Fornicator!' at him. The Bill was passed by 179 votes to 71.

The controversy which raged around the Eliza Armstrong case has somewhat obscured the results of the Maiden Tribute campaign. It was a notable victory, not merely in the specialised history of women's emancipation, but also in the story of the development of nineteenth-century liberal democracy. For a thousand years it had been tacitly accepted that the daughters of the lower orders were freely available for the sexual enjoyment of the privileged. The lower orders were now in a position to impose and enforce a denial of this dubious right. But the privileged were still in a position to exact a price for this limitation of their pleasures.

## XXXV

IN exploring the possibilities of avenging themselves on him, Stead's enemies hit upon the idea of exploiting Eliza Armstrong's mother. In one of her brief periods of comparative sobriety, she was persuaded by Cavendish Bentinck's agents into an unexpected, and highly untypical, paroxysm of maternal concern. Appearing at a Marylebone police station, she reported the disappearance of her little girl, admitting quite shamelessly that she had sold her, but declaring that she had believed it to be for a limited time only, and that her husband was missing his little Eliza.

This came as a complete surprise. Nobody, least of all Rebecca Jarrett and Stead, had ever imagined that Eliza Armstrong had a father. To those who wished to prosecute Stead, the emergence of 'Basher' Armstrong (so-called because of the form of affection he customarily displayed towards Mrs Armstrong – he does not appear to have had another Christian name) came as a gift from Heaven. Clearly, Rebecca Jarrett had not obtained the redoubtable 'Basher's' endorsement of the sale of his putative daughter, and as a result, Cavendish Bentinck was able to lay an information against Stead, Bramwell Booth and the wretched Rebecca on the ground that they had committed an abduction. On this basis all three were arrested and brought to trial.

The entire legal corps of the Treasury was assembled to aid the prosecution, which was led by the Attorney-General in person. An equal number of distinguished Counsel offered their services to the Defence, presumably in happy expectation of law offices under the Crown in the event of a Liberal victory in a general election. Stead declined their services, undoubtedly in the fallacious belief that 'the pure in heart need no lawyers'; he was, after all, secure in the knowledge that the Archbishop of Canterbury, the Bishop of London, the Cardinal-Archbishop of Westminster, his old colleague, John Morley, the rising star of the Tory Party, A. J. Balfour, and the radical scourge of homo sexuals, Henry Labouchère, were all prepared to testify in his defence.

He had forgotten that he would be tried on a point of law, not of morality, and that the law could be harsh – the law could be 'a ass'. An experienced counsel would have seen immediately the point on which the whole case for the prosecution should have foundered, a point which he, in his inexperience, completely missed. 'Basher' Armstrong was not married to Mrs Armstrong; 'Basher' Armstrong had not set eyes on Mrs Armstrong at the time Eliza was born. There was, therefore, no case to answer under existing law.

Neither Bramwell Booth, who was acquitted, nor Stead, whose ensuing imprisonment was far from arduous, could be said to have suffered as a result of the verdict. Real suffering was reserved for Rebecca Jarrett and for Eliza, who was dragged weeping from the arms of her Salvation Army guardians, and was restored to the unlovely care of an alcoholic mother and a brutal step-father. It was not long, however, before Eliza ran away from home – her mother does not seem to have been in a condition to have cared about her second departure, 'Basher' having sought comfort in the arms of a more desirable co-habitant before the case had ever begun – and restored herself to the protection of the Booths. She was happily married a few years later, became the mother of six children and corresponded regularly with Stead until his death on the *Titanic* in 1912.

Commentators on the Maiden Tribute affair have accorded an importance to the Eliza Armstrong case quite beyond its actual significance. The two columns in the *Pall Mall Gazette* devoted to the exploit were a minimal part of the whole series, and had little effect on the fate of the Criminal Law Amendment Act, which was passed, of course, as a result of what was *not* in the series rather than because of what *was*.

Many of Stead's most active supporters, including G. B. Shaw and Bramwell Booth, had been disturbed at the little melodrama performed in the house of Madame Mourez. Josephine, to whom the words 'medical examination' were anathema, was highly displeased at it. She had greater cause to feel uneasy. Rebecca Jarrett had been made the scapegoat of the entire business, so that an embarrassed Prosecution, all too aware that public opinion was turned against the whole proceedings, could exculpate Stead and Bramwell Booth. Josephine, who gave evidence on her behalf, was appalled to find that she herself was being used to this end. Categorically she had declared:

'I do not wish to make any excuse for my own share in the hardihood and imprudence to which I am ready to confess, and of which I was guilty in asking Rebecca to undertake this difficult work.'[1]

The result was that she sat in the courtroom and heard Mr Justice Lopes, in his summing-up, describe her as 'an amiable but foolish lady'. The judge went on to explain to the jury that if Mrs Butler had not been so charitably disposed, 'she would have known what sort of a woman Jarrett is, and would never have trusted her'.

Josephine became more and more indignant on Rebecca's behalf, and felt greater and greater remorse at the part she had played in her fate. For there can be little doubt that the real begetter of the Eliza Armstrong case was Josephine. From the moment the idea of a 'Secret Commission' was first mooted by Stead, Josephine, remembering how her old anti-slavery friends had bought slaves in order to deliver them from bondage, had proposed that the same principle should be applied to the victims of white slavery, and that this would prove more forcibly than anything else that actual slavery existed in Britain.

Certainly she was responsible for volunteering Rebecca's services to Stead, though she indignantly denied that she had exerted any pressure on her, or that Rebecca had agreed through fear of being dismissed by her:

> We were as sisters together, not employer and employed, as reiterated by the Attorney General and the Judge. She never received one penny from me, nor from Mr Stead. . . . She had nothing to lose or gain by undertaking the work for Mr Stead, which proved to be too hard for her. I had her with me for several hours previous to her going to London, and we talked the matter fully over; we asked God to guide us; and to this hour, I believe He did guide us, in spite of our mistakes. If Rebecca had said, on leaving the room that day, 'Mrs. Butler, I cannot undertake this work,' I should have replied, 'All right, dear Rebecca, don't attempt it. Go back to your work at the cottage.' She would not have incurred one moment's displeasure from me, and she knew it.[2]

This was undoubtedly true. But what Josephine forgot, or was, perhaps, completely unaware of, was that by asking Rebecca to undertake the task, she was putting moral pressure on her, if only because Rebecca was emotionally utterly dependent upon her. Even after she had agreed to co-operate, Rebecca showed little enthusiasm for the task. She wrote to Josephine from London: 'I feel there is some trouble coming. I could wish now I had never left my home and undertaken this other affair. I love you all very much. . . . I wish I had you with me this afternoon, to hear your loving words.'[3]

The trouble had come. Nobody had warned her of the possibility of arrest and imprisonment for what she had done. Now, in the dock, she was being made the scapegoat by a judge and prosecution anxious to evade the public contumely which would be heaped upon them if they were to victimise Stead or Bramwell Booth. It was far from what Cavendish Bentinck and his associates had planned, but the entire blame for the Eliza Armstrong abduction was being heaped on Rebecca's head. Mr

Justice Lopes, in a summing-up worthy of his great predecessors Coke or Jeffreys, referred to her as 'this disgusting and abominable woman', who had 'returned to her old haunts as a dog returns to its vomit'.[4]

George Butler *fils* wrote to his mother: 'What bullying it seems to pitch into the poorer agents in the case, like Mrs Jarrett.'[5]

Not everybody felt the same. Stead, as Josephine acidly observed, 'speaks of having had a fair trial; compliments the prosecution; confesses himself to have been to blame; hopes that nothing will be done to reverse the sentence. Perhaps Mr Stead may think that he himself was courteously treated; but what of the courtesy, or even decent fairness shown in regard to Rebecca?'[6]

Rebecca's own attitude in the dock exacerbated Josephine's sense of remorse at having imposed her will on her. Except for the one day during which she had been forced to admit under examination that, to protect her old associates, she had told a somewhat trivial lie, her conduct was both admirable and exemplary in its stoicism.

When Josephine returned to Winchester, having seen Rebecca committed to Millbank Prison, she found the girls whom Rebecca had rescued particularly embittered by the verdict. 'I'm sure God doesn't care a bit for us girls,' one of them told her. 'Good people are punished and frightened, and all the work is put an end to; and girls are badly treated as ever. God lets off bad rich men so easily, and doesn't care for us girls a bit.'[7]

Josephine attempted to explain that Rebecca's sacrifice was far from futile, that the cause was won. The girls refused to believe her. 'We've waited too long!' one of them explained.

She attempted to make amends both to Rebecca and to the girls who felt themselves to be deserted and betrayed. She wrote, in a matter of weeks, a life of Rebecca Jarrett, relating her story, rebutting both prosecution and judge in detail. It is more noteworthy for its scarcely controlled indignation than for factual accuracy, but, thanks to the sensation caused by the trial, it sold well and went far to rehabilitate its subject in the eyes of the public.

Rebecca bore her two years' imprisonment with a dignity and fortitude which George Butler saw fit to compare with that of

St Paul. The chaplain of Millbank wrote to Josephine requesting that she might be employed as his housekeeper if Mrs Butler no longer required her services. 'But I *do* want her,' Josephine replied.

In fact, Rebecca did not return to Josephine after her release, but enrolled herself in the ranks of the Salvation Army. She survived until 1929, a loyal, devoted and hardworking member of that society. Throughout the remainder of her long life she spoke of Josephine only with gratitude and love.

# 6. The Years of Bereavement

JOSEPHINE remained in London after the trial, making arrangements for legal costs to be paid and attempting by paying her regular visits in Millbank to make the first few weeks of Rebecca's imprisonment endurable. It was not until the turn of the year that she telegraphed George to tell him that she was at last coming home.

George's health was deteriorating rapidly, a fact which he had kept from her. When she arrived back in the Cathedral Close, Winchester, she found, to her dismay, that he was very ill indeed. The guilt she felt over her part in Rebecca's arrest and imprisonment was increased by her remorse for having so long neglected her husband. She had always promised herself that, at some point in their lives, she would withdraw as far as her temperament allowed from active campaigning, in order that they might enjoy some time together. Now, she believed she had left it too late; as the winter drew towards spring, George remained in his bed, and his doctors were sure that he was dying.

George, however, rallied, though his doctors forbade him to exert himself, and Josephine took him abroad, to Naples, and Hattie's home, in the belief that the warmth of the Mediterranean sun would do him good. She hoped also, rather pathetically, that by letting him escort her round the relics of Hellenic culture in southern Italy, she could, in some measure, make reparation for never having allowed herself the time to gratify his lifelong wish by going with him to Greece itself.

They succeeded in visiting Cumae, where George trotted happily around declaiming Virgil, and tracing to his own satisfaction 'the path by which the Sibyl's cave was reached, and the hollow in which stagnates Lake Avernus'.[1] But only a few days after this excursion, rheumatic fever struck him again, and he was confined to his bed.

On 13 April 1886 a telegram arrived from Sir James Stansfeld: 'The Royal Assent has this day been given to the Repeal Bill.'

The last relics of the Contagious Diseases Acts had been abolished.

'I thanked God at that moment', wrote Josephine some years later, 'that Queen Victoria had washed her hands of a stain which she had unconsciously contracted in her first endorsement of this legislation.'

But elsewhere she confessed to a sense of anticlimax.[2] The wait had been too long, the struggle too bitter, the horrors she had witnessed in London, where there was no regulation, too terrible for her to feel that there was any real cause for rejoicing. The knowledge, which she was too honest to hide from herself, that George, whatever happened immediately, had not long to live, precluded any possibility of joy over the outcome. She regretted that she had brought him to Italy; she knew that if he was indeed dying, he would wish to do so in the quiet of his bedroom overlooking the Close, where he would be able to hear, in the stillness of his room, the sound of the Cathedral music which he loved so well.

As soon as he was fit to travel once more, they set out to return to England. They had managed to reach Berne when George once again collapsed. Josephine was not short of medical advice. She numbered among her friends the most distinguished physicians and professors of medicine in Switzerland. It was after returning from a visit to one of these, Professor Demme of Berne, that she found George lying back on his pillows, the tears streaming down his face, 'depressed as I have never seen him in all his illness in Winchester'.[3] He begged her to write summoning their children, and to the Dean and Chapter at Winchester asking for their prayers. George's sickness lasted for months. Hattie came up from Naples to help Josephine nurse him, and Stanley and Charles travelled to and from England with each new crisis:

He had no more fever, [Josephine wrote to her sons] but the pain has been sharp and constant, and his dear face bears traces of much suffering. He cannot use his hands; he can only look on while we do everything for him. The dressing and moving were painful; a cold perspiration covered his face from weakness.[4]

As she and Hattie raised him from the pillows, he caught sight of the mountains through the open window – the 'pure white Alps. . . . He was silent, but after a time, he drew a long breath, and said, "How wonderfully beautiful!" '

One night, a week later, Josephine woke up at four o'clock in the morning feeling that something was badly wrong, and went into George's room. In his delirium he was trying to pray. Once or twice he whispered, 'Into Thy hands I commend my spirit.' Once he became lucid and whispered to Josephine, 'We wish to have a few more years, do we not, dear?' And Josephine wept, realising how he had missed her during her long absences from home.[5]

She threw herself into nursing him day and night, with that terrible devotion which had characterised her nursing of Stanley when, as a child, he had had diphtheria. She forced herself to remain awake, night after night, kneeling on the bare boards of the floor to pray whenever she was afraid she might yield to sleep. It was under these circumstances, when she herself was close to delirium, that she believed a miracle to have occurred.[6]

A feeling of despair had come over her. 'My strength was failing me, and he was worse.' Once more, she forced herself to kneel on the floor in prayer. But fatigue and depression robbed her even of the ability to pray. At that moment she realised, or believed that she realised, that the physical presence of Christ was with her in the room, and that she heard his voice speaking to her, 'The prayer of faith shall save the sick; call on Me in time of trouble, and I will deliver thee.' Blinded with tears she could only stammer out, 'Lord, I believe. . . .'

A few hours later George was better. According to Professor Demme, George had survived an inflammation of both lungs, pleurisy and a serious heart-attack, 'any one of which should have been enough to have killed most men'.

Josephine was determined never again to be separated from George for longer than a few hours 'during our united lives. I refused all invitations to attend meetings, in London or elsewhere, – sometimes, I fear, to the surprise as well as regret of my fellow-workers in public matters. My choice was, however, deliberate, and I have never had cause to regret it.'[7]

Those last two years of their marriage were, in many ways, the happiest. They travelled abroad, revisiting old haunts, re-capturing past pleasures with none of the disillusion usually attendant on such excursions. George even returned to his old profession of art critic, writing a series of articles for the *Contemporary Review* on art galleries he visited on the Continent.

By November 1889 it was clear to Josephine that George's health was failing once more. She decided that they should spend the winter at Amalfi, in company with the Meuricoffres.

'Hope dies hard in a loving heart', wrote Josephine to her sons. And there seemed to be cause for hope. At Amalfi, George would climb with his old vigour to the cliff tops, Josephine panting after him, and they would sit, arm in arm, and gaze out across the bay to the mountains – 'a deep, rich purple, over which there seems to be drawn a veil of golden gauze'.[8]

Then, unexpectedly, disaster struck. There was an influenza epidemic in the town, and George fell a victim. This time, the doctors assured Josephine, there was not the slightest hope of a recovery beyond a matter of days. George had expressed the wish that he might die at home, in Winchester, and his doctors advised that there was nothing to be lost by taking him there.[9]

As soon as his fever was abated, Josephine started the long, agonising journey. George himself refused to be anything but cheerful, despite the fact that he knew his days were numbered, and could not move without assistance. When they arrived at Boulogne, he seemed so weak that Josephine begged him to desist from his invariable practice of kneeling, when he rose, with her at the bedside to offer morning prayer.

'Oh yes, darling!' he insisted. 'I am quite strong enough.'

But as he was kneeling, praying – 'it was all praise, from first to last; grateful thanksgiving' – he collapsed. She stayed with him, cradling him in her arms until help came.

'When he had been carried to the vessel and was lying quietly in the cabin with closed eyes, and a look of peace and content, I bent over him and said, "We have a beautiful day, dear, and a perfectly calm sea." Without opening his eyes, he said in a low voice, "How good God is to us!" '

They reached their hotel in London on the evening of 13 March 1890. George was by now delirious. As Josephine knelt beside his bed, he kept asking, 'Whose house is this? Where are we?' And Josephine would reply, 'In London, darling, and home tomorrow.' He was contented at this, and would smile. Finally he reached out for her hand and whispered, 'I shall be glad to go to sleep.'

She remained with him throughout the night. When morning came, he did not wake, and a terrible sense of desolation crept over her. At four in the afternoon, he stirred, turned his face towards her and took her hand once more.

'You will go with me, beloved?' he asked anxiously. 'You will go with me, will you not?'

Josephine answered without hesitation, 'Yes, I will! Oh, I will! I will go with you!'

'For I knew,' she wrote later, 'that my heart would follow him whither he was going, and would dwell with him there.' And it was true that, as her eldest son raised her up from the bed where George now lay lifeless, a part of her had died.


## XXXVII

GEORGE's death had not come unexpectedly, and therefore it did not result in the crisis of faith which followed Eva's death. In public, and among her associates, Josephine maintained a dignified calm. In private she surrendered to a grief as terrible as she had expected it would be, committing her deepest emotions to a diary which her children, in a desire to respect her privacy, later suppressed.

Her sense of bereavement was scarcely mitigated by the need to leave her pleasant house in the Cathedral Close at Winchester, to make way for George's successor in the now-vacant Canonry. Nor had she the consolation of being deeply involved in public work; she had, during the previous four years, largely devoted herself to caring for her ailing husband. She never had the heart to attempt to create another home: she put into store the greater part of her furniture and movables, where they remained until her death, sixteen years later. For the first five years of her widowhood she lived with her eldest son, George, in his pleasant bachelor residence overlooking Wimbledon Common. But when he married, and removed to a large country house, Ewart Park, in her own homeland of Glendale, in Northumberland, she retired in a succession of bed-sitting-rooms, preferring a self-imposed solitude to a relationship which could never adequately replace her marriage.

A year after George's death she was still rendered inactive by grief. Her prophecy of fourteen years before was fulfilled:

> If he were to die and leave me, I do not say I could not live or work any more, but I fear I would fall into a state of chronic heartache and longing which would make me rather useless, and perhaps a weariness to others who would never fully understand what and who I had lost.[1]

To George W. Johnson, the editor of the *Christian Socialist*, and later to become her first biographer, she wrote:

> I am terribly lonely now, since my great sorrow. I feel as if I can hardly go on. My husband was more than anyone ever knows of inspiration as well as strength to me. I rejoice that each day brings me one day nearer to him. For the light of my life seems to have quite gone out.[2]

She had been devoting her time to writing her *Recollections of George Butler*, a disorganised, yet very moving account of their marriage. Now, as if to arouse her from her inactive mourning, she received a letter from an American lady, a Dr Kate Bushnell, who was a leading member of the World's Women's Christian Temperance Union. Kate Bushnell described how, one hot summer day, she had fallen asleep and had dreamed that she was being tossed on the billows of the Atlantic on her way to see Josephine Butler. 'It became plain to me that she had something for me to do.'[3] It would have been totally out of keeping with Josephine's character to have found this letter 'faddish' (to use her own word) or to have been embarrassed by the Messianic role in which Kate Bushnell had cast her.

Josephine had become aware of the situation in India through her old colleague and friend Alfred Dyer, who was temporarily resident in Bombay.

The repeal of the Contagious Diseases Acts had been ignored by the Indian Government, and in June 1886 Major-General

Chapman, Lord Roberts's Quartermaster-General, had issued a memorandum instructing senior officers commanding cantonments and military districts in India, to ensure that prostitutes attached to regimental bazaars were medically inspected and that there were enough of them, properly housed, for the requirements of their men.

In July 1888 it was discovered by a commission set up by the Free Church of Scotland that army-regulated brothels had been reopened adjacent to the military cantonments at Peshawar and Rawalpindi, presumably with the tacit consent of the authorities. As soon as the Commission made its findings known, protests were immediately voiced by the Anglican bishops of India. In January 1890 Lord Cross, Secretary of State for India, was forced to intervene, and, as a result of communicating with the new Viceroy, Lord Lansdowne, he assured Parliament that the Government of India had conformed to the instructions of Her Majesty's Government. Lord Roberts, the Commander-in-Chief, took the precaution of writing to Josephine in her capacity as Secretary of the British and Continental Federation, stating that he believed the report of the Free Church of Scotland to be greatly exaggerated.

The arrival of Kate Bushnell's letter, following Lord Roberts's curious, because unsolicited, denial that Regulation was practised in British India, combined with Dyer's obvious unease regarding the situation there, could scarcely be ignored. Since she saw no reason to doubt that the vision vouchsafed to Kate Bushnell was of God, it seemed clear to her that God, through Dr Bushnell, was calling her from the slough of self-pity into which she had fallen, and was summoning her to take up the Cause once more.

She replied to Kate Bushnell saying that she, and the Abolitionist Federation, required the services of a woman who was prepared to tour the military districts of India to 'make careful inquiry into the condition of things there, with a view to ridding that people of the oppressive tyranny and shame imposed on them by the Army authorities'.[4] Kate Bushnell showed this letter to a fellow-member of the World's Women's Christian Temperance Union, a Mrs Andrews, who had been profoundly impressed by W. T. Stead's florid biography of Josephine – *Josephine Butler; a Life-Sketch* – which he had written while incarcerated in Holloway (then a prison for men). Mrs Andrews readily agreed to accompany Kate Bushnell on a tour round the world, which included, in the first three months of 1892, an inspection of the cantonments in India.

Their findings were sufficient to galvanise Josephine into something approaching her former activity. The American ladies had discovered that, not merely was a system of Regulation operated in the cantonments, but that women were actually requisitioned from native bazaars for the use of soldiers, and to substantiate their accusations, brought back to Josephine examples of the official tickets given to Indian women allocating them to certain soldiers or groups of soldiers. Josephine thereupon deposited the evidence with James Stuart and a fellow Member of Parliament, Walter McLaren, drew up a 'Statement of Facts' which she submitted to the India Office and communicated the findings generally to Stead.

Stead, who could be relied on to provide the greatest possible publicity, published Kate Bushnell's report in his journal the *Review of Reviews* under the title 'Masked Mutiny', implying that the Anglo-Indian Army assumed itself to be so far above the Law as to ignore the decrees of Crown, Ministers and Parliament. Lord Roberts had returned to Britain only a matter of weeks earlier. In the *Christian Commonwealth* he promptly denied the truth of the allegations published in the *Review of Reviews* both in interpretation and in substance.

However, on being requested for information by a Departmental Commission, the Government of India confirmed Kate Bushnell's findings without qualification. There remained only the need to ascertain the extent of Lord Roberts's responsibility. Major-General Chapman had been responsible for a circular to cantonment commanders insisting that a sufficient number of women be registered 'in proportion to the number of men who visit them' and sanctioning 'any reasonable expenditure from cantonment funds' for the requisition, housing and hygienic maintenance of such women.[5] This circular was issued after the Indian Government had stated (in 1887) its concurrence with the repeal of the Contagious Diseases Acts, and was based on the entirely independent Special Cantonment Acts which had existed, unnoticed by Josephine and her allies, since the 1850s for the benefit of British troops serving in India.

Josephine witnessed Chapman's examination before the Commission, and her description of him in a letter to her son Stanley reveals that she was very much her old self:

Chapman is a Plymouth Brother and holds prayer-meetings. He is a dark, evil-looking man, lean, dried up like a piece of old tree-trunk, expressionless, with a mouth of a peculiar form – thin, mechanical, which slowly opens like a steel trap to emit the lies he speaks with a face of black night and imperturbable impenitence – then shuts again, like a skeleton's mouth.

Asked by Stansfeld if he had a distinct order from Lord Roberts to draw up the circular, the mouth opened, said 'Certainly' and clanked shut again.

'Did Lord Roberts initiate it?' 'Certainly'.

'Did Lord Roberts see it in proof and read it over?'

'Most certainly. He read it over and entirely approved it.'[6]

As a result of the Commission's report, Lord Roberts was severely reprimanded, the Government, in an unprecedented gesture, paid out eight hundred pounds to Dr Bushnell and Mrs Andrews to cover the expenses they had incurred in India and the Special Cantonment Act was amended. But the victory of Josephine and the Abolitionists was far less conclusive than at first appeared. The peculiar condition obtaining in military service in India – the majority of soldiers being unmarried, cut off from their own countrywomen, finding themselves in a strange land and in a climate peculiarly trying to Englishmen – and the quite appalling incidence of venereal disease among British troops in India led to embittered resistance on the part of both military and civil authorities to the ending of Regulation. By 1897, semi-official organisation of regulated prostitution in cantonments was practised once more, an eventuality gleefully prophesied by the Anglo-Indian press two years earlier:

The religious fanatics who howled until a weak Government gave way to their clamour will probably howl again now at the way the old order of things will be enforced under another name but with very little difference in manner. The way the Indian Government have got over the difficulty is simply by classing venereal diseases in the same category as small-pox and other contagious diseases which the law provides for by segregation, special hospitals, etc.[7]

It was not until towards the end of the First World War that the authorities found the answer to the problem of venereal disease among troops serving in the Far East. It was to make effective prophylactics freely available on request, and to charge soldiers who became infected with V.D. with having committed a military crime.

The painful truth was that Josephine and her friends – including Kate Bushnell and Mrs Andrew despite their three-month tour – had little idea of the conditions obtaining in India, and none of Hindu attitudes regarding sex and sexuality. However, the controversy regarding regulation in India had one decisive result; it convinced Josephine that, with or without George's help and companionship, God still had work for her to do – 'though I am still tired and old, I feel I must stand up at the guns a bit longer'.[8] It was not so much the actual controversy which caused her once again to take full command of the Abolitionist movement after an absence of some eight or nine years, as the memorial praying for the re-introduction of regulation in India signed by 'one hundred and twenty gentlewomen, including princesses and other ladies of title'. This certainly shocked her:

> My heart is wounded with a sense of shame, and I mourn for those whose eyes are blinded to the truth . . . we cannot now, without the constant acting of a lie, pretend that we are now a united womanhood. Our cause will receive deeper wounds than it has ever received yet if we attempt to minimize or gloss over the hideous fact that women, ladies of high estate and honourable names, have publicly petitioned for the re-establishment in a portion of the British Empire of the masterpiece of Satan, that 'covenant with death and agreement with hell'![9]

The pamphlet which she wrote in reply to the hundred and twenty gentlewomen has the same trumpet-ring as the pamphlets she wrote – *The Constitution Violated, An Appeal to the People of England* – proclaiming her adherence to the Repealist Cause twenty-five years earlier, and though it purports to deal with the question of regulation in India, it is in fact a further declaration of the ideals to which she had remained constant over that quarter-century. Regulation remains an infraction of social justice and those chiefly responsible are upper-class, self-styled Purity workers. 'Our race is suffering largely from a species of moral atrophy, from a fatal paralysis of the sense of justice. Many literally do not know what justice is.'[10]

The root cause of this blindness, this 'moral atrophy', is the failure of the prosperous to understand, and to be concerned for, the poor.

'This loss of respect for these high principles and of moral faith, this belief in and appeal to material forces for the moralizing of the people prevails chiefly among the more privileged classes.'

The poor cannot so easily forget the real meaning of Justice: 'They are reminded of what Justice is, too often, by its absence,' she remarked laconically.

## XXXVIII

IN the spring of 1894, Josephine set out for Italy. Reports had reached her to the effect that despite the formal abolition of state regulation of vice in that country, the system was still in full operation, with government supervised brothels and dispensaries in every village. In view of the fact that the Italian parliament was confronting a major economic crisis, massive unemployment, an epidemic of violent strikes in the industrial north, agrarian riots in the south and a series of public scandals involving members of the government, it is relatively easy to appreciate why deputies found the question of state regulation less than urgent. Josephine, however, determined to emulate her heroine, Catherine of Siena, by going to Rome to insist that Pope Leo XIII make an official announcement of support for her cause. She believed that the Papacy, still nursing its grievance over the fall of Rome in 1870, and embracing the self-ordained isolation of Vatican City, would immediately realise the advantage with regard to world opinion to be gained by embracing a cause so palpably righteous. She wrote to Cardinal Manning at Westminster, seeking introductions to members of the Papal Curia. Manning was eighty-two years old, tired and depressed. He failed to provide her with a letter to 'a decent Cardinal', as she had requested, but did

arrange an introduction to a Canon Regular of the church of
St John Lateran, a Father Rousseau, who was a well-known
preacher, and known personally to Leo XIII.

Father Rousseau attended her at her hotel, 'a very striking
man, a sort of modern Saint Dominic . . . bronzed with sun and
weather and outdoor preaching, dark splendid eyes, full of
life, intelligence and kindness'.[1] He appeared, however, to be
more intent on converting Josephine to Catholicism than with
assisting her in attaining her objective:

> He went about it so frankly that I could not help smiling.
> [she reported to Stanley] He said how my heart 'would be
> comforted by the Sacrament.' I said that I have the Sacra-
> ment in *my* Church. He said, 'Ah? but you have not there the
> *Real Presence* of the Saviour!' I replied, 'Pardon me, Father,
> I think I have often been conscious of the real presence of my
> Saviour in receiving the Sacrament.'[2]

Father Rousseau was clearly taken aback. He had imagined
that Josephine would have been prepared to assume a favourable
attitude towards the possibility of reception into the Catholic
Church in order to obtain an entrée to the Pope.

'You are honest and straight,' he told her; 'all who come to
see us are *not.*'

He told her that she must obtain an audience with the Pope
in order to plead her cause. Having discovered something of
the protocol which would attend such an interview, Josephine's
Anglican conscience was troubled:

> You have to be dressed according to order – all in black,
> no bonnet, but with a long black veil from head to foot *and
> no gloves.* You are often kept waiting in a long ante-room.
> Then, when ushered into the Pope's long audience chamber,
> you must *kneel* at the door, then kneel again in the middle
> of the room and again when you reach the Pope, when you
> kiss the sapphire ring on his finger. Now I confess a moral
> objection to practising this subservience. I like nice old gentle-
> men; but I never want to kneel to any man. I should have to
> ask God in my heart to forgive me for doing so. For a good
> cause, however, I would make the sacrifice; but there is a
> material difficulty. My knees are so stiff with rheumatism

that I have had to give up kneeling altogether. I could get down on them; but the getting up again is so difficult, and I fear it would be very ungraceful.[3]

Father Rousseau urged her to set aside all objection: 'His benediction could do you no harm,' he assured her. Josephine agreed that this was true, and, to her delighted astonishment, Father Rousseau assured her that the Pope would 'fix the day and the hour to see me'.

When, however, the invitation arrived, she had less reason to be pleased. It was in the form of a suggestion that she should attend the Pope's private Mass. Despite the fact that her Italian friends assured her that this was the best possible way to introduce herself in person to Leo XIII, and a very rare privilege, Josephine was furious. She believed that it was part of a Vatican ploy to draw her into the Catholic embrace, and unwisely perhaps, she rejected the invitation, stating her regret that the Curia should be so interested in her conversion. 'That was not the business which brought me to Rome,' she remarked to Stanley.[4]

At a dinner party given in her honour she met Count Pasolini and his wife. Pasolini had never previously met her, but admired her by reputation, and had translated into Italian her memoir of John Grey of Dilston. A member of the Black Nobility, he introduced her to one of the Pope's legal advisers, Aicardi by name, who arrived at her hotel room one morning, accompanied by his son, also a lawyer.

At first Aicardi's advice seemed to contain little hope. He explained that the Pope could not issue an encyclical or a public rescript at the request of one lady, and a non-Catholic at that. Although, he continued, the Pope was utterly opposed to state regulation of vice, he could make no public statement on the subject except to a Catholic audience. He recommended that she should 'obtain the opinion of as many *local* Bishops as possible, and that an expression of opinion made by them or Monsignori or other ecclesiastics should be brought to the Pope on the subject of higher morality and of the abolition of State regulation'.[5]

Josephine's reaction to this demonstration of the labyrinthine approach to the Curia was one of scorn: 'Now I hope you see the situation. The Pope is clever enough and *good* enough to see that we are right; but he cannot deal with J. E. Butler, nor with a *mixed* Federation; but he can deal with the faithful; and he desires that the Bishops should *suggest* to him and claim from him precisely what J. E. Butler has claimed from him.'

It was her encounter with Gladstone all over again, made worse by the fact that Leo XIII was not as approachable in the physical sense as George's old friend had been. Once again, however, she was less than just. In February 1894 to her surprise she was invited to private audience with Leo XIII and without any pre-conditions. A few days, however, before she was due to be received at the Vatican, she was struck down by illness.

On this occasion, the danger to her life was real enough: the Pasolinis, on hearing of her condition, rushed to her hotel, arranged that she should, both by day and night, be attended by two Sisters of Charity and telegraphed to her eldest son George, with whom she had made her home in London, to come immediately. Her lungs became infected, and for five weeks she lay between life and death before she recovered sufficiently to be moved away from the unhealthy climate of Rome to the cleaner, more bracing air of Frascate. Her convalescence was a long one, and the depression which was the natural consequence of so severe a sickness was exacerbated by the disappointment resulting from an opportunity missed. For a time she thought God had deserted her:

> I was busy with my Master's work, doing what I could, quietly with faith and prayer, when suddenly – in a moment – I was struck down by this sickness. . . . The spiritual darkness was even greater than the physical suffering. Why the God of Love *allows* a child of his to be so knocked down and stamped upon, I *cannot* understand.[6]

As the tide of depression ebbed away, her normal, intimate relationship with God was restored. Rome and Satan were responsible for what seemed to be her abject failure:

> A strange deadness to present things comes over me. The Ghosts of Rome still follow me. Rome seems to me to have been not only the centre of the world's history for over

2,000 years, but the centre of Satan's machinery for working
the destruction of souls. You know I am no 'spiritualist',
but my awful experience in Rome has taught me some things
of which I scarcely dare to speak – of the power of the Evil
One and his rage against God and his Christ. There is surely
something peculiarly difficult to conquer, or even fathom in the
intricate and deeply rooted evils of an old *effete* civilization.[7]

On her return to Wimbledon, Josephine received an invita-
tation from G. F. Watts to sit for him. He was anxious to paint
her portrait for his projected 'People's Gallery', for which he
had already completed twenty portraits, since he considered
her to be one of those people who had, in his own words,
'made the century', an opinion which she held to be 'dreadful
nonsense'. Nevertheless her own interest in art and the memory
of her husband's enthusiasm for painting caused her to accept,
and for a week she stayed as Watts's guest at his studio home
at Compton in Surrey.
It was a somewhat sad encounter, and the result – now hung
in the National Portrait Gallery – is a sad, and not entirely
truthful, portrait. Josephine was far from well; she was old,
and weary and was still dreadfully conscious of her failure in
Italy. The house at Compton was, according to Josephine,
'very cold and dull'; she had to take with her George's new
wife (his cousin, Mia St Paul) to make sure she did not lapse into
irritability or fall asleep during the sittings. Aged eighty,
Watts was easily tired, and Josephine's sittings, which were
fatiguing enough for her, were punctuated by long intervals
during which he lay down and bewailed to her his poverty and
the futility of his life. 'He said he had never been wakened up
to try to do good till he was seventy; and he said, "What would
I not give to be able to look back upon such a life as yours!"'[8]
Josephine, who as a rule was well aware of the value of her life,
was not, at that time disposed to accept such a valuation of her
own usefulness.
When, at length, she was allowed to see the near-completed
work, she was not entirely gratified by the result. She had never
suffered from false modesty regarding her looks or her appearance, and the gaunt old woman who stared away from the canvas shocked her:

I don't know what to think of it. It is rather terrible. It bears the mark of storms and conflicts and sorrow so strongly. The eyes are certainly wonderfully done. You know I have no brightness in my eyes now . . . it is not at all pretty, and the jaw and head are too strong and gaunt. I don't think my friends will like it.[9]

For all her misgivings, Watts's honesty and integrity, his refusal to flatter, impressed her: 'He reminded me of Father – a sweet courtesy and modesty, not a bit of boast about him. There is a humble Christian spirit in him. I pray God to give him more hope and light.'[10]

For Josephine herself, there was both hope and light. A few months later she received a letter from Cardinal Vaughan telling her that on a visit to the Vatican he had been informed that 'The Holy Father has made up his mind to issue such a document as you desire.' Needless to say, she was overjoyed: 'I have waited some time for the answer to my prayer and am full of thankfulness to God who has been so *mindful* of my request . . . I hardly dared to hope that He would make the Pope do this.'[11]

She even found a good word for the Pope, which, since she was replying to Cardinal Vaughan, was just as well: 'The Pope is an able man, and – I have no doubt – a true and humble Christian, *although* Pope, and God will bless him.'

When she saw the painting of her in its completed state she was undismayed. It was as though it represented another person, and she remarked buoyantly: 'When I looked at the portrait, I felt inclined to burst into tears. I felt so sorry for her.'[12]


# XXXIX

JOSEPHINE'S afflictions for that year were not over. She had removed from George's home in Wimbledon when he married Mia, and had taken a small house in Balham where she was looked after by her devoted cook-housekeeper, Annie. The winter of 1894 to 1895 was a hard one, during which the Thames was frozen over, in places as late as March. The pipes in Josephine's house were frozen up, depriving her both of hot water and of the use of her kitchen-range, so that cooking had to be done over an open fire. Annie fell ill with a severe attack of influenza, Josephine's rheumatism grew worse and, to top everything, George was thrown from his horse, fracturing his skull severely. The need to nurse Annie, to look after herself and to offer considerable moral support to Mia, who was very shaken by George's accident, precluded her from engaging in active work that winter. Despite these vicissitudes and her own weakness of physique she remained obdurately happy. God had answered her prayers to her own satisfaction and had thus restored her confidence in her belief that she was His agent.

She devoted what time she had to writing. In an article for a women's journal she summed up her own view of her experiences over the previous twelve months:

> The central truth to which I have learned to hold fast is this truth – that death must precede Resurrection; that in every cause which is truly God's cause, failures and disappointments are not only familiar things, but even necessary for the final success of the cause. *It is the lesson of the Cross.*

At the same time she engaged herself in writing a short book which was ostensibly a series of unrelated meditations on passages from the Bible, but which was in fact a discussion of the problem of evil, inspired by her own recent experiences, and embodying an apologia, always recurrent, for her concern for what seemed to her opponents to be the lowest form of female life: 'It was not with Sarah, the princess, or any other woman, but with Hagar, that ill-used slave, that the God of Heaven stooped to converse, and to whom He brought His supreme comfort and guidance.'

The sections dealing with the problem of evil, while destitute of any constructive theological solution (theology was never Josephine's strong point) nevertheless radiate an optimism which had been lacking from her writings since the death of her husband:

> God certainly suffers His children, even His highest saints, to fall now and again under the power of some of those evil

things which we recognize as having been introduced into the world as the attendants of sin and death. He allows sickness to visit them. In the prolonging of such visitations, however, he is I believe, sometimes only patiently waiting for the sufferer to claim deliverance.[3]

The conclusion to the book is a declaration of that optimistic faith which never again yielded to pessimism and carried her happily through her final years, despite bereavements and ever-increasing bouts of illness. It was in such a frame of mind that Josephine prepared herself for her last, and most ferociously embattled, continental crusade.

Everywhere the Regulationists appeared to be losing ground. Only the Russian Empire – which she held in high contempt anyway, as a Liberal for its political institutions, and as a humanitarian for the anti-semitic Black Hundreds and the pogroms in the ghettoes and the Pale – maintained a nationally controlled system of Regulation. However, Geneva, close to Josephine's heart and, ironically, the headquarters of the International Federation, showed little sign of divesting itself of its system of regulation. The time for the decisive battle had come. She had her house in Balham sold, and prepared to settle in Switzerland to await the outcome. There were practical reasons for her decision. The constitution of Geneva admitted a *Droit d'Initiative* by which any organised body of citizens could petition the Grand Council to hold a plebiscite in order to initiate legislation. In October 1895 two members of the Federation were elected to the Grand Council, and in January 1896, when the newly formed Grand Council held its first session, the question of Abolition was the first matter to be raised. Immediately the President of the Council announced that proceedings would be held in camera, and justified this unusual procedure by stating that arguments for the Abolitionist cause, if publicly reported, might tend to the corruption of youth.

The President had calculated that support for the petition would be confined to the two new Councillors and that by holding the debate in camera they would be unable to appeal to their supporters outside the chamber. In fact, they succeeded in rallying thirty previously uncommitted members to their side, a third of the members present, thus ensuring that the plebiscite would be held. It was at this point in the campaign that Josephine arrived to take up residence with a friend of twenty years standing, Mme de Gingins, who owned a château at Clarens, not far from Geneva.

From the moment of their arrival she threw herself into the fray with all her old enthusiasm – 'the smell of powder is always agreeable to one in a fight on a moral issue'.[4] As always with Josephine, it was not the permissiveness of the Genevans, the fact that 'long lines of gentlemen and their young sons are waiting every night at the doors of these palaces to get in',[5] which impelled her to anger. It was compassion for the victims of gross injustice, which inspired her magnificent wrath:

> The poor girls enslaved there are, week by week, bundled into the hospitals like damaged goods. And when they die, they are buried like dogs. They dare not give them Christian burial! Two girls committed suicide by jumping from the windows of one of these houses into a stone yard . . . I would, with all my heart, stir up a revolution here, if I could.[6]

If she did not succeed in stirring up revolution, she certainly inspired excitement. The principal newspaper of Geneva, *Le Genevois*, reported that the whole campaign was a plot by foreigners to ruin the Geneva trade Exhibition planned for that year, and that the agitators were paid by an English lady who had been sent from London 'with hundreds of pounds in her pocket'.

As Josephine herself remarked, Hell was let loose in Geneva. *Tenanciers* (licenced brothel-keepers) walked the streets brandishing revolvers, swearing that they would shoot de Meuron and Bridel, the leaders of the Abolitionist group in the Grand Council. Gangs of ruffians, predictably hired by the *tenanciers*, threatened the homes of known supporters of Abolition, and broke up meetings.

The plebiscite was fixed for Sunday, 22 March. As the day drew near, Josephine came to see it more and more as the seal on her life's work. She appealed to her supporters all over the world to celebrate Saturday the twenty-first as 'an all-day of prayer . . . If people vote right, it will be so grand for other countries. If the people vote wrong! . . . '[7] She could not bear to think of it.

The Sunday morning augured well. In brilliant sunshine and under a cloudless blue sky, Josephine went to early service in the Protestant church where she was accustomed to worship when staying in Geneva. The Pastor invited her to address a few words to the congregation, an invitation which delighted her – 'all scruples about women speaking in churches vanished like a slight cloud before the midday sun'.[8] On leaving the church she drove through the city to spend at least part of the morning taking her breakfast and walking afterwards on the bank of the river.

In the afternoon she retired to the house of a M. Favre, one of Geneva's most distinguished citizens, there to await the result of the plebiscite. Favre's home was a fortress which had belonged to his family since the fifteenth century, and had been deliberately selected by the abolitionists as their headquarters on account of its strength. The abolitionist scrutineers began coming in from the various polling-stations at seven o'clock and continued to do so until about ten. The news they brought was uniformly depressing. Fairly early on in the evening it was clear that the streets were being taken over by the *tenanciers* and their mobs; scrutineers from the outlying *arrondissements* only narrowly escaped being dragged from their horses and beaten up as they rode to the fortress. Finally de Meuron, her leading supporter in the Grand Council, arrived from the porch of the Church of La Fusterie, where all the votes had been collected and counted. The result was 8,300 for the retention of *maisons tolérées* and 4,068 for abolition. Twenty-two thousand citizens of Geneva had signed the petition to the Grand Council, but only twelve-and-a-half thousand turned out to vote. The reason was obvious. Except at the Church of La Fusterie, the police were conspicuous by their absence, and the polling-stations were almost literally besieged by gangs of the *Lampes Rouges* – the *tenanciers'* hired mobs, so-called after the red lights traditionally hung over brothel doors. There was, however, a more fundamental reason for the Abolitionist defeat which Josephine had never taken into account, and which, when it was explained to her, seemed incomprehensible to her.

The night before the poll she was taken by a Mme Rachonnet to visit the editor of the *Genevois* at his home:

> He received us with much courtesy, and even gentleness, as if grateful for our visit. We had a long conversation. . . . He said, 'But, my dear lady, what an *awful* thing, what a tyranny beyond all other tyrannies it would be, should your party triumph, to have a renewal of the ancient sumptuary discipline, of the prying into the secrets of every household and of family life! It would be the most wicked of tyrannies!'[9]

The old fear of Calvin's reign of godly terror died hard in Geneva.

In the meantime, as Josephine and her allies attempted, in prayer, to reconcile themselves to their bitter disappointment, the *tenanciers* and their *Lampes Rouges* began their triumph in the streets outside. They marched in procession, waving banners bearing the red light motif, with forests of red lamps swinging on poles, screaming, swearing and bawling out obscene songs. They took the Church of La Fusterie by storm, and there celebrated what amounted to a Black Mass – an obscene Communion, at the end of which prostitutes pronounced blessings over their red lamps in a mock consecration. They then charged about the city from one church to another, repeating their blasphemous proceedings in a crescendo of obscenity at each stopping-place. Just as bloodshed seemed inevitable, a torrential thunderstorm was let loose, inundating the streets for an hour, and forcing the *Lampes Rouges* and the aimless crowds which had joined them, to disperse. It was, Josephine decided, a sign from God. She comforted herself with the 'thought of Calvary and that profane mob around the Cross. I am sure they said, "He is dead now; we shall hear no more of Him. Now we shall have peace." But had they peace? Was He dead? Before the words were well out of their mouths, He quietly *rose again*.'[10]

In fact, her last Swiss campaign was far from lost. At the same time as the plebiscite in Geneva, the Grand Council of the Canton de Vaud voted to abolish regulation both in the canton as a whole and in the city of Lausanne. The rioting in the streets of Geneva, and the desecration of the churches, had shaken public opinion in Switzerland, if only because it had been fully reported in most of the leading newspapers throughout Europe.

'*I am glad*', wrote Josephine to her colleagues in London, 'that the gates of this inferno were thrown open, and that the results of a hundred years of government organised and protected vice have been, for once, fully revealed.'[11]

But she was not glad, for all her brave words. She was old, desperately tired and far from well. There was, moreover, no George, from whose sure and constant faith she could draw a renewal of spiritual and mental strength.

## XL

SHE had become restless and lonely, moving from lodging to lodging, and place to place, frequently travelling abroad without real purpose, writing prolifically as always. From the end of 1897 until 1900 she produced a monthly newsletter, the *Stormbell*, named after a poem by John Greenleaf Whittier:

> *The Stormbell rings – the trumpet blows;*
> *I know the word and countersign;*
> *Wherever Freedom's vanguard goes,*
> *Where stand or fall her friends or foes,*
> *I know the place that should be mine.*

It was a brave epigraph, but one scarcely borne out by the contents, which are a random and rambling anthology of autobiographical fragments, meditations and, ever increasingly, obituaries of old friends.

Bereavement had never come easily to Josephine. Friendship, and the love of friends, meant much to her, was indeed necessary to her. The two years or so covered by the *Stormbell* saw the deaths of Sir James Stansfeld, Mme de Gingins, Dr Nevins (the leader of the medical wing of the Abolitionists) and Yves Guyot. And then, in the early spring of 1900, Tell Meuricoffre, Hattie's husband, died. As soon as the news reached her she travelled to La Gardonne, the Meuricoffre's Swiss estate, to be at Hattie's side. She found her sister more reconciled to her loss than she had expected: Hattie had always been the more buoyant of the two, and, as with George, Tell's death had come as no surprise. Josephine and Hattie had always been very close to each other. Now they planned to spend much of what time they had left, together, and to Josephine, though she had always loved Tell Meuricoffre, it was something of a relief. As she was boarding the train to travel home to England, Hattie called out that she would come over as soon as she could. Would March 'be too early for me to come?' And Josephine replied, 'You can't come too early, my beloved!'

Two days later, as she stepped from the packet on to the quay at Dover, she was handed a telegram.

Hattie was dead.

Now all her 'soul-friends' – those who loved and truly understood her – were dead, with the exception of James Stuart, and even he had drifted away from her because of disagreements with her.

Old age had done nothing to blunt Josephine's ferocity when confronted with seeming injustice. In 1896, the jubilation over the conviction of Oscar Wilde filled her with disgust, and she would not have been Josephine if she had made any attempt to conceal the fact:

> I am *so sorry* for him. I dare confess it. Most people are shocked at my feeling pity for him. . . . I long to be allowed to write a letter to him in prison. I suppose he must not receive letters. I hope they will treat him mercifully. I pray for him constantly.[1]

Her advocacy of Dreyfus in 1898 would have been less scandalous; she knew and liked the Dreyfus family. Unfortunately she chose to express most forcibly her opinion on the *Affaire* – 'What an awful state France is in! What will it come to? I should not wonder to see a military dictatorship re-established'[2] – in France, and at the time of the Fashoda Incident, when anti-British feeling was at its height.

Her support for British action in South Africa in 1899, would seem, on the face of it, less than controversial. Most of her friends and allies, both in Britain and abroad, were, however, bitterly opposed to the war, seeing it as an example of that naked imperialism of which Liberals had tended to disapprove throughout the second half of the century. Nor was her attitude one which necessarily commended itself to supporters of the war. For Josephine had little sympathy with the Uitlanders, Alfred Milner's 'helots of old':

> Dr Livingstone rebuked the Boers for contemptuously calling all coloured men 'Kaffirs', to whatever race they belonged. Englishmen deserve still more such a rebuke for their habit of including all who have not European complexions under the contemptuous title of 'niggers'. Race prejudice is a poison which will have to be cast out if the world is ever to be Christianised, and if Great Britain is to maintain the high and responsible place among the nations which has been given to her.[3]

She went on to express the view that the British government should declare it to be part of its war aims to release the coloured peoples from Afrikaner bondage; to defend in South Africa 'the weak, the humble, beings demoted to degradation and contempt, and brought under oppression and servitude'. Great Britain she concluded would be 'judged, condemned, or justified', according to her treatment of coloured peoples under her sway.[4]

When her book *Native Races and the War* was published, her continental allies greeted it with horror and amazement. The views expressed in it, considering the vehement pro-Boer sentiments which were held throughout Europe, were likely to wreck both Josephine's reputation, and the Federation of which she was still the cornerstone. Her reply was as proud and as uncompromising as ever:

> In England itself, many of our Abolitionists, including some of my oldest and most valued fellow-workers, stand on a very different ground from mine in this matter. I value friendship, and I love my old friends. But I love Truth more.[5]

It was not, however, the Boers who excited her deepest passion during these last years of active life, but the Tsarist régime in Russia. Although since her childhood days at Dilston she had enjoyed friendly relations with individual Russians, the refusal of the Tsarist government either to allow the formation of a branch of the Federation in St Petersburg or Moscow, or to allow individual Russians to join the Federation, excited her particular indignation. The fact that, in Russia, women

doctors were made responsible for the examination of prostitutes – 'the preparation of poor peasant girls for the market of
vice' – exacerbated her feelings.

In 1900, a letter written by a Jewish girl, which had been
smuggled out of Russia, was given to her:

> My sister lies dead at my side, tortured and beaten to death;
> also beside me lies my father, alive and groaning, for his
> eyes were put out with hot irons. A little child of our family
> (almost a baby) was drenched with petroleum and set on
> fire, then dragged through the streets – her shrieks of pain
> drowned the oaths and laughter of the Cossacks, and the
> slashing of their whips.[6]

'I cannot weep,' commented Josephine. 'I am beyond tears.'[7]

She had never been touched with anti-Semitism. George,
when he had been alive, had always had great admiration for
Jewish scholars and ministers. For his sake, if for no better
reason, Josephine's wrath at the pogroms in the Byelo-Russian
Pale, and the emergence in Russia of the Black Hundreds, was
as violent as it was impotent. Her indignation resulted in an
untypical and sometimes irrational loathing for Russia and
Russians, which nothing, neither the pleading of one or two
Russian friends, nor her deep admiration and love for Tolstoy,
could dissipate. She was convinced that the wrath of God would
descend upon the Tsarist Empire. She sent what little money
she could afford to the Jewish Board of Guardians in London,
to assist in the settlement of Jewish refugees from Tsarist
persecution, and she begged and urged the Federation to do
what it could to help. There was little more she could have done.

Old age usually results in loneliness, to a greater or lesser extent.
With Josephine, loneliness was acute, and, having always been
a gregarious person whether in her work or her pleasures,
peculiarly difficult to bear. The will to resist the limitations old
age sought to impose on her, and the hypochondria which had
affected her all her adult life, was gone. Thirty years of over-
work and emotional tension were taking their toll unopposed.
She was dreadfully tired, never felt really well and was often
painfully, if not seriously, ill. Her sight began to deteriorate, a
terrible blow to one who loved books and was a compulsive

writer; her hands were becoming crippled with arthritis, and she could deal with her copious correspondence only with the greatest difficulty.

Patience had never been her most apparent virtue, and now her impatience turned to tetchiness. She took a strangely untypical delight in bewailing the extravagance in women's costume, at a time when ladies dressed in a style a great deal more simple and less ostentatious than that in which she had taken great delight in the heyday of her beauty. Particularly she bewailed the tendency for domestic servants to be fashionably dressed, commenting rather cattishly: 'People's maids sometimes come to me with messages, respectable girls. But, at the sight of them, I say, "Excuse me, madam, I have not your card. May I know your name?"' [8]

Nor was there any solace to be found in the churches. 'O! the Churches! They are a nightmare to me; and with all their deadness, they seem to be growing more conceited. It is always the Churches, and seldom the poor lost world outside.' [9]

Unable to take an active part in public life, she elected to retire to Cheltenham. The reasons for this extraordinary choice for her home are obscure. Her previous stay in Cheltenham had not been particularly fortunate. Perhaps she associated the town with her life with George. Perhaps it was because Eva had been buried there: Eva, whose memory had haunted her throughout her life. Perhaps it was an old lady's attempt to mitigate the loneliness of the present with a dream of the past.

Whatever the reasons it proved an unhappy choice. She knew nobody, and remained unknown, save by reputation. The atmosphere of priggish respectability she found stifling, as she had found it stifling forty-five years before. One incident kindled the old fire in her. By some extraordinary chance the rooms below her own were taken by a young, fashionable prostitute, who pursued her trade there, albeit with the discretion of a *demi-mondaine*. This met with little approval on the part of the neighbours – understandably one might have thought – and they put pressure on Josephine's landlady to dismiss the more disreputable of her two tenants. A round robin was circulated to this effect. Josephine refused to sign it (as did Fanny Duberley, that astonishing heroine of the Crimean War, who, unknown to Josephine, was a close neighbour). As the girl left,

Josephine 'watched the gay, graceful creature from the window', with something very close to regret. 'I was not well enough to go to her then,' she added sadly. She discovered later that the girl was in a brothel, 'patronised by gentlemen, and as fenced and protected as a maison tolérée abroad'.[10]

The respectable citizens of Cheltenham did not object to the presence of a brothel in their midst, where girls could be exploited. The presence of a single girl, quietly and unobtrusively following her trade, was what had excited their indignation.

'In my end is my beginning' – Josephine's attempts to persuade the clergy of Cheltenham to initiate a campaign against the sexual double standard as practised in the town, and to fight against the conditions in which the poor were forced to exist, met with as little sympathy as had her similar attempts among the divines of Oxford in the 1850s. But then she had been a girl in her early twenties; now she was an old lady of seventy-five, and confined to her room for long periods of time.

At the beginning of 1903, she finally surrendered to the ill-health which had begun to plague her incessantly. She decided to spend what time was left to her in the peace of her own home-land. In an invalid carriage, accompanied by her maid, Mary, she travelled to Wooler, near Ewart Park, the home of her eldest son, where, from the windows of her lodgings, she could look over Milfield in Glendale, her old, ancestral home, and beyond to her beloved Cheviot Hills. There she was among her own people. There she found the quiet joy which she had been seeking since the débâcle of her hopes in Geneva, since, perhaps, the death of George. Friends, and old retainers of the Grey estates, were only too ready to watch over her, to serve her and to look after her; the wives of neighbouring tradespeople were willing to read to her, and to write letters at her dictation.

Although she was in continual pain, she was happy. The impatience, irritation and restlessness of the past three or four years melted away in the love with which she was received in Wooler. She told her grandson, who had been studying Cicero's 'De Senectute' at school, that she did not find old age and invalidism irksome, rather she took pleasure in it as a preliminary rest after so long a struggle:

Now, if I lie awake in the night, I feel I am not obliged to get up in the morning and can sleep all day if I want to. I turn on my side and *rest*, then turn on my other side and rest again, and *laugh* for joy at the thought that good Mary will bring me a cup of tea in the morning, and that I shall have breakfast in bed! Florence Nightingale is still alive, and *she* has been in bed for *seven years*. Surely I may be permitted to live in mine for seven weeks – or even until the whole spring is past![11]

Those who visited her, her grandchildren and their school-friends, remembered, half-a-century later, not merely 'the tiny figure with wrinkled ivory skin, stretched, as it seemed, straight over the bones', but more significantly, 'the beautiful and serene face, with the vital intensity of the eyes'.[12]

Her interest in world affairs was undiminished. The defeat of Russia in Manchuria, and the humiliating surrender of Port Arthur to the Japanese, combined with the sporadic outbreak of what has come to be known as the 1905 Revolution, filled her with what was, but for the religiosity of her language, unholy glee:

> Behind and beyond all the calculations of some pro-Russian people, there is an infinite Divine Power – the power of Jehovah who, long ago, gave the Israelites victories by a handful of men over countless hosts, all in order to *teach* the nations, by His love and His justice towards the weak, and His sternness towards the proud and greedy.[13]

The fact that there were perfectly sound strategic and logistical reasons for the Japanese victory over the Russians worried Josephine not one whit.

But Russia had a trick to play against Josephine – at least in her own estimation. In 1906 winter came early and with great severity. With the bitter winds from the East came an influenza epidemic, which Josephine believed was blown directly from St Petersburg. Her family, and many of her friends at Wooler, succumbed to the virus; at Christmas she was forced to take to her bed for the last time. She continued to dictate letters, one to de Meuron, begging him to continue the struggle in Geneva, one to her future biographer, G. W. Johnson, in which she prophesied that the new Liberal administration would run into trouble over Irish Home Rule. She received a letter from the Chief Rabbi, which moved her deeply, thanking her for her public expressions of concern about the continued persecutions of Russian Jewry – 'Your sympathy is a true solace to me in these days of sore stress and sorrow.'[14]

As the old year drew to its end, and the fierce winds drove flurries of snow in from Lindisfarne and the Holy Isle, Josephine's breathing became more difficult. She knew she was dying, and though in great discomfort, was cheerfully reconciled to the fact. On the night of 29 December 1906 she called her maid, Mary, to her bedside, thanked her for her loyal and devoted service and bade her goodbye. Then she lay back on the pillows, and waited patiently for the Lord Jesus in whom she had always so entirely believed, to lead her out through the curtain of pain so that she might join all those who had promised to prepare a place for her: the child-prostitute who had died in her arms ('When I get to Heaven, I will be very busy – I will ask for a place to be got ready for Mrs Butler – I will see to it'); little Eva ('Mummy, when the door of Heaven opens to let you in, I will run so fast to meet you!'); and George, always George – loving, kind, patient George, without whom there could be no perfect happiness.

# NOTE ON SOURCES

THE vast majority of Josephine Butler's manuscript letters and journals, etc., which have survived are in the possession of the Josephine Butler Society. A further collection, the property until his death of A. S. G. Butler and consisting largely of her letters to Stanley Butler and to Fanny Forsaith, the friend and confidante of her final years, is now in the possession of the University Library, St Andrews.

A comprehensive – and, as far as I have been able to establish, complete – collection of her published works is to be found in the Fawcett Library, Westminster, where also may be found sets of the religious or abolitionist periodicals – the *Shield*, the *Bee-hive*, *Wings*, the *Stormbell*, etc. – to which she was such a prolific contributor.

Previous biographers of Josephine Butler gave been handicapped by the injunction which she laid upon her descendants and friends who survived her that they should do all in their power to prevent any attempt at a biography. Two works, however, are of some value. W. T. Stead's *Josephine Butler; a Life-Sketch*, written in 1886 while its author was in prison, is an example of Stead at his most fulsome and verbose. At the same time it is based entirely on materials provided by Josephine and can be taken to be the nearest thing we have to an 'authorised' biography. A. S. G. Butler's *Portrait of Josephine Butler* was the first biography to be written in defiance of the ban, but was based solely on those materials the author had in his personal possession; nor is it intended to be taken as a full account of her life and career. During the first eighteen years of his life, however, A. S. G. Butler grew very close to his grandmother, closer, indeed, than any other members of his family – he was its sole representative at her funeral in Kirknewton churchyard, on 3 January 1907. He is therefore a unique witness to the closing period of her life.

# BIBLIOGRAPHY

## A. Josephine E. Butler's published writings

*Works marked with an asterisk are pamphlets*

The Education and Employment of Women (Macmillan, 1868).
Woman's Work and Woman's Culture, Introduction (Macmillan, 1869).
Memoir of John Grey of Dilston (Edmonston & Douglas, Edinburgh, 1869).
*An Appeal to The People of England on the Recognition and Super-intendence of Prostitution by Governments (Banks, Nottingham, 1870).
*On the Moral Reclaimability of Prostitutes (National Association, 1870).
The Duty of Women (Hudson Scott, Carlisle, 1870).
Sursum Corda (Brakell, Liverpool, 1871).
*The Constitutional Iniquity of the C.D. Acts (Bradford, 1871).
*Address in Craigie Hall, Edinburgh (Ireland, Manchester, 1871).
*Address at Croydon (National Association, 1871).
*Letter to the Order of Good Templars (Brakell, Liverpool, 1871).
Vox Populi (Brakell, Liverpool, 1871).
The Constitution Violated (Edmonston & Douglas, Edinburgh, 1871).
The New Era (Brakell, Liverpool, 1872).
*Letter on the Subject of Mr. Bruce's Bill (Brakell, Liverpool, 1872).
*A Few Words Addressed to True-Hearted Women (n.p., 1872?).
*Legislative Restrictions on the Industry of Women (Personal Rights Association, 1873).
*Letter to a Friend on a Recent Division in the House of Commons (Brakell, Liverpool, 1873).
*Speech at Bristol to the Vigilance Association (F. Bell & Co., 1874).
Some Thoughts on the Present Aspect of the Crusade (Brakell, Liverpool, 1874).
*Letter to the L.N.A. (Brakell, Liverpool, 1875).
Une Voix dans le desert (Sandoz, Paris and Neuchâtel, 1875).
*State Regulation of Vice (n.p., 1876).
The Hour Before the Dawn (Trübner, 1876).
*Discours Prononcé a l'Hôtel Wagram (Paris, 1877).
*Discours Prononcé dans la salle de la rue d'Arras (Paris, 1877).
*Discours Prononcé dans la Chapelle Malesherbes (Paris, 1877).
*Discours prononcé dans la salle de la Redoute (Paris, 1877).

*The Paris of Regulated Vice (Methodist Press, 1877).
Adieux à Genève (Geneva, 1877).
Ceux qui prient (Paris, 1878).
Catherine of Siena (Dyer Bros, 1878).
Government by Police (Dyer Bros, 1879).
Social Purity (Morgan & Scott, London, 1879).
*Souvenir des Réunions à Vevey (Fontaines, 1879).
Deposition Regarding Treatment of English Girls in Immoral Houses
    in Brussels (Printed for private circulation, 1880).
*Extrait d'une lettre a l'occasion des investigations de M. X. a Bruxelles
    (Neuchâtel, 1880).
*Address at the Tenth Anniversary of the L.N.A. (Brakell, Liverpool,
    1880).
*A Call to Action (Hudson, Birmingham, 1881).
*Address at the Conference of Women at Geneva (Hazell, Watson &
    Viney, 1881).
Letter to the Mothers of England (Brakell, Liverpool, 1881).
*Lettre d'une mère (Neuchâtel, 1881).
*Lettre à ses amis et compagnons d'œuvre (Neuchâtel, 1882).
*Discours d'Adieux à la Conférence de Neuchâtel (Neuchâtel, 1882).
Life of J. F. Oberlin (Religious Tract Society, 1882).
The Salvation Army in Switzerland (Dyer Bros, 1883).
*Dangers of Constructive Legislation in Matters of Purity (Arrowsmith,
    Bristol, 1883).
The Bright Side of the Question (Arrowsmith, Bristol, 1883).
*Questions morales (Lausanne, 1883).
Le Point de jour: discours à La Haye (Neuchâtel, 1883).
*Allocution aux Femmes de Gènes (Neuchâtel, 1883).
The Principles of the Abolitionists (Dyer Bros, 1885).
The Work of the Federation (Federation Offices, 1885).
Marion, histoire véritable (Neuchâtel, 1885).
Rebecca Jarrett (Morgan & Scott, 1886).
L'Œuvre du relèvement moral (Geneva, 1886).
*Our Christianity Tested by the Irish Question (Fisher Unwin, 1887).
The Revival and Extension of the Abolitionist Cause (Doswell, Win-
    chester, 1887).
*Letter to the International Convention of Women at Washington
    (Morgan & Scott, 1888).
*Zwei Vorträge über das Staatlich Regulierte Laster (Mülheim, 1888).
The Dawn, quarterly (Burfoot, 1888–96).
'Women's Place in Church Work', Review of the Churches, 1892.
Recollections of George Butler (Arrowsmith, Bristol, 1892).
*Letter to the World's Women's Christian Temperance Union (Bristol,
    1892).

*St Agnes* (J. Cox, 1893).
*The Present Aspect of the Abolitionist Cause in Relation to British India* (Federation Offices, 1893).
*The Lady of Shunem* (Horace Marshall, 1894).
*\*The Constitutional Iniquity* (Federation Offices, 1895).
*\*Lettre à Madame Duplan* (Lausanne, 1895).
*\*Two Letters of Earnest Appeal and Warning* (Federation Offices, 1896).
*A Doomed Iniquity* (Federation Offices, 1896).
*\*Address to the L.N.A.* (Arrowsmith, Bristol, 1896).
*Personal Reminiscences of a Great Crusade* (Horace Marshall, 1896).
*Truth Before Everything* (Dyer Bros, 1896).
*Some Lessons from Contemporary History* (Friends' Association, 1898).
*The Stormbell,* monthly (Burfoot, 1898–1900).
*Prophets and Prophetesses* (Mawson, Newcastle, 1898).
*Native Races and the War* (Gay & Bird, 1900).
*Silent Victories* (Burfoot, 1900).
*In Memoriam Harriet Meuricoffre* (Horace Marshall, 1901).
*\*The Morning Cometh* (Grierson, Newcastle, 1903).


# B. Works by Josephine Butler's contemporaries

ACTON, WILLIAM, *Prostitution Considered in its Moral, Social, and Sanitary Aspects* (2nd ed., revised, 1869).
AMOS, SHELDON, *The Contagious Diseases Acts* (William Ridgway, 1876).
BESANT, ANNIE, *The Legalisation of Female Slavery in England* (Annie Besant & Charles Bradlaugh, 1876).
BOREL, T., trans. Joseph Edmondson, *The White Slavery of Europe* (Dyer Bros, n.d., 1876?).
BUTLER, GEORGE, *The Higher Education of Women* (Brakell, Liverpool, 1867).
CHADWICK, EDWIN, ed. M. W. Flinn, *Report on the Sanitary Condition of the Labouring Population of Great Britain* (Edinburgh U. P., 1964).
DAUBIE, JULIE, *La Femme pauvre au dix-neuvième siècle* (Ernest Thorin, Paris, 1869).
DYER, ALFRED, *Facts Are Stubborn Things; a Selection of Cases Illustrative of the Working of The Contagious Diseases Acts* (Dyer Bros, n.d., 1876?).
— *The European Slave Trade in English Girls* (Dyer Bros, 1880).

DYER, ALFRED, *Six Years' Labour and Sorrow; The Fourth Report of the London Committee for Suppressing the Traffic in British Girls for Purposes of Continental Prostitution* (Dyer Bros, 1885).

GOFF, A., *History of the Contagious Diseases Acts* (Moral Reform Union, 1892).

GUYOT, YVES, *Prostitution Under the Regulation System; a Study in Social Physiology* (George Redway, 1884).

HILL, BERKELEY, *Report on the Operation of the Contagious Diseases Acts* (Association for the Promotion of the Contagious Diseases Acts, 1875).

KINGSFORD, DOUGLAS, *A Critical Summary of the Evidence Before the Royal Commissi.* ʾ *upon the Contagious Diseases Acts* ('Kingsford's Summary'), (Tweedie & Co., 1872).

MAYHEW, HENRY, *London Labour and London Poor;* add. vol. IV (Dover Paperbacks, 1969).

NEVINS, BIRKBECK, *Moral, Constitutional, and Sanitary Objections To the Contagious Diseases Acts; including the Case of Caroline Wyburgh of Chatham* (Riby & Russell, Liverpool, 1873?).

PARENT-DUCHÂTELET, A. J. B., *De la Prostitution dans la ville de Paris, considérée sous le rapport de l'hygiène publique, de la morale, et de l'administration*, 3rd ed., revised (Paris, 1857).

SCOTT, BENJAMIN, *Is London More Immoral than Paris or Brussels?* (Dyer Bros, 1881).

STANSFELD, JAMES, *The Validity of the Annual Government Statistics of the Operation of the Contagious Diseases Acts* (Statistical Society, 1876).

STUART, JAMES, *Reminiscences* (printed for private circulation, 1911).

'WALTER', ed. Ebhart and Kronhausen, *My Secret Life* (1969).

WAUGH, BENJAMIN, *William T. Stead; a Life for the People* (Vickers, 1885).

WILSON, H. J. and GLEDSTONE, J. P., *Report of a Visit to the United States* (Leader & Sons, Sheffield, 1876).

WILSON, ROBERT, *Prostitution Suppressible, and Resistance to the Contagious Diseases Acts a Duty* (S. W. Partridge, 1871).

ZOLA, EMILE, *Nana* (Folio Society, 1956).

## C. State Papers

Reports of Inspectors of Factories, for the year ending 1 October 1864.
Children's Employment Commission Reports, 1864, etc.

Commission on the Employment of Children, Young Persons, and
Women in Agriculture, 1867 – 1st and 6th reports.
Select Committee of the House of Lords on the Contagious Diseases
Acts (1867–8).
Royal Commission on the Contagious Diseases Acts (1871).
Select Committee of the House of Commons on the Contagious
Diseases Acts (1879–81).
Select Committee of the House of Lords, to enquire into the law
relating to the protection of young girls (1881–2).

# D. Biographies of Josephine Butler

BELL, E. MOBERLY, *Josephine Butler, Flame of Fire* (Constable,
1962).
BUTLER, A. S. G., *Portrait of Josephine Butler* (Faber, 1954).
FAWCETT, MILLICENT and TURNER, E. M., *Josephine Butler:
Her Work, Principles, and their Meaning for the Twentieth Century*
(Association for Moral and Social Hygiene, 1927).
HAY-COOPER, L., *Josephine Butler, and her Work for Social
Purity* (S.P.C.K., 1922).
HOLMES, MARION, *Josephine Butler, a Cameo Life-Sketch* (Women's
Freedom League, 1911).
JOHNSON, G. W. and L. A., *Josephine E. Butler, an Autobiographi-
cal Memoir* (Arrowsmith, 1909).
STEAD, W. T., *Josephine Butler; a Life-Sketch* (Morgan & Scott,
1887).

# E. Other works consulted

BENJAMIN, H., and MASTERS, R. E. L., *The Prostitute in Society*
(Mayflower-Dell, 1966).
COLLIER, RICHARD, *The General Next to God, the Story of William
Booth and the Salvation Army* (Fontana, 1968).
COMFORT, ALEX, *The Anxiety Makers* (Panther, 1968).
HAMMOND, J. L. and BARBARA, *James Stansfeld; a Victorian
Champion of Sex Equality* (Longman, 1932).
HENRIQUES, FERNANDO, *Prostitution and Society*, 3 vols (Mac-
Gibbon & Kee, 1963).
MARCUS, STEVEN, *The Other Victorians* (Weidenfeld & Nicolson,
1966).

MORTON, R. S., *Venereal Diseases* (Penguin Books, 1966).
PEARSALL, RONALD, *The Worm in the Bud, the World of Victorian Sexuality* (Weidenfeld & Nicolson, 1969).
ROLPH, C. H. ed., *Women of the Streets* (Society for Social and Biological Research, 1955).
STAFFORD, ANN, *The Age of Consent* (Hodder & Stoughton, 1964).
TERROT, CHARLES, *The Maiden Tribute, a Study of The White Slave Traffic in the Nineteenth Century* (F. Muller, 1959).

# REFERENCES

## CHAPTER ONE

[1] 27 Vict. cap. 35.
[2] G. M. Young (ed.), *Early Victorian England* (1934) i. 350.
[3] Mayhew, iv 'Soldiers' Women'.
[4] Ibid.
[5] 29 Vict. cap. 35.
[6] Zola, *Nana* 216.
[7] *Daily News*, 30 March 1875; *An Address to Working Men and Women, relative to a Distressing Case of Suicide at Aldershot* (Westminster, 1875).
[8] *Daily Telegraph*, 15 March 1875.
[9] *Pall Mall Gazette*, 3 March 1870.
[10] J.E.B., journal (undated and unpublished, presumably 1869–70) see *Recollections of George Butler* 218.
[11] Quoted by Stead, *Josephine Butler* 54.
[12] Stafford, *Age of Consent*, 24.
[13] R. A. Butler, in Bell, *Josephine Butler*, 7.
[14] Benjamin Jowett to Florence Nightingale, December 1869; see Chapter Three, note 5.
[15] A. B. Hopkins, *Elizabeth Gaskell: Her Life and Works* (1952) 126, also see Pope-Hennessy *Canon Charles Kingsley* (1948) 123.

## CHAPTER TWO

[1] For this and other references to John Grey in this chapter, see J.E.B., *Memoir of John Grey*.
[2] Butler, *Portrait* 38.
[3] J.E.B., *In Memoriam Harriet Meuricoffre* 2.
[4] Ibid. 6.
[5] J.E.B. to Stanley Butler, 1898.
[6] Butler, *Portrait* 35. This account of the Dipton Wood incident, related by Josephine to her grandson and recorded by him in his biography of her, is the only one left to us. She had always been very reluctant to talk about it, even to her closest and dearest friends.
[7] J.E.B. to Fanny Forsaith, 1900.
[8] J.E.B., *The Hour Before The Dawn* (1882 ed.) 96.
[9] J.E.B. to Fanny Forsaith, 1906.
[10] J.E.B. to her grandchildren, December 1906.
[11] J.E.B. to Stanley Butler, 1898.

## CHAPTER THREE

[1] Virtually the whole of this chapter is based on J.E.B., *Recollections of George Butler* 19–129.
[2] George Butler to J.E.B., 13 July 1856.
[3] J.E.B. to Stanley Butler, 1904.
[4] J.E.B. to John Grey, 1853.
[5] Benjamin Jowett to Florence Nightingale, December 1869. Josephine had written to Florence Nightingale via their mutual friend, Agnes Jones, soliciting her support for a declaration of protest against the Contagious Diseases Acts which was to be published in the *Daily News* (see Chapter Nine). Florence Nightingale wrote to Jowett, seeking his advice on

the matter. Jowett replied, advising her to have nothing to, do with Josephine, though he conceded that she was 'touched with genius'. Florence Nightingale ignored his advice.
⁶ Ibid.

## CHAPTER FOUR

¹ J.E.B., *Recollections of George Butler* 141.
² This account of Eva's death and its aftermath is taken from J.E.B., *Recollections of George Butler* 152–60.
³ Quoted by J.E.B., *In Memoriam Harriet Meuricoffre* 105.
⁴ J.E.B., *Recollections of George Butler* 183.

## CHAPTER FIVE

¹ See J.E.B., *Memoir of John Grey* 288 ff.
² J.E.B., *Recollections of George Butler* 184.
³ Ibid.
⁴ See Butler, *Portrait* 55.
⁵ J.E.B., *Recollections of George Butler* 185.
⁶ Johnson, *Josephine E. Butler* 47.
⁷ J.E.B., *Recollections of George Butler* 187.
⁸ Ibid. 186.
⁹ J.E.B., *Recollections of George Butler* 189–94.
¹⁰ J.E.B. to Fanny Forsaith, undated – 1893?

## CHAPTER SIX

¹ Quoted by Mary Agnes Hamilton, *Newnham, an Informal Biography* (1937) 69.
² David Masson in *Macmillan's Magazine*, October 1867.
³ 'ᾗ καὶ τὴν ἐμὴν ψυκὴν ὀφέιλω': dedication of *St. Paul* by Frederic W. H. Myers (1867). In his preface to *Fragments of Prose and Poetry* (1904), F. W. H. Myers amplified this statement. 'Christian conversion came to me in a potent form, through the agency of Josephine Butler . . . She introduced me to Christianity, so to say, through an inner door; not to its encumbering forms and dogmas, but to its heart of fire.'
⁴ Stuart, *Reminiscences* 180.
⁵ George Butler, *The Higher Education of Women* 35–6.
⁶ See Johnson, *Josephine E. Butler* 57.
⁷ Stuart, *Reminiscences* 181–2; also B. A. Clough, *Memoir of Anne J. Clough* (Edward Arnold, 1903) 129.
⁸ J.E.B. to F. Harrison, 9 May 1868.
⁹ J.E.B. to Albert Rutson, 23 May 1868.
¹⁰ See Stead, *Josephine Butler* 40.
¹¹ J.E.B. to Albert Rutson, 5 March 1868. Albert Rutson, whom she had met during her visit to Cambridge, was shortly to become P.P.S. to H. A. Bruce, Home Secretary in Gladstone's first administration, and author of 'Mr Bruce's Bill'. Josephine's relations with her 'darling Albert', like her relations with Frederic Myers, James Stuart, Sir James Stansfeld and, later, Yves Guyot, were undoubtedly closer than was usual in middle-class circles

in mid-Victorian England. They
did not, however, warrant the
description 'equivocal' which
has been applied to them by a
recent author.

12 Ibid.
13 J.E.B. to Albert Rutson, 22
February 1868.

14 Ibid.
15 J.E.B. to Albert Rutson, 7
May 1868.
16 J.E.B. to F. Harrison, 9 May
1868.
17 J.E.B., *Woman's Work and
Woman's Culture*, Introduction.
18 Ibid.

## CHAPTER SEVEN

1 Mayhew ix 'Seclusives, or Those
that Live in Private Houses
and Apartments'.
2 *Household Words*, 1857, quoted
by Peter Quennell *London's
Underworld* 21.
3 Quoted by Marcus, *The Other
Victorians* 99.
4 Ibid. 100.
5 Taine, *Notes on England*, trans.
Edward Hyams (1957).
6 Marcus 106–10.
7 Children's Employment Commission, 4th Report (1865) 271.
8 Ibid. 91.
9 Elizabeth Gaskell, *Mary Barton*
(1848) Chapter X.
10 Factory Inspectors' Reports for
half-year ending 31 October
1864 90.
11 See Chadwick, *Report* 190–204.
12 Ibid.
13 Ibid. 104–5.
14 Report on Agricultural Gangs;
Children's Employment Commission, 6th Report (1867) 83–4.

15 Quoted by Marcus 137.
16 Children's Employment Commission, 6th Report (1867) 147.
17 Quoted by Marcus 135.
18 Children's Employment Commission, 2nd Report (1864) 94.
In fact, the assistant commissioner, Mr H. W. Lord, who
recorded this statement, was
deceived. 'Madame Elise's Establishment' was a centre of
West End prostitution (see
Terrot, *The Maiden Tribute* 33).
The statement was, no doubt,
representative of the view of
Madame Elise's more reputable
neighbours in Regent Street.
19 Ibid. 119.
20 Andrew Wynter, *Our Social
Bees, or Pictures of Town and
Country Life* (1869) 272.
21 Emily Faithfull, in the *Victoria
Magazine*, July 1872.
22 *Saturday Review*, 12 November
1859.

## CHAPTER EIGHT

1 William Acton, *The Function
and Disorders of the Reproductive Organs, in Childhood, Youth,
Adult Age, and Advanced Life*,
6th edition (1875) 143.
2 Ibid.

3 Quoted by Marcus 112.
4 W. E. H. Lecky, *History of
European Morals*, 10th edition
(1892) ii 283.
5 J. E. Forster, *The Divorce Court*
(1888) 25.

## CHAPTER NINE

1 J.E.B., *Recollections of George
Butler* 218.

2 Ibid. 218.
3 Quoted by J.E.B., *Personal*

*Reminiscences of a Great Crusade* (1896) 8–10.

[4] J.E.B., *Recollections of George Butler* 219.

[5] See Pearsall, *The Worm in The Bud* chap. 3, note 22. Millicent Fawcett, in Fawcett and Turner, *Josephine Butler* 29, tells how in 1927 she met Katherine Furze, Symonds's daughter, who related to her the extraordinary effect Josephine had had upon her father.

[6] J.E.B., *Recollections of George Butler* 218.

[7] J.E.B. to Daniel Cooper, September 1869.

[8] Quoted by J.E.B., *Personal Reminiscences of a Great Crusade* 14.

[9] J.E.B., *Recollections of George Butler* 219–20.

[10] J.E.B., *An Appeal to the People of England*.

[11] J.E.B., *The Duty of Women*.

[12] *Daily News*, 1 January 1870. It was published over the signatures of, among others, Mary Carpenter, Harriet Martineau and Florence Nightingale.

[13] Lujo Bassermann, *The Oldest Profession* (1967).

[14] Henriques, iii.

[15] J.E.B., *Social Purity*.

[16] Ibid.

[17] Ibid.

[18] J.E.B., *On the Moral Reclaimability of Prostitutes*, delivered at the Freemason's Tavern, Manchester, 6 May 1870.

[19] Ibid.

[20] J.E.B. to Albert Rutson, 23 May 1868.

[21] J.E.B., *Personal Reminiscences of a Great Crusade* 43–54. See also, Stead, *Josephine Butler* 51–5.

[22] J.E.B. reported by Wilson, *Prostitution Suppressible* 41–2.

[23] See Frederic Wheeler, *An Authenticated and Shocking History of the Working of The Contagious Diseases Acts* (1876). Also, House of Commons Report on the operation of the Contagious Diseases Acts: evidence taken on 3 April 1873. This contains an account of the Caroline Wyburgh case given by the supervising Examining Surgeon of 'Lock' Hospitals, W. H. Sloggett. Mr Sloggett concluded his statement by declaring that he believed that if the methods used in the Caroline Wyburgh case were not generally employed, 'women would not come for medical examination'.

[24] See note 22 above.

[25] J.E.B. 'to the ladies who signed the memorial', 27 May 1870.

CHAPTER TEN

[1] Royal Commission on the Contagious Diseases Acts (1871), Q. 10, 717.

[2] Ibid. Q. 961.

[3] Ibid. Q. 3,250.

[4] A. J. Mundella, *Address to the Social Sciences Congress at Leeds*, October 1870.

[5] Royal Commission, Q. 20,359.

[6] Ibid. Q. 20,358.

[7] Quoted by Birkbeck Nevins, *An Address to Members of the American Legislature and Medical Opinion, on Recent Proposals to Introduce the System of Regulating or Licensing Prostitution into the United States* (1877) 50.

[8] Quoted by J.E.B., *Vox Pupuli* 34–5.

⁹ J.E.B. to George Butler, 19 March 1871.
¹⁰ Josephine's examination and evidence taken from Royal Commission, twenty-eighth day (18 March 1871) Q. 12,841–13,115.
¹¹ Peter Rylands, M.P., to George Butler, 21 March 1871.
¹² Report of the Royal Commission, section 54.
¹³ Ibid., section 66.
¹⁴ Ibid., section 56.
¹⁵ J.E.B., *Sursum Corda* 23–4.
¹⁶ Ibid. 25.

CHAPTER ELEVEN

¹ This chapter is based largely upon a thirty-five page draft of a letter dated 12 March 1872, in which Josephine explained her objections to 'Mr Bruce's Bill'. The letter is addressed to 'the repealers of the Contagious Diseases Acts'.
² J.E.B., *Recollections of George Butler* 238.
³ J.E.B. to the Liverpool branch of the Repeal Association, 18 March 1872.

CHAPTER TWELVE

¹ J.E.B., *The New Era* 4.
² Ibid. 5.
³ Ibid. 9.
⁴ Ibid. 15.
⁵ Ibid. 16.
⁶ Ibid. 16.
⁷ Ibid. 23–4.
⁸ Ibid. 25.
⁹ Ibid.
¹⁰ *Lancet*, 17 February 1872.
¹¹ *Shield*, 13 July 1872.

CHAPTER THIRTEEN

¹ J.E.B., *Personal Reminiscences* 85.
² Ibid. 85.
³ *Times*, 13 August 1872.
⁴ J.E.B., *Personal Reminiscences* 86.
⁵ *Sheffield Independent*, 14 August 1872.
⁶ J.E.B., *Personal Reminiscences* 88.
⁷ *Northern Echo*, 13 August 1872.
⁸ Stead, *Josephine Butler* 59–63.
⁹ *Times*, 16 August 1872.
¹⁰ *Manchester Examiner*, 16 August 1872.
¹¹ *Saturday Review*, 12 August 1872.

CHAPTER FOURTEEN

¹ J.E.B., *Stormbell*, March 1899.
² Ibid.
³ J.E.B., *Personal Reminiscences* 37.
⁴ Terrot, *The Maiden Tribute* 63–4.
⁵ Stuart, *Reminiscences* 237.
⁶ J.E.B., *Recollections of George Butler* 341.
⁷ J.E.B. to George Butler, March 1878.
⁸ J.E.B., *Recollections of George Butler* 342.
⁹ J.E.B. to George Butler, 31 December 1869.
¹⁰ J.E.B., *Recollections of George Butler* 241.

[11] Fawcett and Turner, *Josephine Butler* 17.
[12] J.E.B., *Recollections of George Butler* 64.
[13] Ibid. 263–4.
[14] Quoted by Stuart, *Reminiscences* 232.
[15] Ibid.

### CHAPTER FIFTEEN

[1] Stuart, *Reminiscences* 221.
[2] J.E.B., *Recollections of George Butler* 271.
[3] Quoted by J.E.B., ibid. 272.
[4] J.E.B. to George Butler, 24 May 1876.
[5] J.E.B. to Stanley Butler, December 1905.
[6] J.E.B., *Personal Reminiscences* 117.
[7] J.E.B. to George Butler, *undated*, 1874.
[8] J.E.B. to George Butler, 17 October 1874.
[9] Quoted by J.E.B., *Personal Reminiscences* 118.

### CHAPTER SIXTEEN

[1] J.E.B. to Edith Leupold, April 1875, on which I have relied for information regarding Josephine's intervention in the case. The account of the inquest on Mrs Percy is taken from the full transcript of the proceedings published in *Sheldrake's Aldershot and Sandhurst Military Gazette*, 3 April 1875, and from the account printed in the *Daily News*, 30 March 1875.
[2] *Daily News*, as above.
[3] J.E.B., *Personal Reminiscences* 199.
[4] J.E.B., *Recollections of George Butler*, 237.
[5] Ibid.

### CHAPTER SEVENTEEN

[1] Henry Wilson to members of the Repeal Association, undated – presumably May 1875.
[2] J.E.B. to Henry Wilson, undated – June 1875?
[3] Report of the International Medical Congress, Vienna (1873) 49.
[4] Quoted (by James Stuart?), *The New Abolitionists* (1876) 4.
[5] Quoted by J.E.B., *Recollections of George Butler* 282.

### CHAPTER EIGHTEEN

[1] Guyot, *Prostitution under the Regulation System* 74.
[2] Ibid. 78.
[3] Ibid. 98.
[4] Ibid. 98.
[5] Ibid. 91.
[6] Ibid. 92.
[7] Ibid. 102.
[8] Ibid. 88.

### CHAPTER NINETEEN

[1] J.E.B. to George Butler, 13 December 1874.
[2] *De Regimine Principum*, trans. I. T. Eschmann (Toronto, 1949) iv 14.
[3] J.E.B. to Sir James Stansfeld, 20 December 1874.
[4] Ibid.
[5] Quoted by J.E.B., *Recollections of George Butler* 284.
[6] J.E.B. to George Butler, 16 February 1875.
[7] J.E.B. to George Butler, 16 December 1874.

## CHAPTER TWENTY

[1] Josephine wrote and published several accounts of her interview with Lecour and the events which led up to it. The version given here is based primarily on a long letter to Sir James Stansfeld, written while Josephine was holidaying at Antibes a few days after the events described, and dated 1 January 1875.

## CHAPTER TWENTY-ONE

[1] J.E.B. to Sir James Stansfeld, 1 January 1875.
[2] J.E.B. to Joseph Edmondson, 7 February 1875.
[3] J.E.B., *Recollections of George Butler*, 287.
[4] J.E.B. to Joseph Edmondson, 7 February 1875.
[5] Ibid.

## CHAPTER TWENTY-TWO

[1] Butler, *Portrait* 119.
[2] J.E.B. to Joseph Edmondson, 7 February 1875.
[3] J.E.B. to George Butler, 10 February 1875.
[4] J.E.B. to Joseph Edmondson, 7 February 1875.
[5] Borel, *White Slavery* 20.
[6] Ibid. 21.
[7] J.E.B. to Harriet Meuricoffre, 5 February 1875.
[8] J.E.B., *Personal Reminiscences* 159.
[9] Ibid. 164-5.

## CHAPTER TWENTY-THREE

[1] J.E.B., *Personal Reminiscences* 165.
[2] J.E.B. to George Butler, 15 February 1875.
[3] Ibid.
[4] Ibid.
[5] J.E.B. to Joseph Edmondson, 17 February 1875.
[6] J.E.B., quoted (by James Stuart?), *The New Abolitionists* 94.
[7] J.E.B. to Joseph Edmondson, 17 February 1875.
[8] See Guyot, *Prostitution* 217-29.
[9] J.E.B. to Sir James Stansfeld, 17 February 1875.
[10] J.E.B. to George Butler, 16 February 1875.

## CHAPTER TWENTY-FOUR

[1] J.E.B., *The Hour Before the Dawn* 35.
[2] Ibid. 34.
[3] Ibid. 95.
[4] J.E.B., *Catherine of Siena* 332.
[5] Ibid. 328.
[6] J.E.B. to Harriet Meuricoffre, 13 August 1876.
[7] J.E.B. to Charles Butler, dated 'The Molt', August 1878.
[8] J.E.B., *Personal Reminiscences* 235.

## CHAPTER TWENTY-FIVE

[1] J.E.B., *Personal Reminiscences* 236.
[2] Guyot, *Prostitution* 290.
[3] *Droits de l'Homme*, 2 November 1876.
[4] For accounts of the trial of

Yves Guyot see Guyot, *Prostitution* 290–92, and J.E.B., *Personal Reminiscences* 236–41.
[5] J.E.B. to Harriet Meuricoffre, January 1877.
[6] J.E.B., *Recollections of George Butler* 308.
[7] Harriet Meuricoffre to George Butler, February 1877.
[8] J.E.B., *Recollections of George Butler* 306–7.

### CHAPTER TWENTY-SIX

[1] J.E.B. to George Butler, September 1877.
[2] J.E.B. to Members of the Repeal Association, November 1877.

### CHAPTER TWENTY-SEVEN

[1] J.E.B. to George Butler, undated – spring 1881?
[2] J.E.B. to Robert Martineau, 2 May 1882.
[3] W. E. Gladstone to George Butler, 19 December 1881.
[4] George Butler to Directors and Council of Liverpool College, 2 March 1882.
[5] George Butler to J.E.B., June 1882.
[6] J.E.B., *Recollections of George Butler* 374.

### CHAPTER TWENTY-EIGHT

[1] Quoted by J.E.B. to Stanley Butler, 27 February 1883.
[2] J.E.B. to George Butler, 14 May 1882.
[3] J.E.B. to George Butler, 16 May 1882.
[4] For an account of the struggles of the Salvation Army 1880–4, see Richard Collier, *The General Next to God* (1965) 88–106.
[5] Ibid.
[6] Quoted by Stafford, *The Age of Consent* 120–1.
[7] J.E.B. to Stanley Butler, 16 February 1883.
[8] Ibid.
[9] J.E.B. to Stanley Butler, 4 March 1883.
[10] Ibid.
[11] Account of the repeal of the second Contagious Diseases Act taken from J.E.B.'s letter to Harriet Meuricoffre, dated Winchester, April 1883.

### CHAPTER TWENTY-NINE

[1] Deposition on Oath of Josephine E. Butler, made before Thomas Stamford Raffles, Esq., J.P., on the 8th day of November, 1880.
[2] Dyer, *The European Slave Trade* 29.
[3] Dyer, *Six Years' Labour and Sorrow* 2.
[4] Dyer, *The European Slave Trade* 14.
[5] J.E.B. to Sir William Harcourt, 8 November 1880.
[6] J.E.B. to George Butler, April 1880.

## CHAPTER THIRTY

[1] *The Shield*, 1 May 1880.
[2] J.E.B. to Dr Carter, 1 April 1880.
[3] Ibid.
[4] Dyer, *The European Slave Trade* 26.
[5] Ibid. 26.
[6] Ibid. 27.

## CHAPTER THIRTY-ONE

[1] Quoted by Dyer, *Six Years' Labour and Sorrow* 15.
[2] Ibid. 19.
[3] Ibid. 13.
[4] Hansard, 3rd series, cclxi, 1610–12.
[5] Report of the Lords' Committee 57.
[6] Ibid. 21–40.
[7] Quoted by Dyer, *Six Years' Labour and Sorrow* 23.
[8] Report of the Lords' Committee 72 ff.
[9] Quoted by J.E.B. to Mrs Priestman, undated–April?1883.
[10] J.E.B., *Recollections of George Butler* 375.
[11] Ibid. 376.
[12] J.E.B. to George Butler *fils*, July 1883.
[13] Quoted by Collier, *The General Next to God* 142.
[14] Ibid. 143.
[15] Ibid. 145.
[16] Ibid. 144.
[17] J.E.B., *The Salvation Army in Switzerland* 110 ff.
[18] Ibid. 233.

## CHAPTER THIRTY-TWO

[1] J.E.B. to Harriet Meuricoffre, 17 September 1883.
[2] Stafford, *The Age of Consent* 126.
[3] Quoted by Waugh, *William T. Stead* 1.
[4] Quoted by Terrot, *The Maiden Tribute* 139.
[5] Ibid. 75.
[6] Ibid. 94.

## CHAPTER THIRTY-THREE

[1] Quoted by Terrot, *The Maiden Tribute* 101.
[2] *Pall Mall Gazette*, 6 July 1885.
[3] Waugh, *William T. Stead* 9.

## CHAPTER THIRTY-FOUR

[1] Dated London, 5 June 1885.
[2] W. Bramwell Booth, *Echoes and Memories* (London, 1925).
[3] Quoted by Catherine Bramwell Booth, *Bramwell Booth* (London, 1933).
[4] J.E.B. to Fanny Forsaith, 1905.
[5] Stafford, *The Age of Consent* 161.
[6] *Pall Mall Gazette*, 9 July 1885.
[7] Quoted by *Pall Mall Gazette*, 11 November 1885.
[8] Quoted by Stafford, *The Age of Consent* 197–8.

## CHAPTER THIRTY-FIVE

[1] J.E.B., *Rebecca Jarrett* 42.
[2] Ibid. 40–1.
[3] Ibid. 29.
[4] *Pall Mall Gazette*, 9 November 1885.
[5] George Butler *fils* to J.E.B., 3 September 1885.
[6] J.E.B., *Rebecca Jarrett* 54–5.
[7] Ibid. 57.

## CHAPTER THIRTY-SIX

[1] J.E.B., *Recollections of George Butler* 417.

[2] 'When the telegram came from Stuart [sic] announcing that the Acts were no more, I hardly felt as if I cared. We had struggled too long.' Quoted by Stead, *Josephine Butler* 97.

[3] J.E.B. to Stanley Butler, 28 September 1886.

[4] J.E.B. to Stanley Butler, 1 October 1886.

[5] J.E.B. to Harriet Meuricoffre, 11 October 1886.

[6] J.E.B., *Recollections of George Butler* 434–6.

[7] Ibid. 446–8.

[8] J.E.B. to George Butler *fils*, 3 November 1889.

[9] Account of George Butler's last journey taken from journal kept by Josephine, 25 February to 23 March 1890.

## CHAPTER THIRTY-SEVEN

[1] J.E.B. to Harriet Meuricoffre, 13 August 1876.

[2] J.E.B. to G. W. Johnson, 18 February 1891.

[3] Johnson, *Josephine E. Butler*, 156–7.

[4] Ibid. 157.

[5] Quoted by Fawcett and Turner, *Josephine Butler* 127.

[6] J.E.B. to Stanley Butler, 8 August 1893.

[7] Quoted by Fawcett and Turner, *Josephine Butler* 129–30.

[8] J.E.B. to Stanley Butler, 30 May 1893.

[9] J.E.B., *The Present Aspect of the Abolitionist Cause in Relation to British India*.

[10] Ibid.

## CHAPTER THIRTY-EIGHT

[1] J.E.B. to Stanley Butler, December 1893.

[2] Ibid.

[3] Ibid.

[4] J.E.B. to Stanley Butler, 9 January 1894.

[5] J.E.B. to Henri Minod, 24 January 1894.

[6] J.E.B. to Fanny Forsaith, undated – 1895?.

[7] Ibid.

[8] Quoted by Butler, *Portrait* 186.

[9] Ibid.

[10] J.E.B. to Stanley Butler, undated – 1895?.

[11] Quoted by Butler, *Portrait* 164.

[12] Ibid. 187.

## CHAPTER THIRTY-NINE

[1] *Wings*, January 1895.

[2] Quoted by Johnson, *Josephine E. Butler* 159.

[3] Ibid. 161.

[4] J.E.B. to George Butler *fils*, March 1896.

[5] J.E.B. to Stanley Butler, 14 March 1896.

[6] Ibid.

[7] J.E.B. 'to various friends', 25 March 1896.

[8] Ibid.

[9] J.E.B. 'to various friends', 7 April 1896.

[10] Ibid.

[11] Ibid.

CHAPTER FORTY

[1] J.E.B. to Stanley Butler, June 1896.
[2] Quoted by Butler, *Portrait* 188.
[3] J.E.B., *Native Races and the War* (1900), pp. 151 on.
[4] Ibid.
[5] *Stormbell*, June 1900.
[6] Quoted by Butler, *Portrait* 189–90.
[7] Ibid. 190.
[8] Ibid. 211.
[9] J.E.B. to Fanny Forsaith, 1902.
[10] Ibid.
[11] Quoted by Butler, *Portrait* 212–13.
[12] Ibid. 217.
[13] Ibid. 190.
[14] Quoted by J.E.B. to G. W. Johnson, 26 December 1906.

# INDEX

# INDEX